Solving Data Mining Problems through Pattern Recognition

ISBN 0-13-095083-1

90000

9 780130 950833

THE DATA WAREHOUSING INSTITUTE SERIES
FROM PRENTICE HALL PTR

Planning and Designing the Data Warehouse, *Ramon Barquín and Herb Edelstein*

Building, Using, and Managing the Data Warehouse, *Ramon Barquín and Herb Edelstein*

Data Mining: A Hands-On Approach for Business Professionals, *Robert Groth*

Solving Data Mining Problems through Pattern Recognition, *Ruby L. Kennedy et al.*

Parallel Systems in the Data Warehouse, *MRJ Technology Solutions*

Solving Data Mining Problems through Pattern Recognition

By:
Ruby L. Kennedy, Unica Technologies, Inc.
Yuchun Lee, Unica Technologies, Inc.
Benjamin Van Roy, Massachusetts Institute
of Technology
Christopher D. Reed, Fidelity Investments and
Unica Technologies, Inc.
Dr. Richard P. Lippmann, MIT Lincoln Laboratories

To join a Prentice Hall PTR Internet mailing list, point to:
http://www.prenhall.com/mail_lists/

Prentice Hall, PTR
Upper Saddle River, New Jersey 07458

Library of Congress Cataloging-in-Publication Data

```
Solving data mining problems through pattern recognition / Ruby L. Kennedy …
  [et al.].
      p.   cm. -- (Data Warehousing Institute series from Prentice
  Hall PTR)
    Includes bibliographical references and index.
    ISBN 0-13-095083-1
    1. Pattern recognition systems.  2. Data mining.  I. Kennedy,
  Ruby L.  II. Series.
  TK7882.P3S65  1998
  006.3--dc21                                        97-42065
                                                        CIP
```

Editorial/Production Supervision: Craig Little
Acquisitions Editor: Mark L. Taub
Manufacturing Manager: Alexis R. Heydt
Marketing Manager: Dan Rush
Cover Design Director: Jerry Votta
Cover Design: Scott Weiss

Published by Prentice Hall PTR
Prentice-Hall, Inc.
A Simon & Schuster Company
Upper Saddle River, NJ 07458

Unica Technologies, Inc.
55 Old Bedford Rd.
Lincoln, MA 01773

Prentice Hall books are widely used by corporations and government agencies for training, marketing, and resale.

The publisher offers discounts on this book when ordered in bulk quantities. For more information, contact:
Corporate Sales Department, Phone: 800-382-3419, fax: 201-236-7141, email: corpsales@prenhall.com or write
Corporate Sales Department, Prentice Hall PTR, One Lake Street, Upper Saddle River, New Jersey 07458.

Printed in the United States of America
10 9 8 7 6 5 4 3 2 1

ISBN   0-13-095083-1

Prentice-Hall International (UK) Limited, *London*
Prentice-Hall of Australia Pty. Limited, *Sydney*
Prentice-Hall Canada Inc., *Toronto*
Prentice-Hall Hispanoamericana, S.A., *Mexico*
Prentice-Hall of India Private Limited, *New Delhi*
Prentice-Hall of Japan, Inc., *Tokyo*
Simon & Schuster Asia Pte. Ltd., *Singapore*
Editora Prentice-Hall do Brasil, Ltda., *Rio de Janeiro*

PRW is made possible by:

Yuchun Lee
David Cheung
Christopher Reed
Ruby Kennedy
Allison Huang
Dmitriy Baranovsky
Benjamin Van Roy
Robert Crites
Robert Swiston
Dorothy Minior

Other Trademarks

The following are trademarks of other organizations:

- MODEL 1™ is a trademark of Group 1 Software.

- Microsoft™, MS™, and MS-DOS™ are registered trademarks, and Windows™ and Excel™ are trademarks of Microsoft Corporation.

- Adobe™ and PostScript™ are registered trademarks of Adobe Systems, Inc.

- Hewlett-Packard™, DeskJet™, HP™, and LaserJet™ are registered trademarks of Hewlett-Packard Company.

- IBM™, AT™, and PS/2™ are registered trademarks of International Business Machines, Inc.

- UNIX™ is a registered trademark UNIX Systems Laboratories, Inc.

Contents

Chapter 1   Introduction

Chapter 2   Key Concepts: Estimation

Chapter 3   Key Concepts: Classification

Chapter 4   Additional Application Areas

Chapter 5   Overview of the Development Process

Chapter 6   Defining the Pattern Recognition Problem

Chapter 7   Collecting Data

Chapter 8   Preparing Data

Chapter 9   Data Preprocessing

Chapter 10   Selecting Architectures and Training Parameters

Chapter 11   Training and Testing

Chapter 12 Iterating Steps and Trouble-Shooting

Appendix A References and Suggested Reading

Appendix B Pattern Recognition Workbench

Appendix C Unica Technologies, Inc.

Appendix D Glossary

Software License Agreement

What's on this CD

FIGURES

TABLES

Foreword

by Dr. Ramon C. Barquín, Series Editor
President, Barquín and Associates, Inc.
Chairman, Advisory Board, The Data Warehousing
Institute

Most intellectual progress takes place in increments, building upon stable platforms of pre-existing knowledge. This is one of those specific instances where we are able to clearly see how work which had been done over the last few decades can now be put to good use in solving new problems.

Its always been a given that data mining depends substantially on statistical methods and techniques. Furthermore, it is difficult to find a definition of data mining that does not in some way refer to finding "patterns in the data."

In this important volume, the authors build on the significant amount of work that has been done in pattern recognition over the years and apply it to solving data mining problems.

Pattern recognition is "the association of an observation to past experience or knowledge," the authors tell us. In the process, they remind us that with advances in computer technology, many pattern recognition tasks have become automated. We must also remember that it is the need to massage the huge amounts of data that we now have the capacity to collect in data warehouses that has forced us into the kind of progress we have also made in data mining. Its applications today are extremely valuable and diverse: fraud detection, risk management, promotion targeting, basket analysis, database marketing, etc.

But I'd like to put this into perspective by alluding to some of the work done by the former Librarian of Congress, Daniel Boorstin. He introduced me to the concept of the "mechanized observer" some years ago in his book of essays called *Cleopatra's Nose*. Since we've been able to collect data about our universe in gargantuan proportions, he concludes, we can no longer simply discover new things in a direct fashion. Now we are in the "age of negative discovery" and need to look through trillions of collected bits of data to reach a conclusion after lengthy periods of analysis whether we have really discovered a new pulsar in space; or whether a specific trace pattern indicates the existence of a new nuclear particle.

Pattern recognition has been with us for some time. Data mining has started to serve us extremely well, recently, in obtaining the meaning from the data we collect. This book does a great job in teaching us how we can use pattern recognition techniques to solve data mining problems.

It is an excellent addition to our series.

Ramon Barquín

Preface

Data Mining   Data mining is a term usually applied to techniques that can be used to find underlying structure and relationships in large amounts of data. These techniques are drawn primarily from the related fields of neural networks, statistics, pattern classification, and machine learning. They are becoming more important as computer automation spreads and as the processing and storage capabilities of computers increase. Widely available, low-cost computer technology now makes it possible to both collect historical data and also to institute on-line analysis and controls for newly arriving data.

Applications   Data mining techniques are being successfully used for many diverse applications. These include paper and sheet metal production control, medical diagnosis and risk prediction, credit-card fraud detection, computer security break-in and misuse detection, computer user identity verification, aluminum and steel smelting control, oil refinery control, pollution control in power plants, fraudulent income tax return detection, automobile engine control and fault detection, electric motor fault and failure prediction, mass mailing and telemarketing, and simplifying world-wide-web usage by predicting useful sites from past user behavior.

**Benefits of
Data Mining**

Benefits in these and other applications include reduced costs due to more accurate control, more accurate future predictions, more effective fault detection and prediction, fraud detection and control, and automation of repetitive human tasks. In addition, services can be improved and extended due to a better understanding of underlying processes and human behavior.

**Outline of this
Book**

This book provides a concise introduction to some of the most important input-output mapping, prediction, pattern classification, and clustering algorithms useful for data mining. This introduction is based on many collective years of experience by the authors, which has led to a focus on practical issues that must be addressed to successfully solve data mining problems. The book provides a basic road map for experts who know much about a specific application, but little about neural networks, statistics, pattern classification, or machine learning.

This road map first helps potential users determine whether input-output mapping, prediction, pattern classification, or clustering algorithms are appropriate for a given application. It then helps users determine which measurements, attributes, or features might be useful as inputs to these algorithms and provides guidance in collecting and formatting this data for computer analysis. Guidelines are then presented for accurately accessing performance using separate training, evaluation, and test data partitions or cross-validation. Finally, each important algorithm is described and guidance is provided concerning settings for parameters used to control the many algorithms.

**Multi-
Algorithm
Approach**

An important truism presented in this book is that data mining is an art and that there is no single simple approach that is best for all problems. Rather, there are many algorithms and data representations, and the best strategy is to interactively experiment to find an approach that works for a particular data set. This human interaction is greatly simplified by the availability of software toolkits which allow users to interactively explore many algorithms on a common data set using the same performance metrics. This book focuses on one comprehensive software toolkit (Pattern Recognition Workbench) that includes most of the algorithms described and has the capability of handling large data sets. Details concerning this software, however, are relegated to the Appendix and to sections at the ends of chapters. These details can thus be skipped or used as examples of the types of information required to apply the various algorithms.

Intended Audience

This book is most useful for persons who have a specific application in mind, but who know little about data mining algorithms. They can use this book to determine whether the algorithms presented can be applied to their application, to learn terminology, and to provide guidance when they try out some of the recommended approaches using a software toolkit. More experienced users who want to understand the theory behind prediction, mapping, control, pattern classification, and clustering or who would like to read detailed descriptions concerning specific data mining applications should explore other more advanced texts.

Richard P. Lippmann

Chapter 1

Introduction

Pattern recognition is the association of an observation to past experience or knowledge. Humans continuously perform perceptual pattern recognition, and the amazing complexity of the cognitive processes involved has made pattern recognition an active area of research in psychology and neurophysiology for many decades.

With the recent advances of computer technology, many pattern recognition tasks have become automated. These include tasks naturally performed by humans, such as speech and handwritten-character recognition, as well as jobs that are unnatural and difficult, such as financial time-series forecasting or seismic event prediction. Today, useful applications of automatic pattern recognition are prevalent. As computers and the methods of automatic pattern recognition progress, more and more fascinating applications are being discovered in fields as broad as finance, manufacturing, and medicine.

This chapter provides an overview of pattern recognition. In particular, we discuss the following topics:

- ❑ Pattern recognition by humans
- ❑ Pattern recognition by computers
- ❑ Classification and estimation
- ❑ Fixed, parametric, and nonparametric models

Chapters 2 and 3 continue by providing a conceptual framework for pattern recognition and nonparametric (or data-driven) modeling.

1.1 PATTERN RECOGNITION BY HUMANS

Perceptual Pattern Recognition

Humans naturally perform a wide variety of perceptual pattern recognition—from understanding spoken languages, to recognizing faces of friends and foes, to distinguishing between the odors of garbage and the perfumes of romance. We often take these abilities for granted, underestimating the complex mental processes involved. However, if asked to explain how one understands a spoken language from the sound waves produced by a speaker, most of us would be dumbstruck, not knowing how to begin describing a formal method for this task we perform effortlessly.

Specialized Pattern Recognition

In addition to standard perceptual tasks, many humans have learned to perform highly specialized forms of pattern recognition. This often requires calculation and analysis beyond immediate perceptual reactions. Specialized pattern recognition serves important roles in virtually all disciplines. Radiologists diagnose diseases by examining X-ray or ultrasound images. Given limited information about a loan applicant, a banker decides whether or not to approve a loan. Football coaches select plays based on constantly changing circumstances during a game. Each of these tasks is an instance of the fundamental pattern recognition problem—immediate observations are assessed based on some combination of innate knowledge and past experience.

1.2 PATTERN RECOGNITION BY COMPUTERS

The phenomenal improvements in speed and affordability of computers over the past decade have inspired many new uses, including the automation of pattern recognition. Although humans readily excel at many pattern recognition tasks, the benefits of computerized pattern recognition are numerous.

Benefits of Automated Pattern Recognition

Automated perceptual tasks such as speech and image recognition enable the development of more natural and convenient human-computer interfaces. Tedious jobs involving pattern recognition, such as forms processing or quality control, can be computerized to function continuously with consistent performance at extremely low cost. Computers also can act as substitutes when human experts are scarce in specialized areas such as medical diagnosis, or in dangerous or inaccessible situations, such as fault diagnosis and automatic error recovery in nuclear power plants. Even when experts are readily available, pattern recognition systems may provide support—particularly when expert decisions are prone to personal biases and human error.

Superiority with Complex Calculations

Computers are particularly useful for pattern recognition tasks humans find complicated. This is common when a task entails complex numerical calculations involving many variables. Computers often can perform calculations and sort out information to recognize patterns far faster and more reliably than humans. For example, both speed and dependability are crucial when a currency trader seeks to recognize potential trends in the market. In such a task, calculations involve numerous variables, and slight delays can translate into tremendous losses.

1.3 DATA MINING AND PATTERN RECOGNITION

Emergence of Data Mining

Data mining has become widely recognized as a critical field by companies of all types. The use of valuable information "mined" from data is recognized as necessary to maintain competitiveness in today's business environments. With the advent of data warehousing making the storage of vast amounts of data common place and the continued breakthroughs in increased computing power, businesses are now looking for technology and tools to extract usable information from detailed data.

Database Marketing Example

Some of the fields where data mining has received the most publicity and success are in database marketing and credit-card fraud detection. For example, in database marketing, great accomplishments have been made in the following areas:

- Response modeling — Predicting which prospects are likely to buy based on previous purchase history, demographics, geographics, and life-style data

- Cross-selling — Maximizing sales of products and services to a company's existing customer base by studying the purchase patterns of products frequently purchased together

- Customer valuation — Predicting the value or profitability of a customer over a specified period of time based on previous purchase history, demographics, geographics, and life-style data

- Segmentation and profiling — Improved understanding of customer segments through data analysis and profiling of prototypical customers

Terms

This text uses the terms "data mining" and "pattern recognition" interchangeably, as both concentrate on the extraction of information or relationships from data. The term "data mining" evolved primarily from the database marketing or database application realms, while "pattern recognition" was derived from engineering fields such as process control and quality inspection. Both phrases deal with essentially the same ideas, but represent the nomenclature developed from different industries.

Discovery

While "data mining" has a very broad interpretation that can include topics such as automatic discovery, exploratory agents, and sequencing, this text concentrates on the more prevalent and *practical* aspects of data mining—namely those areas of data mining addressed through pattern recognition. This text does not address the subject of "discovery" because it lies outside of the bulk of practical data mining applications. The topic of discovery is a fascinating one that often intrigues the imagination, but this book concentrates on applications where pattern recognition technology has been shown to significantly contribute to application success.

Pattern Recognition Terminology

Pattern recognition and its related terminology are more closely related to the underlying technology than terms typically associated with data mining. In addition, the terms are industry independent, allowing the topic of data mining to be applied to many different businesses. As it is more straightforward to think of data mining using pattern recognition nomenclature, the remainder of this book uses primarily pattern recognition terminology.

1.4 TYPES OF PATTERN RECOGNITION

Labeling Observations

Regardless of what is performing pattern recognition—man or machine— the same fundamental process ensues. In an abstract sense, pattern recognition can be viewed as the process of assigning a *label* to an *observation*. The *input* of a pattern recognition system is an encoding of an observation. In the case of automated pattern recognition, the observation is typically encoded as a vector of numerical values, called an *input vector*. The *output* is the label assigned to the observation (see Figure 1-1).

Figure 1-1 An Abstract View of Pattern Recognition

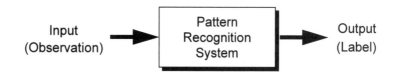

Pattern recognition tasks assume highly varied forms. It is convenient to divide pattern recognition tasks into two categories that, while closely related, have conceptual differences calling for separate treatment. These two categories are *classification* and *estimation.*

Classification vs. Estimation

In the technical literature, the term "pattern recognition" often is used interchangeably with "classification," which is the process of assigning one of a finite set of labels to an observation. However, in this book, we choose a common and broader definition of pattern recognition that also encompasses estimation. Estimation is the process of assigning one of a (typically infinite) number of numerical labels to an observation. The next two sections describe each of these forms of pattern recognition.

1.5   CLASSIFICATION

Classification involves associating an observation with one of several labels called *classes.* One classification problem we solve on a daily basis is handwritten-character recognition. This is the task of recognizing a handwritten symbol as one of the 26 letters of the English alphabet.

1.5.1   Calculation in Classification

Perceptual classification tasks, such as handwritten-character recognition, consist of immediate responses to sensory input. However, classification often requires conscious calculation and analysis. An example is medical diagnosis. In this context, the observation may include patient symptoms and clinical measurements, such as blood pressure and body temperature. Using this information, the doctor makes formal calculations and exploits knowledge and experience to classify the observation as one of many possible medical conditions.

1.5.2   Uncertainty in Classification

Classification problems often entail decision-making in the face of uncertainty. This phenomenon is illustrated by the example in Figure 1-2. The writer of the depicted symbol probably intended to convey either the letter

"A" or the letter "H." However, to a reader, the character may be ambiguous.

Figure 1-2   Character Classification Example

In a borderline case of this sort (and without additional contextual clues), either choice has some chance of being wrong. Thus, a decision must be made in the face of uncertainty. In this event, the character should be categorized as the most *probable* class, even though there is some possibility the classification may be incorrect (i.e., the decision could not be made with high *confidence*).[1]

1.5.3   Computer-Automated Classification

The automation of classification through the use of computers is a common practice today reaping tremendous benefits. One example, manufacturing quality control, involves the detection of defects among components or finished goods at a manufacturing facility.

Quality control is necessary in virtually every industry. For instance, in the computer industry, the detection of faulty solder joints on circuit boards is a critical matter. Consistent early detection can generate immense savings

---

1. Sometimes, it actually may be inappropriate to simply choose the most probable class. Biases due to costs and benefits associated with different classes can influence the criteria for best classification. For instance, a risk-averse mutual fund manager will not classify a stock as a "buy," even when the price will probably increase, if there is a reasonable chance that the company will collapse.

in subsequent maintenance costs, since weak solder joints are a primary cause of computer malfunctions. Detecting defects can be thought of as a classification problem, where each solder joint must be classified as "acceptable" or "defective." The effort required for quality control is tedious and may require precise measurements and calculations suitable for automation. Furthermore, automation's speed and consistency are immune to human factors such as fatigue and pressure to fill immediate orders.

1.6 ESTIMATION

Estimation, the second type of pattern recognition, entails generating an approximation of some desired numerical value based on an observation.[2] One example is estimating a person's age based on his or her physical appearance. This can be thought of as an extended form of classification where each number—say, between 1 and 100—is a "class," and a person must be categorized as one of these 100 classes.

Difference Between Estimation and Classification

The fundamental difference between estimation and classification is that "classes" in an estimation problem follow an explicit ordering (i.e., a sequence of values). In general, similar observations lead to estimates that are numerically close. Furthermore, in estimation problems, there is often an infinite continuum of classes, where in classification, the number of classes is finite.

1.6.1 Calculation in Estimation

As with classification, estimation often involves explicit calculations beyond immediate perceptual reactions. An example of a sophisticated estimation task is a venture capitalist calculating the expected return for an investment. In this case, the venture capitalist gathers relevant information

---

2. More generally, estimation can involve the approximation of a vector of several numerical values, given an observation. In this case the output is often referred to as an *output vector*.

concerning the potential investment as the observation and produces an estimate of the expected profits (the output).

1.6.2   Uncertainty in Estimation

Sequential Outputs

Estimates often are prone to uncertainty. In some sense, the uncertainty inherent in estimation problems is worse than in classification problems. The slightest uncertainty in estimation can seriously affect the chance an estimate is exactly correct. This is certainly true for age estimation—no matter how talented you are, guessing the exact age of a person is nearly impossible. However, estimates can be numerically close enough to true values to be useful. In the context of age estimation, you might be able to generate guesses that are almost always close to the correct ages, even though the guesses rarely correspond to the exact ages.

Classes Are Not Sequential

Sequential relationships are typical to estimation problems, but nonexistent in classification. Classes in a classification problem have no clear concept of closeness or ordering among them. For example, in handwritten-character recognition, if a written character is meant to be an "A," but a wrong classification is made by the reader, there is no clear advantage to having the wrong guess being a "B" rather than any other letter of the alphabet. The answer is either right or wrong.

On the other hand, estimation problems offer a means of computing "closeness" or degree of error. Guessing a person's age as 25 years old is only "one off" if the person's age is 26. This would be a "better guess" than 28, which would be "three off." In classification, one wrong guess is generally as bad as another, while in estimation, a wrong guess close to the correct answer is generally better than a far one. The fact that estimation methods take advantage of ordinal features is the key distinction between estimation and classification.

1.6.3 Computer-Automated Estimation

Estimation often benefits from the speed and reliability of computer auto-mation. Computer automated estimation, for example, has become a crucial tool in financial-market analysis over recent years. Financial-market analysis typically involves *prediction*, the estimation of future numerical quantities. Observations consist of a barrage of numerical quantities (e.g., stock prices, trading volume, indices, etc.), requiring analysis well suited to computers. Consequently, most firms in the financial industry rely heavily on computer-automated estimation to maintain competitiveness.

1.7 DEVELOPING A MODEL

Just as for any other task to be performed by a computer, automated pattern recognition requires a "program" providing detailed instructions. These instructions are typically mathematical equations characterizing the relationship between inputs and desired outputs of a pattern recognition system. Formulating these mathematical equations, or building a *model*, is the central problem in automating a pattern recognition task.

The development process for building a model is often referred to as *modeling*. This section discusses the primary approaches for modeling, the relationships among them, and the merits and shortcomings of each.

1.7.1 Fixed Models

Closed-Form Equations

The most straightforward approach to modeling involves formulating closed-form equations that define how the outputs are derived from the inputs. These equations can then be easily translated into a computer program to automate pattern recognition. A model produced in this manner is referred to as a *fixed model*, since all of its characteristics are fixed when the equations are derived.

Fixed models are suitable for simple, fully understood, pattern recognition tasks. An example is estimating the amount of time it takes for a stone to fall to the ground given its height. Newtonian mechanics dictates an exact formula for this estimation problem. In particular, the time taken for a stone at height h meters to fall is $\sqrt{(2h)/9.8}$ seconds, since the acceleration due to gravity is constant for all practical purposes (9.8 meters per second squared). This provides the model required to automate this estimation problem. Figure 1-3 shows estimated falling time as a function of the height.

Figure 1-3 Time for an Object to Fall from a Given Height

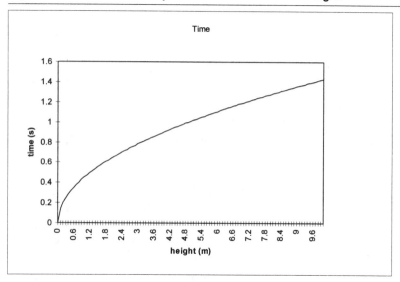

Unfortunately, many common pattern recognition problems are not as well understood as the falling stone problem. Even for pattern recognition tasks we perform effortlessly, such as speech recognition, it is not clear how to define explicit mathematical relationships. The same is true for complex problems relying on "intuition" and "experience." The lack of a formal understanding for many practical pattern recognition problems severely limits the applicability of fixed models.

Expert Systems

Before departing from the topic of fixed models, note that *expert systems* studied in the field of artificial intelligence fall into this category of models. The development of expert systems employs sophisticated techniques for producing explicit rules (equivalent to mathematical formulae) based on the knowledge of domain experts. Once these rules are produced, the model to be used for automated pattern recognition is fixed. As with closed-form equations, this approach is most effective when the problem is well understood.

1.7.2 Parametric Models

When faced with an estimation problem, we might have a very good idea about how inputs and outputs interrelate, but not to the level of precision required by a fixed model. For instance, consider the falling stone example from the previous section, but suppose the stone is dropped on another planet where the gravitational acceleration is different. We know it takes $\sqrt{(2h)/g}$ seconds for a stone at height h meters to fall to the ground, where g is the rate of acceleration due to gravity (on this new planet). In this case, our knowledge does not provide us with a complete model as it did on Earth.

To complete the development of a model, we must assign a value to g. This can be done by experimentation. In particular, we could drop a few stones and measure the time it takes for them to fall. The results would constitute a table of *example patterns* as shown in Table 1-1. An example pattern is defined as an input vector and the *desired output*. In the case of the falling stone problem, the input vector has only one component, the height from which the stone is dropped. The desired output is the amount of time the stone takes to fall to the ground.

Table 1-1   Experimental Results from a Falling Object

Height (m)	Falling Time (s)
0.5	1.9
1.3	0.4
2.8	0.46
4	0.68
7.3	0.7
9.7	1.04

Given the example patterns, a value should be selected for g so the model produces estimates close to the measured times when presented with the corresponding heights as input.

Figure 1-4 illustrates the example patterns (as x's) and some candidate models using different values of g. Clearly, the middle curve is the best of the three models. Note though, the middle curve does not pass through every data point. This could be due to slight inaccuracies in the structure of the model, as well as measurement errors made when collecting example patterns.

Though it may be easy for a human to "eye-ball" a good value for g after seeing the graph for this two-dimensional example, this is not generally possible for more difficult problems involving complex relationships and multiple variables. However, there are computer algorithms that can calculate appropriate values for parameters in such settings.

Figure 1-4   Computing the Best Value of *g* Based on Examples

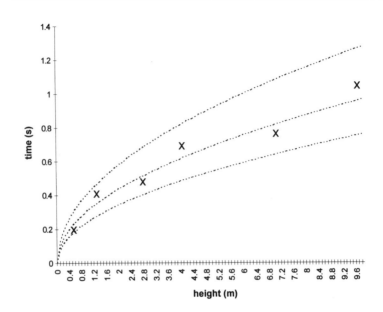

The example described in this section involves a parametric model. In general, the key feature of a parametric model is that explicit mathematical equations characterize the structure of the relationship between inputs and outputs, but a few parameters are unspecified. The unspecified parameters are chosen by examining data examples. Hence, the stage of formulating mathematical equations allows for some flexibility in the model, which is fine tuned by empirical analysis.

Linear Regression

Another example of parametric modeling, widely used for estimation problems in practice, is linear regression. Linear regression hypothesizes a linear relationship between inputs and outputs. In other words, if there is one output variable denoted by y and three input variables denoted by x_1, x_2, and x_3, linear regression uses a model of the form:

$$y = c_0 + c_1 x_1 + c_2 x_2 + c_3 x_3 \qquad \textbf{(EQ 1)}$$

where the coefficients c_1, c_2, and c_3 are chosen to optimize the model's accuracy on a data set. Linear regression models work extremely well with very few data examples when the underlying process is linear. However, when nonlinear behavior is present, linear regression often generates a poor model.

Parametric modeling generally requires a fair amount of knowledge concerning the pattern recognition task at hand, although the degree of accuracy is less than required by a fixed model. However, this degree of understanding is frequently unavailable in real-world problems. Parametric modeling is thus often infeasible or when used anyways, inaccurate.

1.7.3 Nonparametric Models

Large Data Sets

In this modern era known as the information age, technological advances pave the way for collection and storage of increasingly large amounts of data. Data acquisition and analysis are prevalent in virtually every field of study—from manufacturing, to medicine, to market research, to finance. Large data sets are rich in information, and there are many methods for developing models to exploit this wealth.

Models relying heavily on the use of data, rather than domain-specific human expertise, are called *nonparametric* or *data-driven models*. The popularity of nonparametric models has exploded over the past few years, as data has become increasingly available and computers have become fast enough to perform sophisticated analyses on huge amounts of data. Nonparametric modeling techniques have been very successful in solving many complex pattern recognition problems over the past decade—problems that have not been solved analytically. Furthermore, new problems arising today, that would have traditionally required years of study to solve, are now being solved quickly through nonparametric methods.

Using a Data Set

Nonparametric methods generally employ data sets containing large numbers of example patterns. For instance, in a data set used in developing a handwritten-character recognition system, the example patterns may consist of handwritten characters and the English letters they represent.

The basic premise of nonparametric methods is that relationships consistently occurring in the data set will recur in future observations. This is necessary since the model attempts to generalize based on the examples presented in a data set. One important benefit is that nonparametric methods do not require a thorough understanding of the problem. Furthermore, arbitrarily complex models can be produced by nonparametric methods, while fixed and parametric models tend to be limited by human comprehension.

Nonparametric Methods

Many nonparametric methods are discussed in current technical literature. Among these are methods associated with classical statistics, such as nearest cluster methods, as well as more modern machine-learning algorithms, such as neural networks and decision trees. The primary difference between traditional and modern methods is that modern methods are generally geared towards the use of larger data sets and are able to work well with many input variables.

1.7.4 Preprocessing

Complex Problems

Many pattern recognition problems are incredibly complex, and the relationship between inputs and outputs cannot be well characterized by a data set of a reasonable size. For instance, in macroeconomic forecasting, every single microeconomic variable (such as the sales at every firm in the country) could potentially influence the state of the economy. A nonparametric method would require a tremendous amount of data and time if it were to produce a model by sorting out the relationships among all microeconomic variables and the subsequent state of the economy. Though theoretically possible, it is generally not feasible to collect enough data and allow enough time to generate a nonparametric model for a problem of this magnitude.

Key Features

Fortunately, human experts often have an idea of what information is most relevant and what features are key for a pattern recognition problem. This knowledge can be used to transform observations into a more intelligible form. For instance, in the case of macroeconomic forecasting, reasonable estimates might be generated based on a few important macroeconomic indicators such as the gross national product, the unemployment rate, and the status of particular key industries. Though economists do not know the exact relationships, their intuition and experience may suggest that these are the key variables influencing the future prosperity of the economy.

Once all the information about the economy is narrowed down to a reasonable number of macroeconomic indicators, it may be feasible to develop an effective nonparametric model to forecast the economy. Figure 1-5 illustrates the two stages involved in such a model.

Figure 1-5   Macroeconomic Forecasting Example

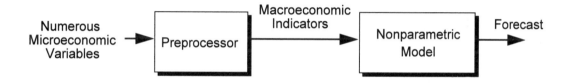

The nonparametric model is produced using a set of example patterns, each consisting of values for the macroeconomic indicators at a particular time and the subsequent performance of the economy. Since there are fewer input variables, the relationship between them and the desired forecast should be less complex, allowing the nonparametric model to be developed using a reasonable amount of data.

The removal of irrelevant information and extraction of key features to simplify a pattern recognition problem (as was done in the macroeconomic forecasting problem) is called *preprocessing*. In a two-stage set-up, including a *preprocessor* and a nonparametric model, the original encoding of the observation used by the preprocessor is referred to as a *raw input vector*. The transformed observation produced by the preprocessor and used by the nonparametric model is called a *preprocessed input vector* or *feature vector*. Figure 1-6 illustrates a generic two-stage model.

Figure 1-6 Two-Stage Pattern Recognition System

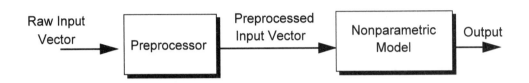

Preprocessing and Fixed Models

Using a nonparametric model with a preprocessor can be viewed as separating the model development into two parts: a fixed portion and a nonparametric portion. Domain-specific knowledge concerning the particular task is incorporated in the preprocessor, while the less well understood aspects of the task are captured using a nonparametric model. The size requirement for the data set is generally reduced as more knowledge is incorporated into the preprocessing stage, thereby simplifying the task of the nonparametric model.

1.7.5 A Continuum of Methods

The fixed and nonparametric approaches to modeling can be viewed as two extremes of a continuum. The fixed model uses only existing knowledge concerning a pattern recognition problem, but no data. The nonparametric approach relies on a large data set, but uses little knowledge that a domain expert may possess.

The combination of nonparametric methods and preprocessors as well as parametric methods can be viewed as hybrids between the two extremes. These hybrid approaches use a combination of domain-specific expertise and data to develop models. In general, the amount of data required is reduced as more knowledge concerning the pattern recognition task is incorporated. Hence, there is a trade-off between the degree of understanding available and the amount of data required to create an accurate model. With this interpretation, all the modeling approaches are located on a continuum. Figure 1-7 presents an intuitive interpretation of this continuum and where various methods fall.

Figure 1-7   Continuum of Modeling Methods

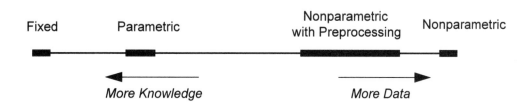

1.7.6   Biases Due to Prior Knowledge

Avoiding Over-Processing Data

Though incorporating knowledge in a nonparametric model through preprocessing is often needed to reduce requirements on computational time and the number of example patterns, unexpected detrimental effects can result from preprocessing. One of the original reasons for using nonparametric methods is to discover previously unknown relationships.

If we do not understand a pattern recognition task well and try to develop a fixed model, the performance is not likely to be good. On the other hand, nonparametric methods can be used to develop models even when we do not have a good understanding of the problem. By using a fixed preprocessor without completely understanding the task at hand, we could introduce misleading knowledge or delete potentially useful aspects of observations. This can lower the accuracy of the resulting model.

When developing a preprocessor, a balance must be struck between introducing too much potentially biased knowledge, and introducing sufficient knowledge for a nonparametric method to perform well given a reasonable number of example patterns. Choosing good preprocessing techniques is an "art" requiring intuition about the task at hand as well as a feel for the richness of information contained in the data and the complexity of the recognition task at hand.

Handwritten-Character Recognition Example

It is interesting to study the trend in the leading approaches to developing automatic handwritten-character recognition systems over the years. A few decades ago, handwritten-character recognition systems were primarily based on man-made models characterizing how the letters of the English alphabet should be written. Only a couple of parameters in these models were actually tuned by real data.

By the middle of the 1980's, nonparametric methods were widely used in the handwritten-character recognition industry, but extensive preprocessing was performed to extract key shape-based features such as curves, loops, and angles. Since that time, the data sets used to develop handwritten-character recognition systems have grown tremendously. Increasingly compute-intensive approaches using less sophisticated preprocessing and "rawer" features have been employed to produce the most successful systems. This evolution reflects a drift along the continuum of methods over the years, as computers have become faster and data has become more accessible.

1.8   THE PURPOSE OF THIS BOOK

Pragmatic Approach

This book presents a pragmatic approach to solving pattern recognition problems, with a heavy emphasis on nonparametric methods. Due to their success in a broad range of disciplines, nonparametric approaches have become standard tools in recent years. Furthermore, the effectiveness of these methods will continue to grow with advances in computation speed and the accessibility of data.

A rigorous treatment of the theory involved in parametric and nonparametric modeling entails an extensive background in several advanced mathematical disciplines, including multivariable Fourier and functional analysis, as well as stochastic processes, statistics, and computational complexity theory. However, the essential ideas most relevant to the development of real-world applications are "intuitive."

Experience Is Key

Nonparametric modeling is an empirical "art." Skills in the application of nonparametric methods can only be developed through experience. Because of this, the most successful practitioners are not necessarily well versed in theoretical foundations of the field, while strong theoreticians are not necessarily skillful when it comes to solving real-world problems. In this spirit, rather than concentrating on the theoretical aspects of nonparametric modeling, this book stresses a *process* for the development of successful nonparametric models.

Structure of Book

In Chapters 2 and 3, we present the basic concepts for an intuitive understanding guiding the use of nonparametric modeling techniques to solve estimation and classification problems. Chapter 4 discusses several types of problems, such as time-series prediction and information compression, that can fundamentally be viewed as special cases of estimation or classification problems.

In the following chapters, we guide the reader through the steps involved in solving pattern recognition problems, illustrating standard difficulties encountered in the process and ways to tackle them. We also provide descriptions of successful recent and classical parametric and nonparametric algorithms, highlighting traits most useful to practitioners.

Chapter Appendices

Chapter appendices describe how the necessary steps can be performed using Pattern Recognition Workbench (PRW), a user-friendly software for developing and deploying pattern recognition solutions. PRW contains many of the most commonly used nonparametric algorithms and provides a complete environment for both preprocessing data and setting up and running experiments. Our hope is that PRW will help to foster the widespread and systematic use of nonparametric methods to solve pattern recognition problems in all fields of study.

Accruing Experience

If you are just getting started with solving pattern recognition problems, keep in mind this *is* an art that, at least for beginners, requires extensive experimentation that can be frustrating at times. However, experience quickly accrues, and skills in this art can lead to numerous exciting applications.

Chapter 2

Key Concepts: Estimation

Due to certain conceptual differences, we will treat estimation separately from classification (discussed in the next chapter). We discuss estimation first because many issues arising in both types of pattern recognition are more natural to describe in this context. Furthermore, as we will discuss in Chapter 3, classification problems can always be transformed into estimation problems, where each estimated value is the probability an observation belongs to a particular class.

This chapter introduces important concepts for thinking about estimation and applying nonparametric methods. We begin by defining several commonly used technical terms. We then discuss the characteristics of a good model, the use of fixed and parametric models, a conceptual framework for thinking about nonparametric modeling, and a widely used practical approach. We conclude by considering the practicality of certain statistical properties on which modeling relies. Chapters 2 and 3 together provide a foundation for the application-oriented ideas presented in the remainder of this book.

2.1 TERMINOLOGY AND NOTATION

Input Vectors and Input Variables

As discussed in Chapter 1, estimation is the process of generating a numerical valuation from an observation. For computational purposes, observations are generally encoded as vectors of numerical values called *input vectors*.

Each component of an input vector is an *input variable* and represents a particular feature or characteristic of the problem. For instance, when estimating tomorrow's peak temperature given today's weather conditions, the input vector may consist of input variables representing various atmospheric measurements such as today's temperature and humidity. It also might include historical data, such as yesterday's temperature, or the average temperature for this date over the last 10 years.

Input Space

The number of input variables (i.e., the number of components in an input vector) is the *input dimensionality*. The set of allowed input vectors (all possible combinations of input variable values), which is typically infinite, is called the *input space*.

Output Variables and Output Space

A model may estimate the values of one or more variables given an input vector. These *output variables* are components of the *output vector*. The number of output variables in the output vector is the *output dimensionality*, and the infinite set of possible output vectors is called the *output space*.

☞ **NOTE:** In statistics, input variables are also known as *independent variables* and output variables are also known as *dependent variables*. In this text, the more general terms of "input" and "output" variables are used because they are domain independent.

Mapping

An estimation model can be viewed as a "functional block" that generates an output vector when presented with an input vector (see Figure 2-1). The model is defined by a *mapping* from the input space to the output space A mapping is a mathematical function assigning one output vector to each possible input vector. For a fixed model, we denote the mapping by a func-

Solving Data Mining Problems through Pattern Recognition

tion F. Hence, the equation $Y = F(X)$ defines the relationship between the input vector $X = [x_1, x_2, ..., x_n]$ and the output vector $Y = [y_1, y_2, ..., y_n]$.

Figure 2-1   Functional Block View of an Estimation Model

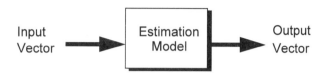

In the case of parametric and nonparametric models, mappings are not fixed *a priori*, but are manipulated upon examination of a data set. A data set can be characterized as containing k example patterns denoted by (X_1, D_1), (X_2, D_2), ..., (X_k, D_k). In this notation, for each index i between 1 and k, X_i is a vector in the input space and D_i is the corresponding vector in the output space. Each X_i is an input vector drawn from an observation, and D_i is the desired estimate. For example, in a temperature prediction problem, X_i could be a vector recording a particular day's weather conditions and D_i would be the temperature on the following day.

Parameter Vector

The dependence of parametric models on data is usually expressed as $Y = F(X|\theta)$, where θ is called a *parameter vector*. This notation implies F is a function of the parameter vector as well as the input vector. Values are assigned to the parameter vector after inspection of a data set, and different parameter values result in different mappings.

Supervised and Unsupervised Learning

Learning algorithms that fine tune parameters using example patterns (input-output data pairs) are called *supervised learning algorithms*. Learning algorithms that cluster data patterns (inputs without corresponding output patterns) are known as *unsupervised learning algorithms*. The majority of algorithms examined in this book fall in the supervised learning category.

2.2 CHARACTERISTICS OF AN OPTIMAL MODEL

Before exploring methods for developing models, it is important to understand what characteristics make a model desirable. In general, the most critical property is that a model generates accurate estimates for future observations. The optimal model is the one expected to produce the most accurate estimates.

When there is no uncertainty (e.g., noise) in an estimation problem, any two identical input vectors have identical output vectors. It is therefore possible to define a mapping that always maps an input vector to the desired output vector. This mapping defines an optimal model for an optimal problem.

Error Due to Uncertainty

When there is uncertainty, as is normal in practical estimation problems, the situation is more complicated. In this case, no model can be error-free, because the same input vector may be associated with different outputs. The optimal model in this case is the one minimizing expected error.

Example

To illustrate the effects of uncertainty, let us consider an example. Suppose the input for an estimation problem is last year's average rainfall in a country and the output is an estimate of this year's average rainfall. The model minimizes expected error and generates outputs equal to its inputs. However, the estimate generated by the model may be very different from the actual amount of rainfall a country will experience this year. Figure 2-2 illustrates discrepancies that might be expected between example patterns and the model. The x's plot example patterns for a particular country—last year's rainfall vs. this year's rainfall.

Figure 2-2 Error of an Optimal Model on Noisy Data

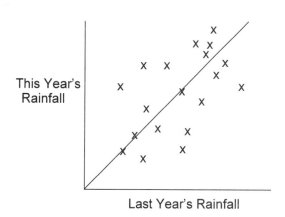

Optimal Models Err in the Presence of Uncertainty

The large errors do not necessarily reflect a deficiency in the model. No other mapping with the same input and output variables would be expected to outperform this one. The errors are due to uncertainty in the problem. For any model—fixed, parametric, or nonparametric—error does not imply that a better model exists. Even the best possible model will err in the presence of uncertainty.

2.3   SOURCES OF ERROR

Modeling Error

From our discussion in the previous section, there appears to be two potential sources of error in estimation. The first is *modeling error*. This is the error due to differences between the model used and an optimal model.

Uncertainty

A second source of error is uncertainty. The example of rainfall prediction exemplifies this phenomenon. Given a fixed set of input and output patterns, even the optimal model is imperfect (error-prone). However, this error might be reduced by redefining the estimation problem as one with additional inputs. For example, using global weather conditions as additional inputs may enable more accurate estimates. This additional information might reduce uncertainty, since rainfall in any particular country over the coming year is influenced by the global climate.

Missing Variables vs. Random Noise

In our example, error may be reduced as more inputs are incorporated. Nevertheless, at some point, additional inputs no longer improve the model's accuracy, and the model may still err. Uncertainty, therefore, can be classified into two types: uncertainty due to missing variables (problem features) and inherently random *noise*. This distinction is important for developing estimation models. The former type of uncertainty can be reduced by adding more information or input variables, while the latter type cannot be avoided.

2.4 FIXED MODELS

Developing a fixed model uses knowledge, intuition, and analysis to minimize error. No data is explicitly used in the process. Such models are typically described by a set of mathematical equations defining how estimates are generated based on an input vector.

Understanding Input-Output Relationships

The development of an accurate fixed model requires a full understanding of the relationships between input and output variables. Our model for predicting rainfall is one example of a fixed model. In that context, our understanding of a simple relationship between last year's rainfall and the expected rainfall for the coming year resulted in a model that generated outputs equal to the inputs. In other words, the mapping was:

$$F(X) = X \qquad \text{(EQ 1)}$$

However, if we want to develop a more sophisticated model by incorporating more input variables in the estimation problem, it is no longer straightforward how a fixed model should be defined. For instance, if we encode global climate features, the relationship of these variables to the desired estimate is unclear. The development of a fixed model using these inputs requires guessing the underlying relationships based on some intuition and simplified analysis. Fixed models of this sort typically oversimplify the relationships which lead to inaccuracy.

2.5   PARAMETRIC MODELS

An alternative that overcomes some of the limitations of fixed models is to tune a model based on data. Parametric and nonparametric modeling methods rely on data to generate the model rather than on an understanding of the underlying relationships. The primary distinction between these two types of modeling is the degree of reliance on data.

Two-Stage Modeling

Parametric modeling involves two stages. The first is similar to fixed modeling. In this stage, knowledge, intuition, and analysis are employed to characterize the nature of relationships involved in the estimation problem. This results in a hypothesized mathematical structure called a *parametric form*. The parametric form is like a fixed model, as it is derived without the use of data. However, it is not an exact description of how outputs should be generated from inputs. Instead, there is a set of free parameters, and thus a parametric form can be viewed as a functional box as in Figure 2-3.

Figure 2-3   A Parametric Form

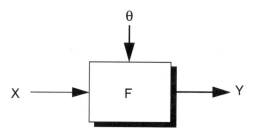

Once numerical values are assigned to these parameters (θ), a parametric form defines a mapping. In general, each possible setting of parameter values results in a different mapping. Hence, the parametric form can be thought of as a way of defining a set of potential mappings for an estimation problem. Ideally, a mapping from this set provides a good model for the estimation problem.

Using Data to Select Free Parameters

The second stage of parametric modeling uses data to select numerical values for the free parameters. In general, the parameters are chosen to minimize error on a given data set. In other words, this second step selects one mapping, from the set of possible mappings defined by the parametric form, that performs well on the data set. Because the search space of possible solutions is limited to a few free parameters, fitting a parametric model to data is often a very efficient solution.

The workings of parametric modeling are probably best conveyed through examples. In Chapter 1, we discussed an example of a parametric model for estimating the time for a stone to fall on a different planet. In that context, Newtonian mechanics were used to derive a parametric form with one parameter—the gravitational acceleration on the new planet. Once this parameter was tuned using data, the model was ready for deployment. We now present a more common parametric form.

2.5.1   Example: Linear Regression

Due to its simplicity and widespread use, linear regression provides a good starting point for thinking about parametric modeling and the use of data in general. As a parametric method, linear regression assumes a definitive parametric form for the estimation problem to be solved (i.e., the data is linear). If nonlinear relationships exist, linear regression may not be an appropriate choice for modeling.

Structure of Mapping

Graphically, for a problem with one input variable and one output variable, linear regression can only produce mappings that are straight lines (e.g., see Figure 2-4). With a two-dimensional input space, the mapping becomes a plane. More generally, for a problem with an n-dimensional input vector $X = [x_1, ..., x_n]$, there are $n+1$ parameters contained in a parameter vector $\theta = [\theta_0, ..., \theta_n]$, and the mapping takes on the form:

$$F(X|\theta) = \theta_0 + \theta_1 x_1 + ... + \theta_n x_n \qquad \text{(EQ 2)}$$

Each setting of the parameters results in a different linear mapping. For cases with more than one output variable, linear regression produces separate models estimating each output (so that $n+1$ parameters are required per output vector).

Choosing Parameters to Fit Data

Given a set of example patterns for an estimation problem with a single input x and a single output y (as denoted by x's in Figure 2-4), linear regression selects parameters so that output values generated by the model are close to desired output values provided by the example patterns. In other words, a line is chosen to best *fit* the data.

Figure 2-4   Example of Fitting a Line to Example Patterns

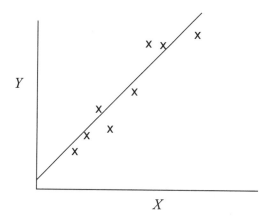

2.5.2   Generalization

Up until now, we have thought of parametric modeling in terms of two stages: designing a parametric form and then choosing parameter values using data. In this section, we will explore an alternative interpretation of parametric modeling, which leads to further understanding and prefaces the use of nonparametric methods.

Consider the problem of producing an estimation model given only a data set. There are an infinite number of mappings that fit a (finite) data set well. Figure 2-5 exemplifies this by showing the output from two models as a solid curve and a dashed line, both of which perform perfectly on the example patterns, denoted by x's.

Figure 2-5 Two Models that Fit the Data

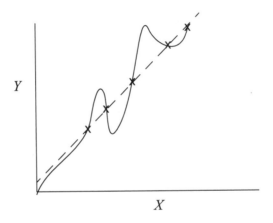

Generalization on Out-of-Sample Data

The coexistence of multiple models performing perfectly on available data is the norm for estimation problems. We are thus faced with the problem of how to choose the most appropriate one. The objective is to select a model that will perform well, not only on the available data set, but also on data not in the data set, or *out-of-sample* data. The ability of a model, tuned based on one data set, to perform well on out-of-sample data is referred to as *generalization*.

Parametric Forms and Generalization

An alternative way of viewing a parametric form is as a definition of how to perform generalization. For instance, consider the case illustrated in Figure 2-6. We originally have access to the example patterns denoted by x's. Two of many candidate models are the linear model (i.e., the dashed line) and a polynomial model (i.e., the swiggly curve).

Solving Data Mining Problems through Pattern Recognition

If we know the underlying relationship in the estimation problem is linear, we would expect typical out-of-sample data of the sort denoted by the o's. Thus, although the squiggly curve performs better on the original data, the linear model performs better on out-of-sample data. Hence, the linear parametric form guides us to good generalizations when the underlying relationships are linear.

Figure 2-6 Linear vs. Arbitrary Model on a Linear Problem

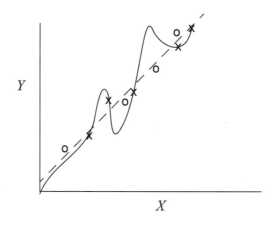

Generalization vs. Memorization

The last example demonstrates that superior performance on one data set does not necessarily translate to another. Due to noise, even the best model—in our example, the linear model—can err on the original data set, while outperforming alternative models on out-of-sample data. One lesson this highlights is that we do not merely want a model that *memorizes* the original example patterns (reducing error on original data set). A good model must *generalize* to provide good estimates for out-of-sample data. In other words, the expected performance of a model must be measured by its accuracy on out-of-sample data, not by its ability to learn the mapping of the original example patterns.

2.5.3   Shortcomings of Parametric Methods

When at least one set of parameter values leads to a good model, parametric methods are extremely effective. However, the choice of effective parametric forms for many real-world estimation problems requires a degree of understanding not available. Practitioners often employ linear regression by default when there is no clear understanding of what parametric model will work well.

Overly Restrictive Parametric Forms

The use of a parametric model, such as linear regression, can lead to poor models when the parametric model does not fit the underlying relationships. Often times, data may be sufficiently informative to generate a superior model. For instance, consider the example patterns denoted by x's in Figure 2-7.

Figure 2-7   Example Where Linear Regression Is Overly Restrictive

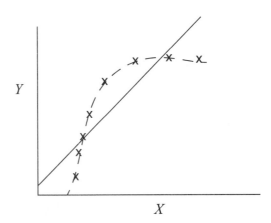

A person might infer a mapping similar to the dashed curve, while linear regression would generate the solid line. Intuitively, the curve seems to capture the relationships inferred by data much better. Unless there is a good reason to believe that the underlying relationships are linear, and the discrepancies between the linear model and the example patterns are purely due to noise, the curve appears to be a better model. In this case, linear regression is an overly restrictive technique leading to a poor model.

2.5.4   Iteration through Parametric Forms

In simple examples, such as the one in Figure 2-7, a person can "eye-ball" the data to detect the inadequacies of a linear model and infer a better one (e.g., a parabolic curve). However, for problems with multiple inputs and more complex relationships, it is hard to even visualize mappings. Thus, determining whether inaccuracies of a parametric model are due to modeling error or noise is not a simple matter. When there is modeling error, it is often unclear what parametric form will produce a better model.

A common approach is to try several different parametric forms. For instance, we might try linear regression first. When it appears that the error of the resulting model on the data is too high, a more complicated parametric form might be tried next. If this still does not produce a model that performs well on the data, yet another parametric form can be hypothesized and tried. This process usually ends either with a model that performs well on the data or with the resolution that the errors are due to noise.

Flaws of the Iterative Approach

In many practical scenarios, either of the above conclusions of an iterative process is unsatisfactory. In the first case, even if the parametric model performs well on the original data set, the ability of the model to generalize is questionable. The reason a parametric model is normally expected to generalize well is because the parametric form is based on an understanding of the underlying relationships. However, when a parametric form is hypothesized without consideration for the true underlying relationships, there is no reason to believe performance on the original data set will translate to equivalent performance on future data sets.

The second conclusion that errors are due to noise also may be unacceptable. The fact that a few attempts of parametric forms could not generate an accurate model is not a strong indication that no accurate model exists. It may be the chosen parametric forms just did not capture key characteristics of the relationships reflected by the data.

Nonparametric Methods

Nonparametric modeling operates in a way similar to the approach of iterating through parametric forms. However, the two deficiencies examined are largely overcome. First, nonparametric methods iterate through parametric forms in a more systematic way, allowing arbitrarily complex relationships to be modeled as long as they are reflected by the data. Second, good heuristics exist for selecting the model that generalizes best. In the next section, we discuss these methods in greater detail.

2.6   NONPARAMETRIC MODELS

When presented with a data set, but little information about the underlying relationships in an estimation problem, assuming a particular parametric form can be overly restrictive. Examples, such as Figure 2-7, suggest it should be possible to infer relationships from a data set without assuming a particular parametric form. This possibility allows the potential discovery of relationships not preconceived by human knowledge. Nonparametric modeling techniques are systematic, computational methods for producing models in this context. They are especially applicable when human visualization capabilities break down in estimation problems involving multiple dimensions and complex relationships.

2.6.1   The Underlying Modeling Problem

Ill-Posed Problem

Like all other modeling approaches, the goal of nonparametric modeling is to produce a model that generalizes well on future observations. Unlike other modeling approaches, however, a nonparametric model is based on a data set with little or no prior understanding of relationships involved. Unfortunately, the problem of generating a mapping that fits a data set without knowledge of an appropriate parametric form is ill-posed. Consider the example illustrated in Figure 2-8. The x's denote example patterns, and all three mappings shown fit the data set almost perfectly.

Figure 2-8 Three Models Fitting a Single Data Set

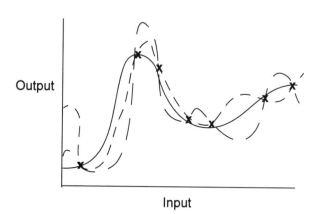

**Infinite
Number of
Mappings**

In general, there are an infinite number of models that fit a finite set of data points. These mappings can differ arbitrarily in any part of the input space not represented by the data set (i.e., where there is no data). Increasing the number of data points often helps in narrowing down the range of candidate models, but there will always be an infinite number of models that fit the data equally well.

2.6.2 Heuristics in Nonparametric Modeling

Heuristics

Since the problem of generating a mapping that fits a finite data set is ill-posed, we must resort to heuristics (i.e., intuitive ideas) for choosing one of the infinite number of candidate models that perform equally well on the data set. The hope is the heuristics will lead to models that will generalize well for most problems. Common nonparametric methods employ a particular set of heuristics for generating models in this context, and their success in numerous applications provides strong empirical evidence for their effectiveness.

Nonparametric methods provide a systematic approach for iterating through parametric forms to arrive at one that generalizes well. Heuristics are used to choose the parametric forms to try in the iterative process, as well as to select the best of those tried.

In the process of developing a nonparametric model, a large number of parametric forms may be tried. For best results, the parametric forms generated should vary in terms of *smoothness* and *complexity*—two heuristic concepts we will discuss in this section.

Smoothness

Smoothness is loosely defined as a measure of how much the output of a mapping changes due to small changes in the input. In general, smoother mappings exhibit smaller changes in their output values in response to a particular change in input values.

Complexity

The complexity of a parametric form can be thought of as a rough measure of the number of different models that can be produced by setting its parameters to different values. For example, the quadratic form

$$F(X|\theta) = \theta_0 + \theta_1 x + \theta_2 x^2 \qquad \textbf{(EQ 3)}$$

is more complex than the linear form

$$F(X|\theta) = \theta_0 + \theta_1 x \qquad \textbf{(EQ 4)}$$

This is because any linear mapping can be generated by the quadratic form by setting θ_2 to zero, whereas many mappings that can be generated by the quadratic form are not linear.

Out-of-Sample Error

In the iterative process of nonparametric modeling, parametric forms are generated, one by one, and then fitted to data. A critical step in nonparametric modeling involves choosing the parametric form expected to generalize best. The most common heuristic used for this involves estimating out-of-sample error—that is, the expected error of a model on data outside of the data used to generate the model. Once out-of-sample error is estimated for each of the parametric forms, the one with lowest error is chosen as the final nonparametric model.

To illustrate how out-of-sample error is estimated and used, consider the example illustrated in Figure 2-9. The available data is randomly divided into two separate sets, referred to as the *training set* and the *test set*. In the figure, these sets are denoted by x's and o's, respectively. Two parametric forms are fitted to the data in the training set, and then the out-of-sample error for each is estimated by computing error on the test set. The model denoted by the solid line clearly yields lower out-of-sample error. By applying the heuristic of choosing the model with the lowest out-of-sample error, we would conclude this model is better.

Figure 2-9   Estimating Out-of-Sample-Error

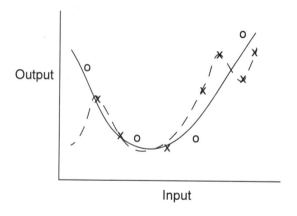

Minimal Complexity

It is not unusual to find the out-of-sample error of many parametric forms to be comparable. In this event, a heuristic that works well in practice is to choose the least complex of the parametric forms.

Maximal Smoothness

An additional heuristic used when competing parametric forms generate comparable out-of-sample error advocates selecting the smoothest model. This follows from the observation that many natural phenomenon exhibit smooth behaviors—that is, a small change in one variable tends to induce only small effects on other variables.

2.6.3 Approximation Architectures

The process of nonparametric modeling requires the generation of a large set of parametric forms from which one will be chosen. In order to ensure at least some of these will be capable of capturing relevant relationships, it is important to choose parametric forms of varying complexity and smoothness. An *approximation architecture* is a way to generate a class of parametric forms. There are many different approximation architectures used in practice, and the trade-offs among different choices is a central issue of current research in the fields of neural networks, statistics, and approximation theory.

Polynomials of Increasing Complexity

To clarify our abstract definition of approximation architectures, let's consider one simple example—polynomials. For simplicity, we choose a problem with one-dimensional input and one dimensional output. Then the set of parametric forms generated by the polynomial architecture are as follows:

$$F(X|\theta) = \theta_0$$

$$F(X|\theta) = \theta_0 + \theta_1 x$$

$$F(X|\theta) = \theta_0 + \theta_1 x + \theta_2 x^2 \qquad \text{(EQ 5)}$$

$$F(X|\theta) = \theta_0 + \theta_1 x + \theta_2 x^2 + \theta_3 x^3$$

$$\dots$$

The first polynomial, with degree zero, generates a mapping that associates a single value with all inputs. The first degree polynomial is exactly the same as a linear regression model. The second degree polynomial generates mappings that are quadratic in shape. Figure 2-10 shows mappings that could be generated by these first three polynomials to fit a set of example patterns. Complexity increases with the polynomial degree, while the smoothness of mappings generated tends to decrease with degree.

Arbitrary mappings can be approximated to any level of accuracy given a polynomial of sufficient degree.[1]

Figure 2-10   Polynomial Mappings of Different Degrees

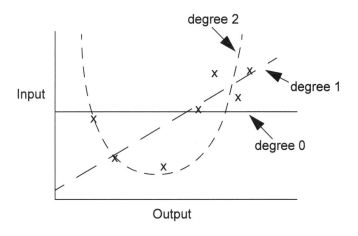

Multi-Dimensional Spaces

Though we have only examined the case with single-dimensional input and output spaces, the polynomial models discussed can be generalized to multi-dimensional spaces. Polynomials thus seem to provide a useful architecture for nonparametric modeling. However, due to certain

---

1. Formally, the approximation error can be made arbitrarily small only under certain conditions (which for practical purposes are satisfied by all problems that are not degenerate). For example, if the underlying function is square (Lebesgue) integrable over a bounded subset of the input space, then arbitrarily good approximations can be made in the sense of mean-squared error over that subset.

complications when dealing with multi-dimensional estimation problems, polynomials are not generally the architecture of choice.[2]

Popular Architectures

There are a number of popular architectures that have demonstrated practical success. These include the K nearest neighbor methods, group method of data handling (GMDH), projection pursuit mappings, multivariate adaptive regression splines (MARS), and architectures associated with the field of neural networks, such as the backpropagation networks (i.e., multilayer perceptrons), radial basis functions, and wavelet networks. All of these architectures are general in the sense that arbitrary mappings can be approximated to any level of accuracy given appropriate degrees of smoothness and complexity.[3]

Choosing an Architecture

Choosing the right architecture for a particular problem relies on an element of art. For many problems, particular architectures may vastly outperform others. The best approach is to experiment with several architectures to select the best one for the problem at hand. This can be done by using multiple architectures to generate the parametric forms used in the iterative modeling process. Data from the test set can be used to estimate out-of-sample error across parametric forms generated by all the architectures being considered.

Practical Characteristics

In addition to trade-offs in the accuracy of models generated by the different architectures, there are many practical characteristics that deserve attention. Among these are differences in the computation time and memory required to generate models, the reliability of training algorithms, and the computation time and memory required to use the models once they are

---

2. There are two problems with polynomial architectures. The first is, empirically, the mappings generated do not generalize well, especially when there are many input variables. A second problem arises when input spaces are multi-dimensional. The number of terms, and thus the number of coefficients, increases exponentially with the number of input variables. Hence, as the number of input variables increases, the number of parameters for polynomials, even of fairly low degree, make them computationally unmanageable. The group method of data handling (GMDH) is a more practical architecture that takes on a polynomial form, but limits the number of terms through use of heuristic rules. This keeps the number of parameters manageable.

3. The mathematical formalities required for this to be true in the case of polynomials also are required here.

Solving Data Mining Problems through Pattern Recognition

ready for deployment. For many applications, the accuracy of models produced by different architectures may be comparable, while there may be vast differences in practical characteristics. In this event, the practical characteristics should dictate the choice of architecture.

2.6.4 A Practical Nonparametric Approach

To place the elements of nonparametric modeling in perspective, this section describes a basic approach. Note, however, we do not include a discussion of preprocessing as part of the approach, although it is often a crucial step in the development of a nonparametric model. This is because the nature of preprocessing is largely problem-specific, while this section concentrates on the problem-independent aspects of nonparametric modeling. We reserve a discussion of preprocessing for the next section.

Basic Approach

Given a set of data, the basic approach to applying nonparametric modeling is as follows:

1. Reserve a portion of available data as an evaluation set to measure final performance.

2. Divide the remaining data set into training and test sets.

3. Generate multiple models with varying degrees of complexity and smoothness using different approximation architectures and tuning parameters to fit the training set.

4. Find the models that perform best on the test set.

5. Of the best performers, choose the model with lowest complexity and/or greatest smoothness.

6. Assess performance of the final model using the evaluation set and then STOP!

Reserving an Evaluation Set

The first step of the approach consists of reserving a portion of the data available for final evaluation. This data set is often called the *evaluation set*. It will be used to generate an unbiased assessment of the final model prior to deployment. A sufficient amount of data should be reserved in the evaluation set for the assessment to be statistically sound; however, the majority of available data should be reserved for model development.

Assigning a portion of data to an evaluation set is unnecessary if there is no need for an immediate accurate assessment of model performance. In particular, if more data will be available prior to model deployment, the new data can be used as an evaluation set. Avoiding the use of available data for an evaluation set is especially important when the amount of data available is prohibitively small. For a further discussion of evaluation sets, see Section 11.1, "Train, Test, and Evaluation Sets."

Dividing Data into Training and Test Sets

The second step of the approach consists of dividing the set of available example patterns into two subsets—a training set and a test set.[4] There are no specific proportions by which the data set must be divided, but the training set generally contains a majority of the data (e.g., 70% for training, 30% for testing). The data in the two sets should be randomly sampled from the original set so neither set is expected to be biased.

Generating Multiple Models

Next, parametric forms are iteratively generated, fitted to the training set data, and assessed using the test set data. The models generated should differ in the degree of complexity and smoothness. In addition, since some architectures may be more appropriate than others for any particular problem, models from different architectures should be generated. It also is helpful if some baseline models (i.e., existing approach to the problem or simple linear models) can be generated for benchmarking.

---

4. We employ this approach of dividing the data set here since it is widely used and it simplifies our discussion. However, when it is critical to maximize the amount of information drawn from a data set, cross-validation methods, discussed in Chapter 11, can lead to much better results than this simple scheme.

Solving Data Mining Problems through Pattern Recognition

Effects of Complexity and Smoothness

It is interesting to note the importance of varying complexity and smoothness. For a given architecture, the error of the models on the training set generally decreases as their complexity increases. The error on the test set, on the other hand, only diminishes to a certain point after which error plateaus or increases with complexity. Figure 2-11 illustrates this phenomenon.

Figure 2-11   Model Complexity vs. Training and Test Error

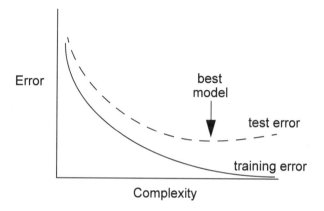

A simple example illustrates the cause underlying this behavior. Consider the example patterns for a single-input-single-output estimation problem illustrated in Figure 2-12. The x's denote the example patterns in the training set and the o's denote those in the test set. The mappings associated with three models (numbered in order of increasing complexity) are depicted. The parameters of all three models have been tuned to fit the training data. Clearly the performance of model #2 on the test data is best. Model #1 is not complex enough to capture relevant relationships, while model #3 is too complex and generalizes poorly.

Figure 2-12   Models of Varying Complexity

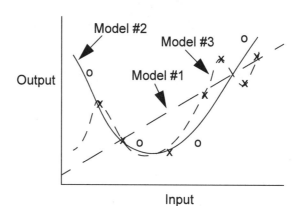

Smoothness provides an additional dimension along which different models should be generated. By enforcing greater degrees of smoothness, models can often generalize better since the effects of noise are filtered out. However, opting for too much smoothness can cause inaccurate modeling of relationships that are not smooth.

Selecting the Best Model

The model that performs best on the test set should be selected from all those produced in the iterative process. However, there are often multiple models that perform almost equally well on the test set. In fact, performance differences may be statistically insignificant (i.e., if we generate another test set, the relative ordering of these models may be changed). In this event, we can apply our heuristics to select a model with the least complexity and/or the smoothest mapping.

Assessing the Final Model

Performance of the chosen model can be assessed by computing error on the evaluation set. It is crucial that the model's performance is assessed using an evaluation set independent of the training or test sets, because the training and test sets are used in the process of model development. In general, errors on the training and test sets will be smaller than those on an independent evaluation set.

Computation of error on the evaluation set should be performed only after all modeling has ceased. Any additional improvement to the model (or selection of alternative models) will implicitly use information given by the evaluation set. If this rule is violated, the error of a new model on the evaluation set will be biased, just as are errors on the training and test sets.

☞ **NOTE:** We cannot stress the importance of this point enough! *The evaluation of a model's performance must be completely independent of and come after the model development process!* Numerous practitioners, perpetuated by badly designed processes and flawed commercial software products, are guilty of incorporating the results from the evaluation set into their modeling process.

Note, however, that we do not advocate stopping all improvements to solving a problem. It is simply that the evaluation set should not be reused to assess model performance. When new data is available, the evaluation set can be incorporated into training and test set data, while the new data can serve as a new evaluation set.

2.6.5   The Role of Preprocessing

Preprocessing aims at simplifying the relationships to be inferred by a model. Though nonparametric methods can infer arbitrary relationships from data, as the relationships become more complicated, more data and computational time are required. Because of this, preprocessing is crucial when the quantity of available data is a limiting factor.

Though preprocessing plays an extremely important role with nonparametric methods, there is not much conclusive general advice. The development of an effective preprocessing scheme usually exploits a combination of problem-specific knowledge and iterative experimentation. The process can consume considerable time and effort, often up to

ten times that required to produce nonparametric models once a preprocessor has been developed. Furthermore, the quality of preprocessing
often produces a huge difference in the accuracy of the ultimate solution.

Reducing the Size of the Input Space

One commonly used type of preprocessing aims at reducing the number of
input variables (i.e., reducing the size of the input space). The premise is
that nonparametric methods typically make better generalizations from a
fixed-sized data set if the dimensionality is lowered while maintaining the
most significant relationships reflected by data. This aspect of preprocessing is illustrated by the example of reducing economic data to a set of key
macroeconomic indicators, as discussed in Chapter 1. In addition to
approaches using problem-specific knowledge, there are several generic
preprocessing algorithms that attempt to reduce dimensionality without
losing significant information. These include principal component analysis (PCA) and clustering techniques, among others.

Smoother Relationships

A second type of preprocessing involves transforming a problem so that
the relationships of the resulting problem are simpler, usually in the sense
that the associated mappings become smoother. These transformations are
usually generated using intuition about the problem. An example of this
type of transformation used when analyzing audio signals, involves transforming time-waveforms into frequency representations (i.e., taking a
Fourier transform). Though both representations of an audio signal carry
the same information, the frequency representation often leads to simpler
relationships with desired estimates.

Normalization

For many practical problems, the artificial units used to measure each of
the input variables can skew the data, making the range of values along
some axes much larger than others. This causes relationships to be unnec-
essarily complex by making the nature of the mapping along some dimensions much different from others. This difficulty can be circumvented by
normalizing each of the input variables so the variance of the each variable, as reflected be the data, is equal.

Developing Good Preprocessors

The development of a preprocessor combines the intuitive notions we have
described with problem-specific knowledge and generic dimensionality-
reduction techniques. Figuring out exactly how intuitive notions should be
mathematically formulated and how the elements of preprocessing should

be combined is an art. Practitioners often experiment with different forms of preprocessing in order to arrive at one that works well. Some successful rules of thumb are described in Chapter 9.

2.7 STATISTICAL CONSIDERATIONS

Representative Data

In our discussion of estimation, we assume that example patterns in our data set are representative of those we will encounter when deploying the model. This requires that the input-output relationships satisfy some statistical properties. Since these properties are prerequisite to modeling, it is worthwhile to clarify what they are and to raise awareness of certain difficulties that may arise when they are not satisfied.

Time Invariance

The statistical framework guiding our discussion has implicitly assumed relevant probability distributions are time-invariant. In particular, the distribution of inputs can take on any probability distribution, but example inputs, including those in the initial data set as well as those to be observed in the future, must be drawn from the same probability distribution.

An additional assumption concerns the time-invariance of output distributions. We have implicitly assumed that, for any particular point in the input space, the outputs associated with that point are sampled independently from a time-invariant distribution over the output space.

Practical Considerations

These statistical assumptions generally are not perfectly satisfied by pattern recognition problems arising in practice. However, they are almost satisfied such that solutions relying on these assumptions can be extremely useful. For instance, an estimation model used for weather forecasting may become obsolete over the years as the environment permanently changes due to ozone depletion and global warming. However, a model that works well today will still be expected to work well for many years. On the other hand, more care is needed in the case of modeling behaviors in the stock market, where properties change much more rapidly. In such an event, only very recently observed data should be employed in model development.

Chapter 3

Key Concepts: Classification

Classification is similar to estimation in that a label is assigned to an observation. However, in classification, the labels do not take on continuous numerical values as they do in estimation. Instead, there are only a finite set of admissible labels, typically with no logical sequential ordering.

Types of Models

Estimation models are virtually always defined in terms of a mapping. In classification, on the other hand, there are three general approaches to defining models:

- Decision-region boundaries
- Probability density functions
- Posterior probabilities

Fixed, parametric, or nonparametric modeling techniques may be employed in producing any of these three types of models.

In this chapter, we discuss the three types of models and the use of fixed, parametric, and nonparametric modeling techniques for generating each of the three types of models. However, we go into less detail in discussing fixed, parametric, and nonparametric modeling, since most of the ideas here are analogous to the case of estimation.

3.1   TERMINOLOGY AND NOTATION

Inputs and Outputs

Like estimation, the input space for a classification problem is typically infinite and consists of all n-dimensional vectors with numerical components. The output space, however, consists of a finite set of possible classes. One example of a classification problem is handwritten-character recognition. For this problem, each input variable (or independent variable) might be the intensity of a pixel on an image, measured in terms of a gray scale. The output (or dependent variable) would be the character of the alphabet to which the bit-map corresponds.

Classifiers

A classification model, or *classifier*, can be viewed as a functional block, as in Figure 3-1. A classifier assigns one class to each point of the input space. The input space is thus partitioned into disjoint subsets, called *decision regions*, each associated with a class.

Figure 3-1   Functional Box View of a Classification Model

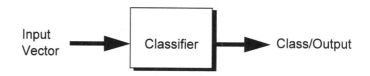

The way a classifier classifies inputs is defined by its decision regions. Figure 3-2 illustrates decision regions for a classifier with two input variables and two output classes, class A and class B. Typical example patterns of class A are denoted by x's, while those of class B are denoted by o's. The two decision regions are distinguished by shading. In practice, however, the example patterns of different classes are rarely so neatly distinguishable. Due to uncertainty, areas of the input space can be clouded by a mixture of example patterns of different classes. In the case of handwritten character recognition, this portion of the input space may correspond to characters that are not clearly written and thus cannot be classified with certainty.

Figure 3-2   Decision Regions for Two-Input Two-Class Problem

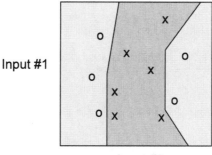

Input #2

3.2   CHARACTERISTICS OF AN OPTIMAL CLASSIFIER

The optimal classifier is the one expected to produce the least number of misclassifications (i.e., classification of an input as an incorrect class). When there is no uncertainty involved in a classification problem, any two example patterns with identical input vectors are associated with the same class. Because of this, it is possible to define decision regions such that there are never any misclassifications. These decision regions define an optimal model.

Error Due to Uncertainty

When there is uncertainty, as is the norm in practical classification problems, the situation becomes more complicated. In this case, any model is expected to misclassify at least some of the time. This is because multiple example patterns can have the same input vector and yet be associated with different classes. The optimal model, in this case, minimizes the expected number of future misclassifications. This classifier would associate an input with its most probable class.

**Optimal
Models Err**

Just as large errors do not necessarily reflect a deficiency in an estimation model, large misclassification rates do not mean a classifier is not optimal. Figure 3-3 illustrates optimal decision regions for a simple problem where classification takes place under uncertainty. The x's and o's denote typical example inputs from each of the two classes. The errors are due to uncertainty in the problem, rather than a deficiency in the decision regions. Like in estimation, the errors caused by such uncertainty are referred to as noise.

Figure 3-3   Optimal Decision Regions with Misclassifications

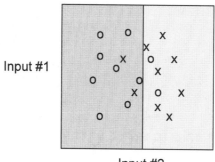

Input #2

3.3   Types of Models

There are three different, but related approaches to defining models widely used for classification. The first approach involves specifying boundaries for decision regions. The second approach involves modeling probability distributions for inputs of each class and then using these distributions to derive the probability that an input belongs to any particular class. The third and final approach develops estimation models that output the class probabilities associated with an input. Any one of these types of models can be generated using fixed, parametric, or nonparametric modeling techniques.

Solving Data Mining Problems through Pattern Recognition

3.3.1 Decision-Region Boundaries

The simplest type of model defines decision regions by explicitly constructing boundaries in the input space. These models attempt to minimize the number of expected misclassifications by placing boundaries appropriately in the input space. The examples we have discussed so far—including those illustrated in Figure 3-2 and Figure 3-3—have characterized models in terms of decision-region boundaries.

3.3.2 Probability Density Functions

The distribution of example patterns associated with any single class can be modeled by a probability density function (PDF). The PDF is a mapping from the input space to probability density values reflecting the statistical distribution of points in the input space. The PDF for a class C evaluated at a point x in the input space is denoted by $p(x|C)$. Figure 3-4 depicts typical example patterns (denoted by x's) associated with one class of a single-input classification problem and the associated PDF.

Figure 3-4   Example Probability Density Function

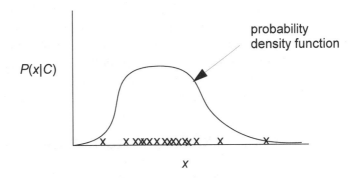

Prior Probabilities

PDFs are not sufficient to generate a classification model. Quantities called prior probabilities (also known as *a priori* probabilities) must be used in tandem. The prior probability for a class C, denoted by $P(C)$, is the probability a random example pattern will belong to the class. In other words, the prior probability represents the probability that should be assigned to a class before observing the input vector of an example pattern. Given a large database, the fraction of examples of class C should be approximately $P(C)$.

Given PDFs and prior probabilities for each class, an optimal classification model can be produced. This model assigns the most probable class to an input vector x by selecting the class maximizing $P(C)p(x|C)$. The optimality of this procedure follows from Bayes' rule and, intuitively, is due to the fact that the probability an input x is of class C is proportional to the probability an arbitrary input is of class C, as well as the probability an example of class C would have an input vector x.

Developing PDFs

There are several widely used parametric and nonparametric methods for modeling PDFs. These methods translate directly into methods for developing models for classification. Once models of PDFs for each class are generated, prior probabilities can be approximated using a database, and a pattern classification model can be produced as described above.

Note, however, this method does not directly minimize the number of misclassifications on a data set. Instead, the method aims at approximating PDFs and prior probabilities. Though error-free models of PDF and prior probabilities lead to optimal classification, the relationship between errors in these models and misclassification rates is not perfectly clear. Nevertheless, models of this type have been successful in practice.

3.3.3 Posterior Probabilities

To minimize the expected number of misclassifications, each observation should be assigned to the most probable class. The probability that an input x belongs to class C, denoted by $P(C|x)$, is called the posterior probability (also known as *a posteriori* probability). Given an input vector, if we could compute the posterior probability for each class, we would classify the input as the class with the highest value.

Estimating Posterior Probabilities

For any class C, there is a posterior probability $P(C|x)$ associated with each possible input vector x. If the classification problem has m possible classes, denoted $C_1, ..., C_m$, we can think of the posterior probabilities associated with an input vector x as a vector with components $P(C_1|x), ..., P(C_m|x)$. The generation of this probabilities vector based on an input vector can be thought of as an estimation problem, as illustrated in Figure 3-5.

Figure 3-5   Estimation Model of Posterior Probabilities

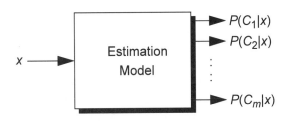

Using Posterior Probabilities for Classification

Since the outputs of this estimation problem are probabilities, they should have values between zero and one, and they should sum to one. Since classification can be performed by identifying each input as the class associated with the maximal output of the estimation model, solving this estimation problem poses a third approach to producing a classifier.

Example Patterns

It may at first seem impossible to produce parametric and nonparametric estimation models that output posterior probabilities, since we do not have appropriate example patterns. In particular, it seems as though we would need example patterns consisting of input vectors and vectors of posterior probabilities. However, the example patterns normally obtained for classification problems, which consist of input vectors and classes, are sufficient.

Transforming Classes to Output Vectors

Examples patterns for a classification problem can be transformed into example patterns for constructing an estimation model for posterior probabilities. Each transformed example problem consists of the original input vector and an output vector with one variable for each output class. An output variable has the value one if the example pattern belongs to that class. All other output variables are set to zero (see Figure 3-6).

Figure 3-6 Output Representation for an Estimation Model

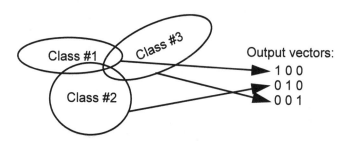

Though the components of this vector are not actual posterior probabilities, the mathematical expectation of an output vector associated with a particular input *does* have components equal to posterior probabilities. Therefore, the estimation model expected to perform best on example patterns not in the training set will output posterior probabilities. Once the example patterns from the classification problem have been transformed as discussed, any estimation modeling method can be used to produce a classification model.

Relationship of Posterior Probability Estimation to Classification

It is important to note that, just as in the PDF approach to classification, models estimating posterior probabilities do not explicitly minimize the number of misclassifications on a training set. Instead, this approach attempts to model the posterior probabilities as accurately as possible. Though perfect modeling of posterior probabilities leads to optimal classification, the relationship between errors in posterior probability estimation and misclassifications is not always clear. Nevertheless, this approach to generating classification models has been immensely successful in practice.

Summary of Classification Model Types

Before departing from the topic of classification models, we summarize the three types of models discussed. Decision-region boundary models partition the input space into regions associated with different classes and aim directly at minimizing the expected number of misclassifications. Class PDF models aim at characterizing the distribution of inputs associated with each class. Posterior probability models estimate the probability each point in the input space corresponds to each class. Figure 3-7 illustrates the three types of classification models for comparison.

Figure 3-7   Comparison of Three Classification Model Types

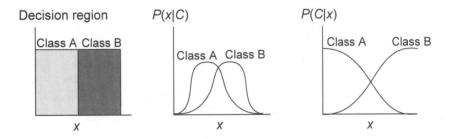

3.4   APPROACHES TO MODELING

Fixed, parametric, or nonparametric approaches can be used to produce models of any one of the three types discussed in the previous section. The ways in which each of these developmental approaches work are analogous to those in the case of estimation. In this section, we briefly describe each of these approaches and mention some popular methods in this context.

3.4.1   Fixed Models

If enough is understood about a classification problem, a fixed model can be produced. Fixed models can be defined in terms of decision-region boundaries, densities, or posterior probabilities, depending on how a developer understands the problem.

Decision-Region Boundaries

If intuition leads to an understanding of what ranges of input values correspond to particular classes, then decision-region boundaries can be derived. For instance, if we wanted to classify cookies as "overbaked" or "underbaked," we might take as input the darkness, and if the value is above a certain threshold, we would classify the cookie as "overbaked." By specifying a threshold we are producing a decision-region boundary for this problem.

Densities

If there seems to be an independent source for examples of each class, characterizing each class's PDF independently may be more natural than constructing decision-region boundaries. For example, if we wanted to classify kinds of fish based on their length from head to tail, a model based on PDFs may be most appropriate. This is because we might have an idea of how the lengths of any particular kind of fish are distributed. We could then formulate the PDF for each distribution independently and then combine them to produce a classifier. This process implicitly draws decision-region boundaries, but may be an easier approach than directly selecting boundaries.

Posterior Probabilities

In some classification problems, it may be difficult to construct appropriate decision-region boundaries or densities, while it is still possible to assess the probability that any particular observation belongs to each class. This is particularly true when there are many features of an observation, each of which increase or decrease the chance that it corresponds to a class. In this event, defining a classifier in terms of posterior probabilities may be most appropriate.

3.4.2 Parametric Models

Parametric modeling for classification is analogous to its counterpart in estimation. The development process consists of two stages. The first is to derive an appropriate parametric form. This parametric form can be defined in terms of decision-region boundaries, densities, or posterior probabilities. As in fixed modeling, choices between these three types of models should be based on what is most natural given the available information. Once a parametric form is chosen, the parameters are tuned to fit data.

Decision-Region Boundaries

One example of a parametric form is the linear discriminant function, which produces boundaries partitioning the input space into two half-spaces. The boundary is in the form of a hyper-plane, and parameter values specify the position and orientation. Algorithms for tuning parameters of such a parametric form focus on finding a set of values that minimizes the number of misclassifications. Many other types of hand-tailored parametric forms for boundaries can be used in a similar fashion.

Densities

Any parametric form for PDFs can be used to generate classifiers. One common parametric technique employs multivariate Gaussian as a parametric form. Parameters are typically selected using the method of moments. The laws of large numbers make this technique theoretically appealing. However, it often generates poor results for realistic classification problems, especially when there are multiple input variables.

Posterior Probabilities

Logistic regression is a parametric technique commonly used in statistics. This is effectively an estimation method, similar to linear regression, that uses a sigmoid instead of a linear parametric form. The reason for this is the sigmoid is more natural for estimating probabilities since it takes on values between zero and one and smoothly transitions between the two extremes. Other parametric forms appropriate for estimating probabilities also are used for classification.

3.4.3 Nonparametric Models

Nonparametric techniques are used to solve classification problems for which relationships between input vectors and classes are not well understood. These methods operate in a manner similar to their counterparts in estimation. Models of varying smoothness and complexity are generated, and the one that generalizes best is chosen using out-of-sample testing and other heuristics.

Smoothness in Classification

One difference from estimation that is worth noting is the way in which smoothness is defined. In estimation, smoothness characterizes the behavior of a mapping. In classification, the meaning of smoothness varies among different types of models. When dealing with decision-region boundaries, smoothness refers to the fact that the boundaries themselves are smooth as well as the fact that there are few decision regions. In the case of PDFs, smoothness refers to the nature of the mapping defining the PDF. In probability estimation, smoothness carries the same meaning as in estimation.

Nonparametric Methods

Each approximation architecture used for classification generates parametric forms of a particular type—boundaries, PDFs, or posterior probabilities. In fixed and parametric modeling, an understanding of the underlying problem serves as a guide for choosing an appropriate type of model. When underlying relationships are not understood, however, it is not clear which type of model should be used. Therefore, in the nonparametric modeling process, it is common to use multiple architectures and generate parametric forms of all three types.

There are many approximation architectures that are commonly used for classification. Architectures for constructing decision-region boundaries include learning vector quantization (LVQ), K nearest neighbor classifiers, and decision trees. Architectures for modeling PDFs include Gaussian mixture methods and Parzen's windows. Any estimation architecture can be used for modeling posterior probabilities. Some of the most commonly used include multilayered perceptron (backpropagation neural network), radial basis functions, and the group method of data handling (GMDH).

3.4.4   The Role of Preprocessing

The situation with preprocessing for classification problems is very similar to that for estimation problems. In estimation, preprocessing is geared towards reducing dimensionality of the input space, transforming the problem into one with a smoother mapping, and properly scaling input variables. The tasks of reducing dimensionality and scaling input variables in classification problems is essentially the same—to provide inputs that differentiate the classes. The only difference is in the concept of smoothness when it comes to how preprocessing should transform problems.

3.4.5 The Importance of Multiple Techniques

**Why Use
Multiple
Techniques?**

Many techniques or algorithms are available for solving any particular pattern recognition problem, be it classification or estimation. Some techniques will always work better on *some* problems, but it is often impossible to know in advance with great certainty, which technique or algorithm is best for a particular problem.

One way of addressing the problem is to try different approaches on the same problem or data set and see which one performs the best. Because building a more accurate model is typically of paramount importance, the cost of additional compute time generally pales in comparison to the benefit of a better model (assuming, of course, that you have access to tools that can test modeling across different algorithms easily). Since compute power is abundant and inexpensive, it is to your advantage to try multiple techniques. Using multiple techniques and comparing their results always gives you more flexibility to consider other trade-offs in selecting the ultimate model. For example, you can consider:

- Practical constraints (memory usage, performance, etc.)
- Algorithm complexity
- Ease of understanding of model results

**Biases and
Assumptions**

As introduced in Section 1.7.5, "A Continuum of Methods," there is a continuous spectrum of algorithms spanning the space between knowledge and data. Some algorithms use more knowledge about a problem to derive a solution with little or no data. Some algorithms require very little knowledge about the problem and deduce an answer based purely on data examples.

Many fields have biases towards particular approaches in this spectrum, mainly for historical reasons. For example, in database marketing, statisticians favor logistic regression. This bias has evolved because of two primary reasons. First, logistic regression has been widely available in practical software tools for some time. Second, logistic regression models have been easier to understand than Nonparametric algorithms (e.g., neural networks). For example, the coefficients of the logistic regression model inherently provide information on the odds ratio relative to each input variable.[1] The problem with the widespread use of logistic regression is that the underlying assumptions of the algorithm are usually violated in practice. For example, logistic regression is designed to deal only with binary inputs and outputs, where the inputs are all statistically independent (rarely the case in real-world, database marketing problems).

The traditional method of understanding a model (like logistic regression) and forcing it on the data is not the only viable approach to modeling. Instead of forcing data onto a potentially unsuitable model or trying to develop a model that fits the world perfectly, it is more practical to view models as simply a stable mapping of inputs to outputs that can generalize well to new data. Then the primary objective is to develop robust models with high predictive accuracy. Of secondary importance is the ability to understand the model relationships (e.g., as interpreted by an odds ratio in logistic regression). The burden of model validity is then critically placed on the model's ability to generalize well and not on the modeler's understanding of the model.

Understanding Modeling Results

To gain the same confidence in models, the following method can be used to examine the relationships learned by the model.

Analyze the relationship between the output variable and an input variable (e.g., in response modeling, look at response rate versus an input variable, AGE). This type of analysis cam be quite revealing in that it shows the actual relationships mapped between the input and output. By looking at this relationship, the user can validate the model against common sense and an understanding of the business. Also note that this approach can be used to validate models across all modeling algorithms.

To reiterate: *Use multiple algorithms without bias and let your specific data help determine which model is best suited for your problem.*

---

1. The log of the coefficient gives the odds ratio. However, many more assumptions are required before this information is completely valid. Namely, all independent variables must be statistically independent and in binary form, etc.

3.5 STATISTICAL CONSIDERATIONS

Just as with estimation, we have implicitly assumed that some statistical properties are satisfied by the classification problems we address. Since these properties are prerequisite to any modeling problem, it is worthwhile to clarify what they are and to raise an awareness of certain difficulties that may arise when they are not satisfied.

Time Invariance

The statistical framework guiding our discussion has implicitly assumed that relevant probability distributions are time-invariant. In particular, the distribution of inputs can take on any probability distribution, but example inputs, including those in the initial data set as well as those to be observed in the future, must be drawn from the same probability distribution.

An additional assumption concerns the time-invariance of posterior probabilities. For any particular point in the input space, the class associated with that point should be drawn according to a set of posterior probabilities that do not vary over time.

Practical Considerations

These statistical assumptions generally are not perfectly satisfied by classification problems that arise in practice. However, they are almost satisfied so that solutions that rely on these assumptions can be extremely useful. An example is response modeling in database marketing, where the underlying input distributions and posterior probabilities (i.e., response rate) may change over time due to global economic changes, changes in competition, or changes in how a company is perceived by customers. However, basic purchase patterns and underlying purchase behaviors are expected to remain relatively constant, such that purchase data from an advertising campaign run three months ago should be useful in constructing a response model for this quarter's campaign. On the other hand, more care is needed for classifying behaviors in the stock market (e.g., buy/sell), where properties change much more rapidly. In this event, only very recently observed data should be employed in model development.

Chapter 4

Additional Application Areas

There are many different names given to problems that are actually special cases of classification and estimation. Because these terms can be confusing and their relationship to classification or estimation may not be obvious, this chapter discusses these relationships. The problems discussed in this chapter include:

- ❑ Database marketing
- ❑ Time-series prediction
- ❑ Detection
- ❑ Probability estimation
- ❑ Information compression
- ❑ Sensitivity analysis

Since these problems are special cases of classification or estimation, the methods described later in this book naturally lend themselves to these additional application areas.

4.1 DATABASE MARKETING

Database marketing is a field where pattern recognition technologies have been tremendously successful. Two example areas, response modeling and cross-selling, are discussed in this section.

4.1.1 Response Modeling

What Is Response Modeling?

The basic idea behind response modeling is to improve customer response rates by targeting prospects that are predicted as most likely to respond to a particular advertisement or promotion. Instead of mailing to or calling (in the case of telemarketing) every prospect on a list or in a database, you select only the ones with a high probability of responding positively. This is achieved by building a model to predict the likelihood that an individual will respond based on demographic, life-style, psychotropic data, as well as previous purchasing behavior. The process of applying a model to a database or list is called *scoring*.

Benefits

The benefits of response modeling are widely recognized as the following:

- Improved return on investment (ROI[1]) for marketing dollars
- Improved inventory control and supply-side management
- Improved customer relationships and retention

By "scoring" potential consumers in a list using a model and then mailing only to those that are likely to respond, you can either:

---

1. Return on investment (ROI) is a widely used measurement of investment effectiveness. It is typically computed as a ratio of generated profit (return) over the cost of program implementation (investment). A value of one represents a break-even campaign. Values greater than one represent profitable campaigns and values less than one mean losses were incurred.

- Save on communication (mailing, printing costs, telephone calls, etc.), or

- Spend the same amount of marketing dollars, but generate more leads/business.

In addition, by targeting your communications more effectively to prospects and existing clients, you improve and strengthen customer relationships. The customer can perceives more value in your communications (i.e., they receive information only on products/services of interest to them).

Lift Chart

A *lift chart* is often used to visualize and measure response modeling performance. The x-axis represents the percentage of prospects (say in a mailing list) to whom you might send product literature. The y-axis indicates the percentage (relative to all potential responses) of responses achieved.

For example, if a mailing list of 100,000 prospects generated a 2% response, there were 2,000 responses. If we randomly selected names from this list, we would expect two responses for every 100 prospects contacted (represented by the diagonal line in the lift chart in Figure 4-1).

Figure 4-1 Example Lift Chart

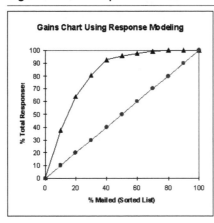

Lift Curves

By using a model to score prospects (i.e., assigning a numeric value to each prospect), we can sort them by their predicted likelihood of responding. We can then concentrate our advertising campaign on the top prospects and avoid the bottom prospects. By plotting the number of respondents versus the number of prospects contacted, we can generate a "lift curve" like the one in Figure 4-1.

If the model performed perfectly, it would identify the exact 2,000 people to target. However, since the input data representing the prospects is typically limited (and not exact) and human behavior has an uncertainty element, the lift is less than perfect. This gains chart shows that you can mail to the top 40% of the sorted mailing list and expect to receive over 90% of the total responses. Instead of the 2% response rate expected by mailing to the entire list, using the model has resulted in an over 100% improvement in the response rate (4.5%)!

4.1.2 Cross Selling

What Is Cross Selling?

The basic idea behind cross selling is to leverage your *existing* customer base by selling them additional products and/or services. By analyzing the groups of products or services that are commonly purchased together and predicting each customer's affinity towards different products using historical data, you can maximize your selling potential to your existing customers. Cross selling is very similar to response modeling, except that you are targeting only existing customers (not new prospects) and you are creating a model that predicts a customer's affinity level to multiple products. Cross selling is one of the important areas in database marketing where predictive data mining techniques can be successfully applied.

Using historical purchase data of different products from your customer database along with demographic, life-style, psychotropic data, you can identify the products that are most likely to be of interest to each customer. Similarly, for each product or product group, you can generate a ranked list of the customers that are most likely to be attracted to that product. Then, instead of mailing to or calling (in the case of telemarketing) every customer in your database, you select only the ones with a high likelihood of responding positively.

This is achieved by building a model to analyze the relationships among the various products as well as other predictive variables. Then for each customer, the model predicts the relative likelihood of that customer buying each of your other products and/or services. The process of applying a model to a database or list is called *scoring*. The customer scores generated by the cross-sell model also can be used to generate a list of the most likely customers to purchase each specific product. Targeted marketing campaigns can then follow two different courses:

- To promote a specific product, contact only those customers that are most likely to purchase that product based on their prior purchases and demographics, etc.

- To create specialized mailings customized for each customer, mail the top ranked products that the model has identified as the products to which the customer is most likely to be attracted.

Inputs and Outputs of Cross-Sell Models

In cross-sell modeling, the inputs are customer attributes, which can include purchase history (e.g., specific products purchased, purchase dates, number of purchases to date, dollar amount of purchases to date, etc.), demographics (e.g., age, gender, household size, etc.), and other relevant information that may influence purchase decisions (e.g., whether they requested information, number of solicitations sent, how they heard about your company, etc.). The outputs in cross-sell modeling are scores that can be used to rank current customers by the affinity level with which they are expected to purchase other specific products or services.

The purchase information for products can be represented in a number of different ways. It can be as simple as a binary purchase flag (i.e., 0 = product was not purchased, 1 = product purchased). It also can be a value representing the number of items purchased or the amount of money spent on the product.

Data to Use   One of the most appealing aspects of cross-selling is that you probably already have the data required for modeling. The minimum data required is purchase information (which can be a buy/no-buy flag, number of purchases, or amount of money spent) for each of your products or services. Of course, models can be augmented by adding demographic, geographic, and life-style data.

Benefits   The benefits of cross sell modeling are widely recognized as the following:

- Improved return on investment (ROI) for marketing dollars
- Improved inventory control and supply-side management
- Improved customer relationships and retention

By "scoring" your current customers using a model and then contacting only those that are likely to buy your other products/services, you can:

- Maximize cross-sell opportunities, minimizing the higher costs of procuring new customers,

- Save on communication (mailing, printing costs, telephone calls, etc.), and

- Generate more sales while spending the same amount of marketing dollars.

In addition, by targeting your communications more effectively to prospects and existing clients, you improve and strengthen customer relationships. The customer may perceive more value in your communications (i.e., they receive information only on products/services of interest to them).

4.2 TIME-SERIES PREDICTION

A time series is a sequence of numerical vectors collected over time. The sequence of locations comprising the trajectory of a thrown baseball is one example of a time series. Another might be the sequence of Dow Jones Daily Industrial Averages, or the sequence of daily values for any collection of financial indicators.

Time-series prediction involves the estimation of one or more values appearing later in a sequence, given past and present values. In the context of a thrown baseball, an example time-series prediction problem is to estimate where the ball will be two seconds from now given the ball's trajectory up until the present. This task is a special case of estimation since it involves the approximation of a value (the future location of a baseball) based on an observation (the past trajectory). Time-series prediction also can be a special case of classification, if it involves the prediction of a coarse characteristic (e.g., whether the Dow Jones Industrial Average will go up or down) rather than a numerical value (e.g., tomorrow's value for the Dow Jones Industrial Average).

Stream of Information

The characteristic distinguishing time-series prediction from general estimation problems is that, as time progresses, each new value generated by the time series is incorporated into the stream of available information. Hence, a quantity that was once of speculative interest becomes part of an information stream on which new predictions are based. This results in a collection of information that can grow indefinitely.

Discarding Irrelevant Information

An important aspect of time-series prediction is discarding the bulk of this information while storing and using the relevant portion to generate desired predictions. For instance, a good prediction of a future location of a baseball may be generated using the locations of only a few recent points in the trajectory. Hence, records of points in the distant past may be safely ignored, limiting the number of components used for the input vector of the estimation problem.

Complex Time Series

As with other forms of estimation, time-series prediction tasks can be extremely complex. One example is the forecast of future financial market conditions based on those of the present and past. Market conditions generally follow long-term trends while exhibiting short-term cyclical behavior. The existence of such patterns in the fluctuations of market conditions makes time-series prediction viable. However, making precise predictions is an extremely complicated task, and it is not always clear what information is required in an observation.

Time-Varying Dynamics

An additional complication often arising in complex time-series prediction, especially in the context of financial analysis, is time-varying dynamics. Because of this, often only very recent data is sufficiently representative of the future. Nevertheless, data from the more distant past also can often be useful in the modeling process (e.g., modeling the price of a crop, which exhibits an annual seasonal pattern). In particular, bootstrap validation methods, discussed in Chapter 11, aim at capitalizing on the use of old data even when that data is not representative of what is expected in the future.

4.3 DETECTION

Detection is a term used to describe the process of identifying the existence or occurrence of a condition. This can be viewed as a special case of pattern classification involving two classes where the "condition exists" or the "condition does not exist."

Two-Class Pattern Classification

What generally sets detection apart from generic, two-class pattern classification is that the condition of interest usually appears on only a very small fraction of the total number of observations. Fault diagnosis in quality control and medical diagnoses are examples of detection. The detected condition here is a defect in a product or a condition in a patient. By treating detection as a special case of classification, it becomes obvious that classification methods are applicable to detection problems.

Costly Errors

In many detection problems, a failure to detect a condition is far more costly than a mistaken detection of the condition's presence when it is actually absent. For example, a smoke alarm can be viewed as a device for detecting hazardous fires. It is not serious if the alarm occasionally errs by sounding when there is actually no fire. However, to prevent severe damage, it is crucial for the alarm to sound whenever there is any possibility of fire.

In the event that detection of a condition is crucial, decisions should take relative costs into account. This can be done by employing an approach to classification involving the estimation of posterior probabilities, and then using these probabilities and relative cost assessments to arrive at a solution that minimizes expected cost. A model estimating posterior probabilities can generate a probability P the condition is present, given a current input vector. Suppose there is a cost K_1 associated with a mistaken detection and a cost K_2 (which is generally much larger than K_1) associated with not detecting the condition's presence. Then, the detection system that minimizes expected cost signals detection in the event that $PK_2 > (1-P)K_1$.

Multi-Class Situations

In some types of defect-detection applications, it may be useful to further classify defects into different classes. Identification of the "type" of defect can be used to route the defects to different destinations. For example, in quality control of chocolate-chip cookies, broken cookies might be distributed to a thrift shop for sale as "seconds," under-baked cookies might be rerouted for additional baking, burnt cookies might be scrapped. Collecting information on the frequency of particular defect types also can be used to monitor or help improve the production process.

In this cookie quality control example, detection becomes a standard classification problem. Output classes might include "good—no defect," "broken," "under-baked," "over-baked," "too small," "too few chips," etc.

4.4   PROBABILITY ESTIMATION

Probability estimation involves approximating the likelihood of an event given an observation. An example is weather prediction. After observing various environmental conditions, such as barometric measurements, humidity, and temperature, it is possible to generate an estimate of the probability of rain on a given day.

Difference from General Estimation

Probability estimation differs from general estimation problems because the estimated output is not generally representative of the final result. In the context of estimating the probability of rain, an estimate may be one-half (50%), while the actual result will be either zero or one (it will either rain or not rain). The value provided by the probability is the statistical expectation of the actual result. Probability estimation models can be produced in the same manner as described in Chapter 3 for modeling posterior probabilities in classification.

4.5 INFORMATION COMPRESSION

A photograph or image often contains a lot of redundant information. For economical storage, redundancies should be removed. However, we must have the ability to regenerate this information if the picture is to be viewed again in its original form. This process of reducing data without actual (significant) data loss is called compression.

Information compression can be cast as a special type of estimation problem. The inputs and outputs of this estimation problem are identical, but the model to be used is constrained. In particular, the model should consist of two stages, as illustrated in Figure 4-2. The space (i.e., number) of outputs from the first stage should be much smaller than the input. These outputs are the compressed version of the input, and the compression clearly must maintain important information if the entire two-stage model is to produce accurate estimates.

Figure 4-2 Two-Stage Estimation with Compressed Inputs

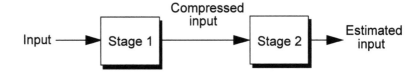

4.6 SENSITIVITY ANALYSIS

In many applications, it is useful to understand how changes in one variable affects another. In particular, if it is possible to change the first variable, a desired effect may be induced on the second (particularly of interest in manufacturing control). The study of such dependencies is called *sensitivity analysis* and is a simple extension to estimation. Once a mapping is generated to model an estimation problem, taking partial derivatives of the outputs with respect to the inputs produces the information required for sensitivity analysis.

Linear Models

Sensitivity analysis has traditionally been achieved using linear models. However, the use of linear models in this setting is especially limiting since the partial derivatives of the mapping are constant over the entire input space. This means the analysis will indicate that, no matter what the current inputs are, the sensitivity of an output to the input variables is the same. Nonlinear models, on the other hand, allow much more interesting analysis, since they reflect how sensitivities may differ in different regions of the input space.

Optimal Set Points

Sensitivity analysis can be used as a means for selecting optimal set points for a controlled system such as a chemical process. In this event, the model should take some set point values as input and generate the performance of the system as output. To achieve optimal performance, we start with a guess for the best set points. Then, using the derivative of the mapping with respect to the set points, we can figure out how we should tweak the set points in small amounts in order to incrementally improve estimated performance. By iterating this process until no changes in set points would increase performance, we have reached a local (and possibly global) maximal level of performance.

A user of this approach to optimizing set points should beware that results may be unreliable if the trajectory taken through the input space during the iterative optimization procedure leads to a region for which there was no data. The model may be arbitrarily inaccurate in that region, since it has no data on which to base relationships.

Chapter 5

Overview of the Development Process

Data-driven pattern recognition has achieved many remarkable successes over the past decade. However, data-driven (or nonparametric) methods are generally heuristic, and rigorous theoretical understanding of such methods is limited. Because of this, the development of nonparametric models often involves an iterative, experimental process. Nevertheless, the process requires far less work than analytical, problem-specific approaches, and practitioners have found nonparametric modeling to be an invaluable tool.

The first four chapters introduced conceptual and theoretical issues concerning the topic of pattern recognition. The remainder of this book presents a practical approach for developing pattern recognition solutions. This chapter introduces the basic steps involved in the development process (see Figure 5-1). Each step is then discussed in greater detail in a separate chapter.

Figure 5-1 Pattern Recognition Solution Process

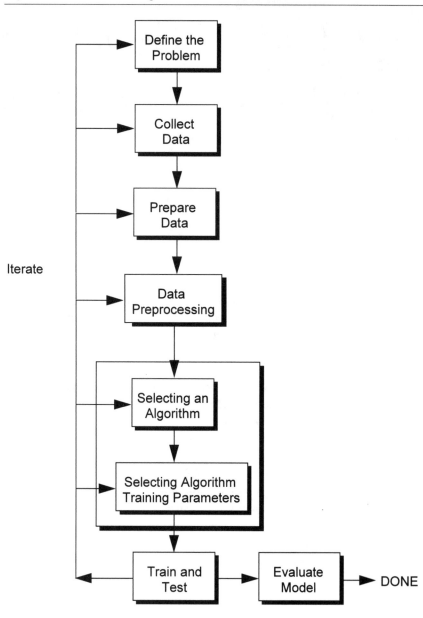

5.1 DEFINING THE PATTERN RECOGNITION PROBLEM

To get started, you will need to think carefully about your problem area and define your specific pattern recognition problem. To do this, you will first need to determine if your problem is suitable for a data-driven modeling solution. You will then need to assess how the solution will be evaluated and what defines success. Finally, you need to define the pattern recognition problem by specifying its inputs and outputs and determining whether it is a classification or an estimation problem.

5.2 COLLECTING DATA

Oftentimes, you will already have a wealth of data to work with. However, if you are collecting the data, there are a number of issues to consider. For example, the amount of data you will need, how you should collect the data, data sampling rates, and the potential use of simulation data to supplement existing data or, in the case of classification, to help define boundary conditions between classes.

5.3 PREPARING DATA

The data preparation step is basically one of "cleaning up" the raw data. It includes basic steps required for data analysis—removing inconsistent data or outliers, handling missing data, converting non-numeric inputs to numeric values, discarding bad data, etc. If your data is in good form, this step may not be necessary.

5.4 PREPROCESSING

Data preprocessing is a major step of the development process. This step transforms the data into its final form for input to a model. Here is where you have the ability to incorporate your domain expertise to simplify the modeling problem. Often times, preprocessing is the key to developing a highly successful pattern recognition solution. Typical preprocessing steps include normalizing the data and reducing the number of input variables.

5.5 SELECTING AN ALGORITHM AND TRAINING PARAMETERS

There are many perspectives for considering available training algorithms. In Chapter 10, we will look at algorithms using the following categories:

- Parametric vs. nonparametric
- Classification vs. estimation
- Type of kernel functions

Selecting an algorithm[1] must satisfy hard constraints (e.g., you have an estimation problem vs. a classification problem), as well as optimize other constraints (e.g., speed performance, training time, etc.) Such practical constraints differ widely among different models, even though accuracy (i.e., error rate on the test set) may be statistically equivalent.

Once an algorithm is selected, experimentation begins to find the optimal parameter settings. Chapter 10 describes a number of commonly occurring

---

1. Actually, in practice, you will need to select an architecture and an algorithm. However, for simplification purposes, since this book only discusses one algorithm for each architecture, we do not make the distinction here.

algorithms in detail, along with suggestions on how to tune their various training parameters.

When employing the nonparametric method of trying different models of varying complexity and smoothness, it is always a good idea to benchmark results against simple parametric methods or existing solutions.

5.6   TRAINING AND TESTING

During training, free parameters are chosen to fit input/output pairs in the training set. In most models, some kind of error (e.g., RMS) is minimized by adapting internal "weights." Once training is completed, testing refers to the step where the trained model is evaluated using a separate data set.

During the training and testing stage, you use several data sets to:

- Tune the architecture free parameters, typically minimizing error.
- Tune algorithm training parameters (or select the best algorithm).
- Evaluate expected performance and accuracy.

Typically, the available data is divided into three disjoint sets (training, test, and evaluation). A separate data set is used for each of the above tasks to avoid biases towards a particular data set.

Validation is an important method for maximizing the amount of information drawn from a data set. It is especially important when the amount of data available is small. Model validation techniques basically divide the available data into a number of folds, generating multiple models using different folds for training and testing. By combining the results of each of the models, you end up with a model that captures more characteristics of the data. By providing an average error rate and variance, validation techniques can prevent the potentially misleading results from a single train-and-test model. These validation techniques can be used in place of the simple train/test approach when data is limited.

5.7   ITERATING STEPS AND TROUBLE-SHOOTING

Once you have generated a baseline model, the bulk of the work begins by trying to improve on your solution. Iteration through the development process can take on many forms from trying different training parameters, to trying different algorithms, to using different data preprocessing, to collecting more or different data, to redefining the original problem.

Experimentation is inherent in this data-driven modeling process. It is often the challenging part of the development where you get to "solve the puzzle."

5.8   EVALUATING THE FINAL MODEL

One of the best ways to assess the performance of a final model is to use an evaluation set. An evaluation set, randomly chosen and expected to represent future data, not used for training or testing of the model, can be used to generate a final expected error for the pattern recognition problem.

Solving Data Mining Problems through Pattern Recognition

Chapter 6

Defining the Pattern Recognition Problem

The first step to solving a pattern recognition problem is to define the problem. Formulating the actual problem involves a number of concrete steps that will be discussed in this chapter. However, there are also a number of other significant issues that must be considered in the practical application of data-driven methods. This chapter identifies some of the salient issues for your consideration:

❑ What problems are suitable for data-driven pattern recognition?
❑ How do you evaluate results?
❑ Is it a classification or estimation problem?
❑ What are the inputs and outputs?

Where possible, we provide guidelines or rules of thumbs to follow in defining a pattern recognition problem. These guidelines will help you get started with a small problem, which you can continually tune and refine. While the details in this chapter may seem overwhelming, surprisingly good results can be achieved without spending significant time or effort addressing most of these issues. If you are new to solving pattern recognition problems, you may wish to skim this chapter without attention to the details. You can always review the tips in this chapter later, once you have generated some initial results.

6.1 WHAT PROBLEMS ARE SUITABLE FOR DATA-DRIVEN SOLUTIONS?

The first question you should ask yourself is, "Are data-driven modeling methods the right approach for my problem?"

When Not To Use

If the problem has a complete, closed-form mathematical solution (e.g., estimating the time it takes a dropped ball to hit the ground given the height) or is well understood and has a good analytic or rule-based solution (e.g., classifying eggs as "medium," "large," or "extra large" by weight), then use that solution instead. If the relationships in the problem are well understood or you know the form of solution is, say, linear or Gaussian, you can use parametric modeling to achieve good results.

When to Use

So when should you try data-driven approaches to modeling? Ideally, when there are no good existing solutions *and* the problem has the following characteristics:

- Lots of historical data on the problem is readily available.

- The problem or behavior is not understood or not easily characterized.

- The problem can be characterized as an input-to-output relationship (i.e., the problem can be thought of as mapping input patterns to output patterns).

- Existing models have strong and possibly erroneous assumptions or are incomplete.

The presence of these characteristics increase the probability of successfully developing a data-driven pattern recognition solution. It doesn't hurt to try data-driven approaches with any particular problem; these are just the characteristics common to highly successful applications.

Combining Data-Driven Solutions with Other Approaches

It can often be advantageous to combine data-driven methods with known methods. For example, let's say there exists a good solution for a given estimation problem. You might want to calculate the residual error and try modeling that error. If the error can be at all modeled, you have just incrementally improved the performance of an existing solution (see Figure 6-1). Instead of defining your problem as using the same inputs (independent variables) and outputs (dependent variables) as an existing model, you may want to consider modeling the residual error instead.

Figure 6-1   Modeling Residual Error to Improve an Existing Solution

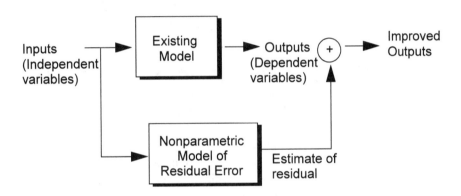

As discussed in Chapter 1, almost all solutions lie somewhere between the two extremes of fixed and purely nonparametric models. The more you know about a problem, the more of an advantage you have. Your knowledge of the problem can often be incorporated in a preprocessing stage (discussed further in Chapter 9). The remainder of the model is then generated using nonparametric methods. This two-stage approach of preprocessing followed by nonparametric modeling often yields results superior to either one singly.

6.2 HOW DO YOU EVALUATE RESULTS?

It may be tempting to rush ahead and proceed directly to experimentation with data-driven modeling. However, it is often beneficial to first contemplate how you might evaluate the results. Here are some questions you might want to consider:

Questions to Consider
- What level of accuracy do you *need* to achieve?
- What level of accuracy would be considered successful?
- How will you benchmark the performance of a developed solution?
- What existing alternatives will you compare against?
- What kind of data will you use to evaluate the various models?

The answers to these questions may help you through the development process as you continually refine your solution.

6.3 IS IT A CLASSIFICATION OR ESTIMATION PROBLEM?

As introduced in Chapter 1, classification is the process of assigning an observation to one of a number of known categories (or classes). Classification problems typically have a finite number of discrete, non-sequential outputs. Estimation, on the other hand, generates an approximation of a numerical value based on an observation. Estimation models map inputs to continuous-valued outputs. Before continuing further, you need to decide whether your problem is a classification or an estimation problem.

Examples
Some examples of classification and estimation problems are shown in Table 6-1.

Table 6-1   Classification and Estimation Examples

Examples of Classification	Examples of Estimation
• Predicting the likelihood of a prospect responding to a marketing offer	• Predicting the value or profitability of a customer over a specified period of time
• Automatically classifying bitmaps of handwritten characters as a letter "A"–"Z"	• Modeling electrode charge variables of electric-arc furnaces in power-generating plants
• Identifying solder joint defects as "good," "missing solder joint," "solder off the die pad," "misaligned joint," "wire bent," or "insufficient solder"	• Estimating the market price for an option based on time-to-expiration, current price of the underlying security, and the strike price of the option
• Predicting the up or down movement of the Dow Jones Industrial Average 10 days in the future	• Estimating the mean time to failure for manufacturing equipment
• Classifying a bank mortgage loan applicant as a "good risk" or "bad risk"	• Estimating tomorrow's peak temperature based on various barometric measurements

Borderline Cases

Note that some borderline problems can be formulated as either a classification or an estimation problem, depending on the desired granularity of the output. For example, suppose we wanted to predict the full-grown size of farm-raised shrimp based on their feed, crowding conditions, water temperature, use of various nutrients, etc. To pose this as a classification problem, the output classes might be "medium," "large," "extra large," and "jumbo." As an estimation problem, the output might be the weight of an individual shrimp in ounces. After estimating the weight, simple rules can be used to classify the weight into one of the "medium," "large," "jumbo," etc. classes. Formulating the problem as one or the other is neither right or wrong. It merely depends on what level of granularity you desire.

☞ **TIP:** Classification may be a better choice than estimation if there is some natural grouping of the outputs, and you assign a class to each group.

Here are some questions you can ask to help decide if your problem is a classification or estimation problem:

- Is there a finite number of categories into which I wish to map the inputs?

  In most cases, if you have a finite number of classes, you are looking at a classification problem. However, if the classes have a logical, sequential ordering, you may want to frame the problem as an estimation problem. For example, guessing a person's age based on their appearance may be considered a classification problem (there would be a finite number of "age classes" 1–125 years). However, since a "guess" of age 25 is close to an answer of 26 based on a sequential ordering of the years, this problem really is an estimation problem.

  Another example might be predicting the amount of time it will take to service a customer given the number of customers waiting in line. Even though there are discrete outputs, there is a natural cardinality with many possible outputs. This problem is better framed as a function estimation problem.

  A classification problem should have a finite number of "independent" classes, where class #1 is no closer to class #2 than class #3, etc. However, if you have a small number of categories and you don't care about any finer distinctions, posing the problem as a classification problem may be perfectly fine. For example, you might pose a problem with large granularity to classify inputs into a three-output classification problem of "low", "medium," and "high."

- Do you have discrete or continuous outputs?

    If you have discrete outputs, you most likely have a classification problem. If you have continuous outputs, it is most likely an estimation problem. Just as a classification problem can be thought of as an estimation problem as the granularity of the outputs approaches infinity, you also can choose to simplify a problem by turning an estimation problem into a classification problem. For example, instead of predicting the exact price of a stock, you might want to predict whether it will move up or down (a two-class classification problem). This problem is simpler and may require less data or provide more accurate results than defining it as an estimation problem. Reducing the problem from estimation to classification also helps to alleviate noisy data problems.

If you are still having problems determining if your problem is a classification problem or an estimation problem, try rereading some of the definitions and examples in this chapter. Remember that some problems are borderline and can be posed as either a classification or an estimation problem. It just depends on the actual outputs you define for the problem.

6.4   WHAT ARE THE INPUTS AND OUTPUTS?

Terminology   The "outputs" or "dependent variables" of a pattern recognition system represent the answer to the problem you are posing. In a classification problem, the outputs might be the labels with which you want to categorize your inputs. In an estimation problem, the output might be the variable you want to model. For example, in an estimation problem where you are trying to predict an option price, the output variable might be the option's price in U.S. dollars. In a classification problem where you are trying to select good candidates for extending credit, the categories might be "good risk" and "bad risk."

So what are the "inputs" or "independent variables" to a pattern recognition system? In the most general sense, the inputs are any data related to the problem that can help determine the desired output value(s). In the option pricing estimation example, input variables might be time-to-expiration, current underlying asset price, the strike price, the interest rate, market volatility, etc. In the banking loan classification example, the inputs might be current salary, outstanding liabilities, bank account balances, other income, number of years employed, etc.

Start with a Small Problem

By defining the inputs and outputs of the model, you are in a sense, defining the problem to be solved. A good strategy is to start with the smallest problem that will provide useful results. For an estimation problem, consider a single output variable that you would like to model. For classification, define a small set of (easily) distinguishable classes.

Starting small has a number of advantages, including the following:

- Smaller problems (fewer number of inputs and outputs) train faster.
- Smaller problems do not require as much data (example patterns).
- Small problems allow you to quickly benchmark preliminary results.
- Small problems provide early successes.

Once you gain some insights with a small problem, you can then expand and improve on your existing system. For example, you can add more output variables to model, more inputs, or more output classes. Plus, the experience you gain from tackling the small problem will be invaluable in experimenting with a larger problem, where long turn-arounds in training times are common.

Decide on the Level of Granularity for Classification Problems

In classification, deciding on the "granularity" of your classes is important. It is easier to classify samples as "good" or "bad," rather than "good," "defect 1," "defect 2," ... "defect n." Start with a small number of classes. This usually requires less data to distinguish among the selected output classes. You can always add more output classes afterwards.

One important consideration in selecting the granularity of your outputs for classification is the amount of data you have available. Generally, the more data you have available, the finer distinctions the pattern recognition system will be able to learn. If you do not have very much data available, it is advisable to start with coarse classes and refine the system as more data becomes available. For example, if you have 500 data patterns available, trying to distinguish among 100 different classes may be excessive. After dividing the data into a training set, a test set, and perhaps an evaluation set, there may not be sufficient examples of each class to provide statistically reliable inferences. Training, testing, and evaluation sets will be discussed further in Chapter 11.

Deciding on the Input Variables

Theoretically, with an infinite amount of data and an infinite amount of time, a computer could sort out all relationships among any number of inputs and outputs. In this process, it may discover that many of the input variables are irrelevant. However, because we are often limited by the data we are able to collect or have access to, and the amount of computation time available, the model may learn incorrect relationships on some variables. To avoid this, we want to simplify the pattern recognition problem as much as possible (e.g., by discarding irrelevant input variables). You can do this by experimenting with key features of the problem, combining features (e.g., the ratio of two input values), and applying intelligent data preprocessing. Data preprocessing is discussed in Chapter 9. See also Section 12.2, "Automated Searches," for ways to intelligently search for the optimal set of inputs.

Quite often, you may think, "Ah yes, the system should have X, Y, and Z as inputs." However, if your current database of collected data contains X, Y, Q, and P, then those are the pieces of data you will have to use for your pattern recognition system. There is nothing wrong with this approach—it simply does the best job it can with what existing data is readily available. The model may be able to extract the same information from Q and P that was available in Z. On the other hand, you may find the resulting error rates unacceptably high, so you may hypothesize Z must be collected and presented as input. It may be more affordable or practical to collect other variables closely related to Z in order to gain most of the information content at a fraction of the price. However, if you have the luxury of deciding what key input variables would be ideal for a particular problem and then collecting the data, that is the optimal approach.

Input Variables Should be Causally Related to the Outputs

The key is to provide the pattern recognition system with the smallest number of critical features that are useful for determining the desired output(s). While correlation between the inputs and outputs is sufficient for pattern recognition, ideally, the input variables should be causally related to the output variables. If input variables are merely highly correlated with the output variable, there is no guarantee that the correlation will always be present in the future. Therefore, there may be times where the model will be inaccurate (i.e., when the inputs are not correlated with the output). Causality, therefore, is an issue in decision-making—if you try to manipulate input variables to determine the corresponding output, the output values will only be valid if causality is inherent.

A good example of correlation vs. causality is shown in the documented "Super Bowl effect." Basically, the correlation is that when an NLF team wins the Super Bowl, stock prices go up. When an AFL team wins, the stock prices go down. While this is a statistically validated correlation, it is easy to see that it is merely a correlation, but has no causal effect on the movement of stock prices. In fact, this is most likely a lucky correlation which will not continue as more data points are collected.

Another example of non-causal and unintentionally biased data is recognizing the gender of a person based on a photo. One study achieved surprisingly accurate results. However, it was later determined that the pattern recognition system had identified gender based on the presence or absence of a neck tie. A person wearing a tie was classified as "male," otherwise "female." While the wearing of a neck tie is highly correlated with gender, it is obvious the pattern recognition system will err when men are not wearing ties.[1] This is an example of a strong correlation that breaks down in cases not seen by the system.

Data Considerations

It is important to consider how much data is available when you define the inputs to your problem. Unfortunately, the size of input spaces for many practical problems grows exponentially with the number of input variables

---

1. Another important issue that this example brings up is that of representative training data. The training data must be representative of future data to be presented to the pattern recognition module. Otherwise, the results may be unpredictable.

involved. This is often referred to as the "curse of dimensionality." Because of the enormity of the input space of interest, general computational requirements can quickly grow to be infeasible. In a practical sense, this means that the more input variables you have, the more example data patterns you will need in your training set to learn the proper mapping of inputs to outputs.

This brings us to two important data sufficiency issues.

- The input data must contain enough information to be able to generate the desired output or distinguish among the desired output classes.

- The data examples provided in the data set must be representative of future patterns presented to the model.

Information Content

Basically, the first caveat says you have to provide "reasonable" inputs to the system. You can't expect to provide your aunt's age and favorite color as inputs and expect to predict tomorrow's weather. These inputs, however, might be useful for identifying customers in a clothing store's database for mailers on an arrival of new red sweaters. In other words, if the inputs don't provide good "clues" to the information you're trying to extract (i.e., the outputs), the pattern recognition system cannot succeed.

Representative Patterns

The second caveat has two important implications. First, since the system learns the input/output mapping from the training data, if you later present an input vector that is significantly different from any pattern in the training set, the model is forced to extrapolate. Essentially, presenting an input vector in an "uncharted" region of the input space can result in unexpected (and sometimes disastrous) results. Since the pattern recognition system has not seen examples in that area of the input space before, this can result in unexpected or seemingly random outputs. Therefore, it is important to make sure your training data will be representative of future input vectors. If not, you must be sure to detect this condition and disregard the model's outputs for these cases.

The second implication is that sufficient data examples are provided for accurate interpolation. This means that (assuming the mapping is smooth) there are enough examples in the regions of the input space of interest so that the mapping of inputs to outputs is constrained. If insufficient examples are provided (i.e., input vectors are few and far between), significant variation can occur in the values generated by the system for those inputs.

If all future input vectors will be very close to provided examples in the training set, a small amount of interpolation may not carry negative effects. However, if future input vectors lie far from example patterns, inaccurate interpolations may result. Generally, the more data, the better chance that the data adequately meets these criteria.

APPENDIX: DEFINING THE PROBLEM IN PRW

**Declaring a
Classification
or Estimation
Problem**

Problem definition is fully encapsulated in the PRW experiment manager. All experiments configured and run within this experiment manager will use these settings. The setup (first) screen of the experiment manger (see Figure 6-2) allows you to declare the problem as a "classification" or a "function estimation" problem.

Figure 6-2 The Experiment Manager Setup Screen

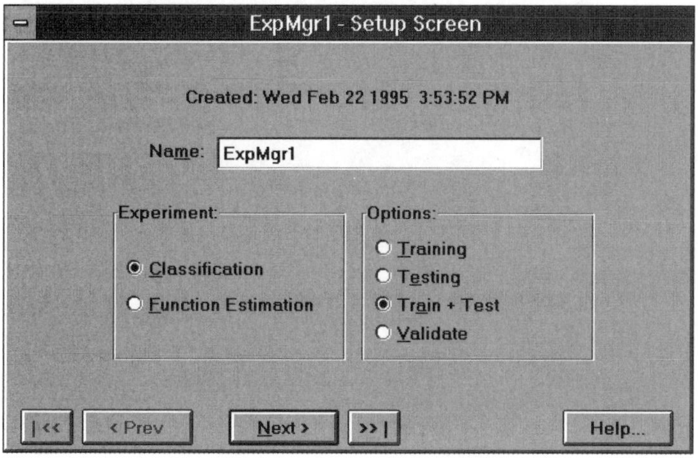

Defining the Inputs and Outputs

The input/output (second) screen of the experiment manager allows you to define the input and output variables (see Figure 6-3). All of the variables (columns) of all of the PRW spreadsheets are listed in the center list box. These variables can be easily designated as input variables by moving them to the left list box, or as output variables by moving them to the right list box.

Figure 6-3   The Experiment Manager Input/Output Screen

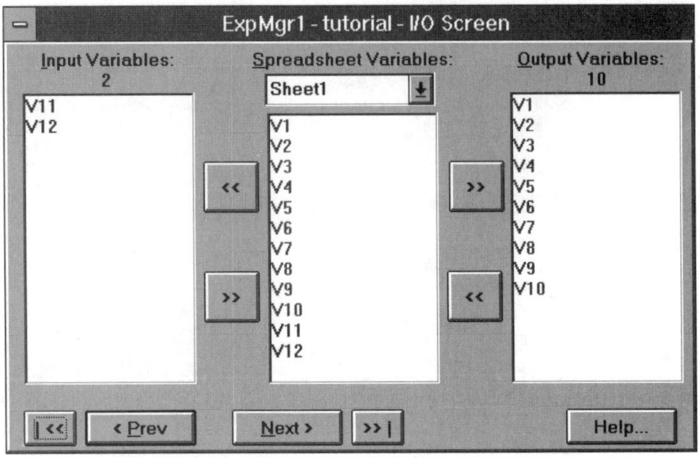

For more information on the setup and input/output screens of the experiment manager, see the *PRW User's Guide*.

Chapter 7

Collecting Data

This chapter discusses the data collection step of the development process. While collecting data is usually straight-forward, several issues should be considered. This chapter covers the following topics:

❏ What data to collect
❏ How to collect data
❏ How much data is enough
❏ Using simulated data

7.1 WHAT DATA TO COLLECT

After defining the pattern recognition problem, the next step is to collect the required data. In many cases, you will already have existing data that can be used. Even if this is the case, you may want to skim through the remainder of this chapter to help you gauge the quality of your data. This is important to understand, since once you begin iterating through the steps of the development process, you may want to consider returning to the data collection step.

Collecting Example Patterns

In order to train a supervised learning algorithm, you will need to collect samples of data consisting of the input values and the corresponding desired output values. This pair of inputs and outputs is called an example pattern. These example patterns will be divided into a training and test set for building the model and an evaluation set for assessing the final model.

For each example pattern, you will need to capture a numerical value for each input or output variable. If one or more input variables are unavailable or cannot be cost-effectively captured, you can go back and redefine the problem without the input or substitute another related, but available input.

More Data Is Better

In general, with stationary processes, you cannot have too much data (i.e., too many example patterns). It is always easier to discard extra data than to try and generate more data in a pinch. An abundance of data can ameliorate a multitude of problems. The more data you have available, the higher the probability of the data being representative of future data and the easier it will be for the model to distinguish between noise and true underlying relationships.

Recent Data and Time-Variant Systems

Since it is important that the example patterns you use to train, test, and evaluate your model are representative of future data patterns presented to the system, usually recent data is desirable. If you are trying to model a highly non-stationary system, the more recent the data, the better. If you are modeling a static system or a slowly changing system, you may be able to successfully use data that is a few years old, yet still representative of inputs and outputs generated by the system today.

For example, a static model might predict the time it takes for a baseball to hit the ground based on the height from which it is dropped. Because physical laws are constant, it doesn't matter whether you use data collected 20 years ago or data collected yesterday. Another good example of a static problem is handwritten-character recognition. Unless handwriting has evolved significantly over time, handwriting samples from 10 years ago will be equally valid and applicable to future data.

An example of a slow time-varying system might be a rolling mill process in metals manufacturing. Modeling the roll force might change slowly over time due to equipment wear and tear, but otherwise, the system's behavior is fairly consistent.

An example of a rapidly time-varying system is the stock market. Any known information that can be used to make money from the market quickly becomes "discounted." Therefore, conditions are always changing, and any predictive system needs up-to-date information for continuous, accurate modeling.

Begin with an Elementary Set of Data

Even though more data is generally better, if you are beginning with a small problem, you should be able to generate preliminary models with a limited amount of data. In most cases, you can begin by collecting a cursory set of example patterns, generate some models, and then go back and collect more data after analysis of the preliminary results. You may find results are very promising, or you may discover that you will need additional inputs to attain the desired level of accuracy. The point is to quickly produce some models to generate data for analysis and then further refine the model.

7.2 HOW TO COLLECT DATA

Whether you are collecting data for your pattern recognition problem or using existing data, there are several simple rules that should be followed.

- For time-series data, choose an appropriate sampling rate.[1]

  If you are collecting data from a dynamic system, you must choose an appropriate sampling rate for data collection. A common mistake is to sample too slowly for a fast-changing system (losing critical indications of change in the system). Sampling too quickly for a slow-changing system may produce lots of repetitive, low information-content data, but you can always condense this data (e.g., by taking an average over several points in time) in the preprocessing step.

  Knowing when and how often the system changes can help you choose an appropriate sampling rate. For example, sampling stock market prices once a day (e.g., the daily closing prices) may be adequate for modeling weekly price changes, but sampling from a manufacturing process that produces 1,000 widgets an hour for modeling product defects might require 1,000+ samples an hour.

  If you have data that samples at too high of a rate, you can try reducing noise by averaging values over a number of example patterns. If you do not sample often enough to capture essential features, you will probably need to go back and recollect the data using a higher sampling rate.

- Make sure the data measurements units are consistent.

  As most systems change over time or data is accumulated from different sources, it is important to check and ensure that all data for a particular input or output variable is consistent. For example, if collecting pressure data from a manufacturing process, make sure that all data for that particular sensor (input variable) is always reported in the same units (e.g., not pounds per square inch for some example patterns and Newtons per square meter for others).

---

1. If appropriate, you can refer to engineering theorems (e.g., the Nyquist sampling theorem) for bounds on the required sampling rate to completely determine a signal function at all points in time.

Another example might be modeling the U.S. dollar against the Mexican peso. You must make sure that all example patterns are using either the "old" peso or the "new" peso (1/1000 of the old peso), but not both.

In most cases, if your data is not consistent, it is merely a problem of identifying the inconsistent data and performing simple data transformation or preprocessing. For example, in the manufacturing example, we could simply convert all pressure measurements to pounds per inch squared.

- Keep non-essential variables not in the input vector as constant as possible.

In general, you want to simplify the problem by holding as many factors as possible constant or taking measurements under the same conditions. (These conditions must be reproducible in the future.) Reducing variation reduces noise in example patterns. For example, in an imaging application, common variables that may be easy (and important) to make constant during data collection and future use might include light intensity, light source location, distance of camera from the object, etc.

- Vary variables not in the input vector if they are expected to vary in the future.

For example, in the imaging application, if the system will be used under varying light conditions, capture examples with as many different light sources as possible. This will force you to capture many more patterns than when using a constant light source. However, this is essential so the learning algorithm will learn correctly in the presence of shadows and varying illumination. Note that the light source is not an explicit input variable to the learning algorithm, but implicitly affects the training patterns. You may find it incrementally aids the learning system to understand the different images by explicitly making the light source an input variable.

- Make sure no major structural changes have occurred during the time period of the collected example patterns.

  In manufacturing processes, it may be common to replace machinery or retool a process. If these changes introduce significant changes to the system you are modeling, it may invalidate data collected prior to the change. If such an event has occurred in your problem, make sure that all data is collected after the event. If the machinery or process may change back to the old method, it may then be best to explicitly encode the machinery or process change as an input variable and use all of the data.

7.3   HOW MUCH DATA IS ENOUGH

How much data is necessary depends on the complexity of the problem and the amount of noise in the data. Although there are a number of theoretical bounds on this topic, they are often based on worse-case scenarios or on restrictive assumptions. The truth is, most of the time, you end up just experimenting and determining the amount of data needed by trial and error.

One simple method for determining if you have sufficient data is to perform your training and testing using a subset of the available data. If performance does not increase when you use the full data set, that is an indication you have enough data. However, it can be dangerous to draw conclusions based on a test this simplistic, since a model may drastically improve its performance by getting certain example patterns, but not others (e.g., getting patterns from a region of the input space where no previous example patterns existed vs. getting example patterns that are essentially duplicates of existing example patterns). Because of these potential pitfalls, it is important to statistically validate your results. Validation methods are discussed in Section 11.2, "Validation Techniques."

Solving Data Mining Problems through Pattern Recognition

Relationship Between Model Accuracy and Amount of Training Data

Generally, the accuracy of a model increases as the number of example patterns available for training increases. Figure 7-1 depicts some example curves from a handwriting-recognition problem, showing how accuracy increases with the number of training patterns [Martin, 1990]. The numbers in parentheses in the legends indicate the number of weights trained for each MLP architecture.

Figure 7-1   Relationship Between Accuracy and Number of Training Patterns

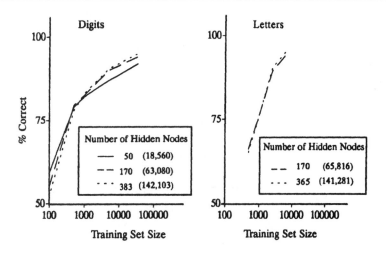

When all said, there are no hard and fast rules for how much data is required to successfully solve any given pattern recognition problem. It is often easiest to just go ahead and use whatever data is easily available and evaluate the preliminary results. You can always go back and fine tune the solution later.

7.4   USING SIMULATED DATA

If you have access to or can collect real data, that is always preferable to generating simulated data. However, since it is not always possible to obtain sufficient samples of real data for training purposes, we must sometimes resort to simulated data. Using simulated data also may be a good way to gather preliminary results and evaluate pattern recognition technology without undergoing the sometimes expensive data collection process.

Generating Simulated Data

When generating simulated data, the following factors are important:

- Make the simulated data as realistic as possible.
- Make the simulated data as representative as possible.

Remember that the overall performance of your model will only be as good as the data used to generate it.

Simulated data can come in many forms. In some cases, real data may be scarce, but a human expert can easily and quickly generate many representative patterns. For example, in a medical diagnosis problem for a relatively rare disease, there many be few case histories of actual patients. However, a doctor may be able to quickly provide examples of patient data representative of real data.

In fault diagnosis problems, a company may produce a new circuit board for manufacturing and shipment. Since no boards have yet been returned from customer sites for repair, simulation can be used to populate a diagnostic database. For example, certain pins can be artificially pulled high or low, shorts can be simulated, defective or burnt-out chips can be simulated, etc.

In other cases, it may be possible to generate a computer simulation of a complex dynamic process, even though it is difficult to generate a closed-form model for an associated input-to-output relationship. An example of this might be a re-entrant line problem, where a product has to visit a number of manufacturing machines in a particular sequence during manufacturing. The same physical machine might have multiple queues of products waiting to be serviced, where at each queue, a slightly different variation of the service is performed (e.g., in semi-conductor wafer manufacturing). Different control costs may be associated with storing components at various stages of production. For example, storing a near-end-product component may incur greater opportunity losses since costly resources have been invested into its production. A simulator of such a re-entrant line problem can be constructed, even though estimating when a finished product will appear at the end of the manufacturing process may be difficult.

Using Existing Simulators

Sometimes a simulation of a process already exists. You can add noise to the simulation data to create a more robust model.

Using Simulated Data to Supplement Data

Simulated data also can play an important role in improving performance of a model with respect to boundaries of the input space of interest. In this case, simulated data is used to supplement real data. By generating example patterns for regions of the input space for which no examples or very few examples exist, you can establish the desired behavior in those regions. This allows the model to generate reasonable, rather than random, behavior in these regions.

APPENDIX: IMPORTING DATA INTO PRW

**Data
Collection**

Data collection is the only development step performed outside of the PRW environment. The data you will need to collect and how it will be collected will be very problem-specific. Once that data is collected (typically into data files), PRW can be used to begin tackling your problem.

**Importing
Data into PRW**

Once you have collected data into files, you can import them into PRW for use. PRW can import fixed-width flat files, binary files, delimited ASCII text files, MS-Excel spreadsheet files, and Dbase 3 files using the data import wizard.

To start the import data wizard:

1. Select an empty column into which to import data.

Click in an empty column where you wish to begin importing data. The currently active cell is highlighted and its cell address is displayed in the **Address** area.

2. Select the Import Data... command.

🖰   Select the **File➔Import Data...** command.

———————————————— *or* ————————————————

⌨   Enter ALT-Z-I or CTRL+I.

If you are creating a new data group, The **Import Wizard - Select Files** window appears. If you are importing data into an existing data group, you are prompted for a file and it is imported directly using the data dictionary for the existing data group. If no files have been selected for import, the **Import Data File** window (a standard file selection dialog box) appears automatically.

Figure 7-2   Select Files Page of the Import Wizard

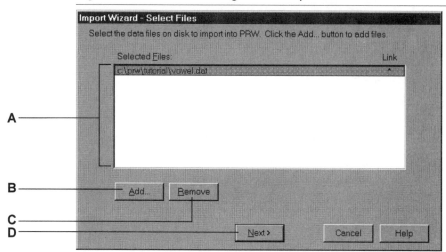

A. The files to import are listed here. Files are imported in the order they are listed. An asterisk (*) to the left of the filename indicates the file is linked to the original data file (Link to File option enabled).
B. Click here to add a file to the Selected Files list.
C. Select a file in the list box and click here to remove it.
D. Click here to advance to the next page.

Specify one or more files to import (see Figure 7-2) and step through the remaining screens of the data import wizard to import your data.

**Fixed Width
Data Files**

Fixed width data files require to you to provide a data dictionary specifying how columns of data are interpreted. You can enter a data dictionary directly or import a saved data dictionary on disk in the Data Dictionary Definition screen of the data import wizard (see Figure 7-3).

Figure 7-3 Data Dictionary Definition Window

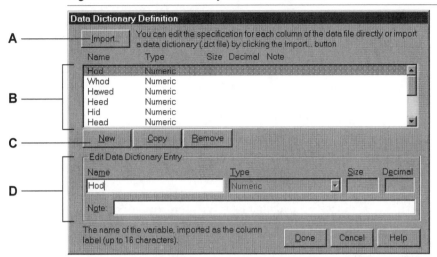

A. Click here to import a previously defined data dictionary definition (.dct file) saved to disk.
B. Each column of the data file is listed/entered here. Select an entry to modify values in the Edit Data Dictionary Entry area.
C. Use the New button to create a new entry, the Copy button to copy the selected entry, and the Remove button to delete the selected entry.
D. Edit the column data for the selected entry here.

ASCII Text Data Files

If you specify a delimited ASCII text file, you can specify format options in the **Text File Conversion Options** window (appears when you click the **Options...** button). Using the available options, you can parse virtually any ASCII data file (see Figure 7-4), including files where the first row of data are labels. You specify how to parse a data file by selecting one or more field delimiters (characters that separate values in different columns) and pattern delimiters (characters that separate one example pattern from the next). Special options allow you to:

- Specify a qualifier (indicates that no parsing should be performed for text within the qualifier characters).

- Enable **Merge consecutive delimiters** (automatically strips multiple delimiters like spaces from each text string) or disable the option (allows import of data with missing column values).

- Import the first row of data as column labels in the spreadsheet with the **Treat first row as labels** option.

- Specify the maximum string length for text strings (extra characters are automatically truncated).

- Specify a pad character for short rows of data and missing data.

Figure 7-4   Text File Conversion Options Window

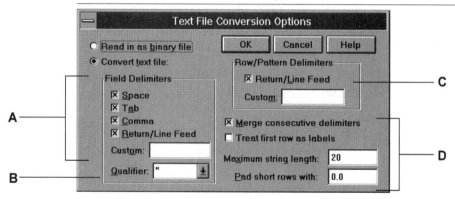

A. Specify field delimiters here or specify custom characters.
B. Specify a qualifier character (text delimited by a qualifier character are imported without parsing).
C. Specify pattern delimiters here.
D. Select other parsing options here.

**Data Formats
in the
Spreadsheet**

Once you have imported one or more data files, you can control how each column of data is displayed using the **Display Formats** window (see Figure 7-5).

Figure 7-5   Display Formats Window

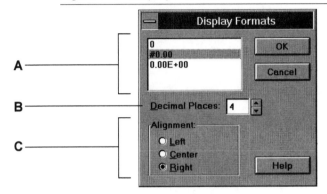

A. Select a display format here.
B. Specify the number of decimal places to display here.
C. Select how the data is aligned in the column here.

**Importing
Multiple Files**

PRW provides tremendous flexibility in importing multiple data files. Column operations, such as source data formats and display formats, are performed once and automatically applied to all files in the data group.

Chapter 8

Preparing Data

The third step of the development process is preparing the data. This step is necessary because most real-world data is not ideal for training a pattern recognition system. For example, it is very common to encounter example patterns with missing data, non-numerical values, and erroneous or inconsistent data.

This step includes a lot of common sense processing to clean up raw data. If you have already initiated analysis of the data, many of these steps may already have been addressed. This chapter covers the following topics:

❑ Handling missing data
❑ Choosing numerical encodings (transforming categorical data)
❑ Discarding erroneous data

Model-related preprocessing issues are discussed in the next chapter.

8.1   MISSING DATA VALUES

In many data sets, example patterns are incomplete (i.e., they do not have a value for every input variable or output variable). For example, in a medical diagnosis classification problem, the inputs might be results from medical tests A, B, C, D, and E. The example patterns would be the test results and diagnoses for different patients. However, it is rare for a patient to have undergone every test. A significant percentage of the time, you may have data values for only three or four out of the five tests. You could "throw out" incomplete example patterns, but often times, you

- Want to be able to predict or classify other example patterns with missing data values, and

- Have too few example patterns to throw out a significant portion of the available data.

Handling Missing Data

There are many different ways to handle missing data. We will explore some of the options here:

- You can manually examine example patterns with missing data values and intelligently enter a reasonable, probable, or expected value. This method can be straightforward if you do not have many missing data values. However, if there is not an obvious plausible value for each case, you may be introducing noise into the system by manually generating a value.

- You can use automated methods to generate a missing value. Some popular methods are to use an average value computed from the example patterns with that value, a modal value (the most common value in the example patterns), or to fill in a fixed value outside the normal data range (e.g., -1 for data normally falling within 0–1). By filling in a missing data value with an average or modal value, you are providing a normal value in the data range. Using a fixed "abnormal" value indicates the data value is missing or contains no information. The fact that a data value is missing, thus, becomes a feature. A model should take into account the fact that particular variables are missing when presented with example patterns in the future.

- You can encode the missing value explicitly in your problem definition. For example, let's say we have three inputs, A, B, and C to our pattern classification module. You could then define the problem as shown in Figure 8-1.

Figure 8-1 Explicit Encoding of Missing Data Values

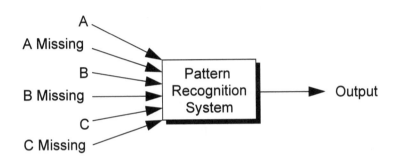

With this definition, you explicitly encode each value is present (0) or missing (1). You might then have the input patterns shown in Table 8-1.

Table 8-1 Example Input Patterns for Explicitly Encoded Missing Values

A	B	C	Preprocessed Input Pattern					
101	0	120	100	0	0	0	120	0
?	1	140	0	1	1	0	140	0
97	?	200	97	0	0	1	200	0
96	2	?	96	0	2	0	0	1
98	1	160	98	0	1	0	160	0

In this table, input A might be the patient's temperature, input B might be the number of weeks since the onset of symptoms, and C might be blood pressure. By encoding the presence or absence of a value explicitly, the pattern recognition system can learn to ignore an input if the corresponding valid indicator is one.

One danger of this approach is that a model may erroneously correlate a missing value with the output. For example, if 90% of the patients that died did not have their temperature measured (perhaps because they were brought into the emergency room), then the resulting model may suggest that the best way to prevent death is to avoid measuring the patient's temperature! One way of avoiding this pitfall is to use sensitivity analysis on the missing input variable to ensure it does not have a much lesser effect than other input variables (see the discussion in Section 9.4, "Reducing the Input Space").

- You can generate a predictive model to predict each of the missing data values. For example, in our simple diagnosis problem, you could use A and B to predict C, B and C to predict A, and A and C to predict B. Once you have trained a model for each of these, you can present the example patterns with missing values and generate a "predictive" value. If a missing data value is correlated with any of the other known variables, this will generate the best missing values.

☞ **NOTE:** If you can always predict a missing variable with certainty, this means the missing variable is not necessary. All relevant information is already provided via the other inputs. Therefore, in correct usage, you should expect imperfect correlation between the missing variable and other inputs.

Typically, you will want to begin with whatever method is easy and reasonable for your problem. After generating some preliminary models, you can evaluate the performance of the model on example patterns with missing values in both the training and the test set. If you discover their error is significantly higher than on the rest of the data, you can try some other preprocessing methods to try to improve results.

8.2 TRANSFORMING DATA INTO NUMERICAL VALUES

Almost all data-driven algorithms utilize numeric inputs. From a computer processing point of view, handling computations with numbers is easier and more efficient. Therefore, if any of the input values are non-numeric (e.g., text strings), they should be intelligently converted to meaningful numerical values.

Categorical Inputs

Categorical input variables contain values that represent a finite number of distinct groups. If there is a logical sequential ordering of the values of a categorical variable (e.g., the categories "low," "medium," and "high"), they can usually be converted to a numerical representation in a straight-forward manner. However, in many cases, categorical variables have no obvious and meaningful ordering of the values (e.g., a variable represent-ing gender, city, sales representative, or ZIP code). In these cases, there are a number of options for converting the values into a numeric representa-tion.

If there are a small number (n) of distinct categories, you can encode the input variable as n different binary inputs. This is known as the "one of n" representation. Each input now represents a single value of the original input and has a value of one if the new input represents the original value, otherwise, it has a value of zero. This encoding preserves the independent nature of each categorical value (i.e., assumes no ordering of the values). However, this representation can be unwieldy or prohibitive as the number of distinct values (n) grows.

If the number of distinct values (n) is too large, then different values must be grouped together somehow to reduce the number of inputs in the new encoding. Once the number of values have been reduced, you can use the simple "one-of-n" decimation method described above. Reducing the number of categorical values can be accomplished in a number of ways:

- Manually — You can manually group similar values together. For example, instead of using an input variable SKU, which might identifies individual products and contain many thousands of different values, you might group SKU's into different product categories.

- PCA-based reduction — You can use principal components analysis (PCA) to reduce the one-of-n representation to a one-of-m representation where m is less than n (see Section 9.4, "Reducing the Input Space"). Through a vector multiplication of the categorical inputs to the weights associated with each eigenvector, a new (smaller) vector of scalars are generated. This will transform the original representation to a lower dimension through a linear combination of the original inputs.

- Eigenvalue-based reduction — You can use principal components analysis (PCA) on the one-of-n representation of categories. Then to reduce the number of inputs, simply choose the top m eigenvectors as sorted by descending eigenvalues and assign each original input value to the eigenvector for which the input has the highest weight. Each eigenvector representing one or more input categories becomes a new category. Since not all eigenvectors are expected to be represented, the number of input categories can be significantly reduced. This approach has the advantage of being easier to interpret than the PCA-based reduction, although some information may be sacrificed in the data reduction process.

- Output variable-based reduction — You can use the output variable to help group values of the categorical input variable together. Values of the input variable that trigger similar output variable values can be grouped together, reducing the number of unique categories.

☞ **NOTE:** It is important to know that if you are applying any of the above methods, especially the output variable-based reduction, you *cannot* use the out-of-sample test set to form these groups. Using information from the test set or hold-out validation set is *cheating* as it gives the model access to characteristics of that data set, which will help it generalize better to that data. Make sure that if this method is used, the reduction process has access only to the training data.

Exploiting Sequential Relationships

When translating ASCII text or non-numeric data values into numeric values, sequential relationships should be exploited whenever possible. For example, let's look at an example where a restaurant is trying to predict how customers will rate their omelettes. Our inputs might be:

- The omelette size (small, medium, and large)
- Optional ingredients (onions, peppers, ham, and anchovies)
- The person's gender (male, female)
- The time of day (based on a 24-hour clock)

Assume we randomly cooked different omelettes for customers entering the restaurant and asked them to rate how much they liked the omelette with a value between 1 (hated it) and 10 (loved it).

Converting Non-Numeric Values into Numbers

The first preprocessing step is to convert non-numeric values (like the omelette size) into some numerical representation. The omelette size can be transformed into the number of eggs used in that omelette as follows:[1]

Small = 2
Medium = 3
Large = 4

Each of the optional ingredients (onions, peppers, ham, and anchovies) can be a binary input. The value will be 1 if the ingredient was used or 0 if it was omitted from the omelette.

---

1. Of course, we could have chosen any of an infinite number of representations. We could have used {-1, 0, 1} or {4.6, 4.7, 4.8} or even {1, 10, 100}. The key is to order the values in ascending (or descending) order. Mapping small to 3, large to 2, and medium to 1 does not take advantage of the sequential size of the omelette. In addition, if we assume that the size difference between a small and medium is the same as a medium and a large, it makes sense to use evenly distributed numerical values (i.e., using {1, 10, 100} does not correspond well to the actual differences in size). But if we were encoding the power (wattage) of a light bulb, using values like {60, 75, 100, 300} would make more sense than simply {1,2,3,4}.

A person's gender does not have any sequential nature. Though we could choose to encode this information as:

Male = 0
Female = 1

in so doing, we are really imposing a sequential order on independent inputs. An alternative way to represent this input that does not imply any sequential relationship is to use two binary inputs. For example, we might choose:

Male = 1 0
Female = 0 1

Cyclical Inputs Finally, we need to encode the time of day into a meaningful numeric value. Using a twenty-four hour clock, we might have values like 9:30, 10:30, 14:15, and 23:00. A first thought might be to translate all times into minutes (i.e., time = hours * 60 + minutes). This would give us 570, 630, 855, and 1380, respectively. This representation gives us the correct differences in time between one value and another as long as you do not compare values over the midnight boundary. However, while time is purely sequential, our representation of time is cyclical (i.e., after 24 hours, the hours go from 23 to 0 hours). This cycle causes problems in calculating time differences over the cycle. For example, 23:59, represented as 1439, is very far away from 00:01 which is represented as 1, when the difference should only be 2.

To eliminate this discontinuity, we could make a simple change to our representation of time. We could simply define time to be the number of minutes elapsed from a fixed point in time (e.g., January 1, 1995). Then all times (although much larger in value) will have a correct sequential and scalar relationship to all other times. However, since we suspect that more people will like omelettes served during the morning breakfast hours than during the dinner hours, we do not want to lose the cyclic nature of our first representation. The fact that the 23:59 to 00:00 discontinuity exists becomes minor compared to this problem. They will be treated as two disjoint ends, but at least the same times of day are clearly evident.

Another alternative, if we want to maintain the cyclical nature of an input, is to map the values onto a circle in two dimensions. This is illustrated in Figure 8-2.

Figure 8-2   Mapping Values onto a Two-Dimensional Circle

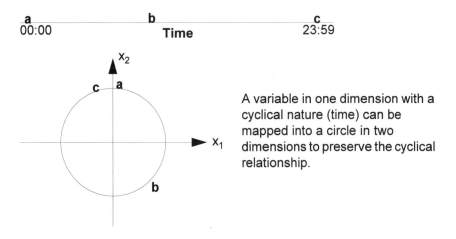

A variable in one dimension with a cyclical nature (time) can be mapped into a circle in two dimensions to preserve the cyclical relationship.

Resulting Model

Once all of the data has been preprocessed, our pattern recognition system might be used to help us plan the menu, optimize the ingredient inventory, and produce higher customer satisfaction. For example, we might learn no one likes anchovies on their omelettes, or omelettes are liked best between 6:00 am and 10:30 am *and* between 11:00 pm and 3:30 am (as a late-night snack). We also might learn most men like large omelettes with ham, and most women like small omelettes with peppers and onions.

8.3   INCONSISTENT DATA AND OUTLIERS

Removing Erroneous Data

Part of preparing data should include a cursory inspection of the data to identify and discard erroneous data. Erroneous data can be due to sensor faults (e.g., a pressure sensor that always outputs zero), machine break down periods, etc. Remove any data that falls into these categories, or remove the input variable if all data for that variable is erroneous.

Since classifications should be consistent and mappings should be smooth, you may find some example patterns that are just incorrect. These "errors" can be due to data-entry problems, measurement errors, human errors, or other sources. You should remove these from your data set to avoid confusion. However, if you have many examples of valid data and only a few examples of invalid data, most nonparametric methods will essentially learn to ignore (or place very little weight) on the invalid data examples.

Identifying Inconsistent Data

Inconsistent data may be easy or difficult to identify, depending on the particular problem. If you have a low-dimensional problem (i.e., three or less input variables), you may be able to display your data in a graph and visually identify bad example patterns. For example, if you have a two-dimensional classification problem, you can plot each of the input patterns in a scatter graph and use a different color to represent each output class. You can then easily identify "misclassified" example patterns by picking out points that are interspersed among points of a different color.

In problems of higher dimensions, you will probably need to use thresholding or filtering of the data to automatically identify bad data values. For example, in a manufacturing process, a sensor may have been working properly, and then failed, generating all zeros thereafter. You could choose to discard these example data patterns, or in this case, you could use any of the methods for handling missing data values to generate replacement values for the failed sensor. Simple line graphs of each input variable usually illuminate erroneous values.

Outliers

Outliers are simply data points that lie outside of the normal region of interest in the input space. Outliers may represent unusual situations that are "correct," but sometimes outliers can be misleading or are just incorrect measurements.

An easy way to spot outliers in data is to plot a histogram of each of your input variables. In most cases, the majority of your data will occupy some range of values in the middle of the histogram. If you have outlier data values, they will fall on the tails of the histogram. You can then easily use a threshold filter to identify the outlier data values. For example, if your input value is a person's age in years, you can filter and eliminate example patterns where the data value is less than zero or greater than 130. These data patterns can be safely assumed to be erroneous (perhaps due to improper data entry).

Another way to identify outliers is to calculate the mean and standard deviation for each input variable. You can then easily define outliers to be data points falling outside of, say, three standard deviations from the mean.

Including or Excluding Outliers

Once you have identified outliers, you need to decide whether or not you want to include them in your data set. If you remove the outliers, the assumption is that you do not care about the part of the input space where the outliers reside. If the outliers are important (e.g., if you are trying to predict the probability of an outlier occurring at any given point in time) and you leave the outliers in the data set, you will need sufficient examples of the outlier data to be able to accurately model them.

If outliers are not critical to your problem, you should initially eliminate all outlier data points to simplify the modeling problem. An alternative is to "winzorize" the outliers. Winzorizing simply sets an upper and lower threshold for a particular variable. All values greater than the upper bound are set to the upper value. All values less than the lower bound are set to the lower value. This allows you to keep the outlier example patterns without keeping extreme data values. Once you are satisfied with your success on the "normal" data points, you can always re-introduce the outliers to study the changes in the performance of the model.

APPENDIX: PREPARING DATA IN PRW

PRW's spreadsheet functions make it easy to clean up your data. This appendix describes how to deal with missing data values, convert non-numeric data to a numerical representation, and handle inconsistent data.

A.1 Handling Missing Data

Replacing Missing Data with a Constant

PRW supports several of the methods discussed for handling missing data. To automatically replace missing data with a fixed value is extremely easy. When you import a text file, just specify the value you wish to use for replacing missing values in the **Pad short rows with** text box (default value of zero).[1] For example, Figure 8-3 shows how to insert the value -1 for each missing value in a text file.

Figure 8-3   Replacing Missing Data Values with a Constant

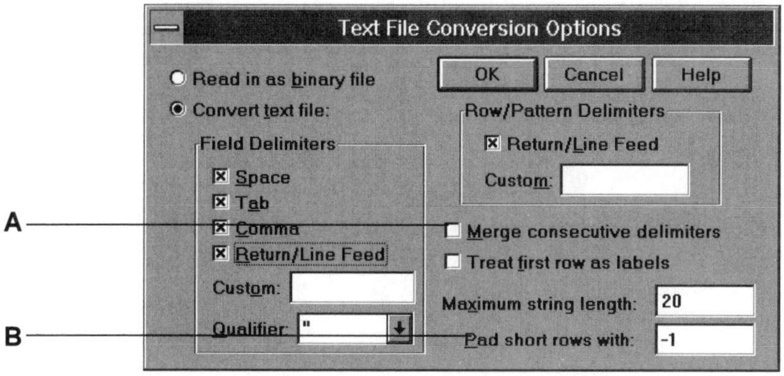

A. Click here to disable the Merge consecutive delimiters option. This will allow missing values to be registered by two consecutive delimiters.
B. Enter the constant value replace missing values with here (also used to pad short rows).

---

1. This value also is used by PRW to pad the end of short rows.

Replacing Missing Data with the Average

To replace missing values with the average of the remaining data values is a little trickier. This is done in several steps. First, you will import the text file and replace missing values with some unique value that will not otherwise appear in the data range (e.g., for a variable that falls within the range 0–1, you could use -1). Then, in the spreadsheet, you will compute the average of all data values that are not equal to the replacement value for the missing data points. This can be easily calculated using a function definition program as follows:

```
V2:
;First create a column containing a 1 for every
;valid value in column V1 and a 0 for each missing
;value. This program assumes the missing values were
;imported as -1's.
Valid = IF(V1 = -1, 0, 1)

;Now add up the valid values.
ValidSum = SUM(Valid*V1)

;Count the number of valid values.
NumValid = SUM(Valid)

;Compute the average, sum divided by the number of
;valid values. Use the CONSTANT macro function to
;preserve this value regardless of how column V1
;changes.
V2 = CONSTANT(ValidSum/NumValid)
```

Finally, you will create a new column which copies the data values in V1, except the missing data values are replaced with the average:

```
V3 = IF(V1 = -1, V2, V1)
```

The new column V3 can now be used in place of column V1. If you wish to delete columns V1 and V2 in the spreadsheet, you can wrap V3 with the CONSTANT macro function (as shown below). Then you can delete columns V1 and V2 without affecting the values in V3.

```
V3 = CONSTANT(IF(V1 = -1, V2, V1))
```

Explicitly Encoding Missing Values

Creating an independent input and encoding missing values is similar to replacing missing values with the average. First, you import the text file and replace missing values with a unique value that will not otherwise appear in the data. Then create a new column that indicates valid values with a 1 and missing values with a 0:

```
V2 = IF(V1 = -1, 0, 1)
```

You would then define both V1 and V2 as input variables in the I/O screen of the experiment manager.

Generating a Predictive Model

Generating a model to predict the missing values is easy in PRW. It simply involves solving a "mini" problem before tackling the real problem of interest. Let us assume we have inputs in columns V1–V5 and that only column V1 contains missing data values. In this case, we want to train a model to predict V1 using the inputs V2–V5. The steps are as follows:

1. **Extract data without missing values.**

   In the spreadsheet, you will need to extract the input patterns with a valid value in column V1. This can be accomplished by using the EXTRACT macro function:

   ```
   V6:
   ;Determine which rows contain valid data.
   Valid = IF(V1 = -1, 0, 1)

   ;Extract only the valid rows.
   V6 = EXTRACT(Valid, V1:V5)
   ```

2. **Define the problem as function estimation with training and testing.**

   In the setup screen of an experiment manager, enable the **Function Estimation** and **Train + Test** options.

3. **Specify V7–V10 as input variables and V6 as the output variable.**

   In the I/O screen of the experiment manager, put the variables V7–V10 in the input variables list box. Put the variable V6 in the output variables list box.

4. **Set up train and test parameters.**

   Use 70% of available data patterns for training and 30% for testing. Use the **Remaining Data** option in the Test Set parameters.

5. **Create, configure, run, and evaluate experiments in the control screen.**

   In this step, you will be solving a "mini" function estimation problem. Once you are satisfied with your results, proceed to the next step.

6. **Build a user function from the selected trained experiment.**

   Select the desired experiment in the experiment icons area of the control screen and invoke the **Build→Function...** command. Select the **An Experiment** option in the **Build** window. Enter a user function name if desired. Then click the **OK** button in the **Build Function From Experiment** window.

7. **Apply the user function to the input columns V2–V5.**

   In the spreadsheet, run the estimator model (user function name of USER1) by using columns V2–V5 as inputs to predict column V1.

   ```
   V11 = USER1(V2:V5)
   ```

8. **Now integrate the predicted values for column V1.**

   Create a new column V12 that substitutes the predicted values for the missing values in column V1:

   ```
   V12 = IF(V1 = -1, V11, V1)
   ```

You can now use column V12 instead of column V1 as an input variable for the pattern recognition problem.

You can repeat this basic process for each data column containing missing data values. When you extract patterns for the training set, just use the OR operator to choose complete patterns. For example,

```
V6 = EXTRACT(IF(V1 = -1 | V2 = -1 | V3 = -1 | V4 = -1
     | V5 = -1, 0, 1)
```

A.2   Converting Non-Numeric Inputs

Another necessary part of preparing data is converting non-numeric inputs into meaningful numeric values.

Automatic Conversion Using NUMBER

Transforming dates, times, prices, and percentages into numerical values is simple using the NUMBER macro function. This macro automatically converts common time and date formats into numerical values. The macro function WEEKDAY converts days of the week into the numerical values 0–6. Figure 8-4 shows some sample data in PRW converted using the NUMBER macro function.

Figure 8-4   Text Conversion Using the Number Macro Function

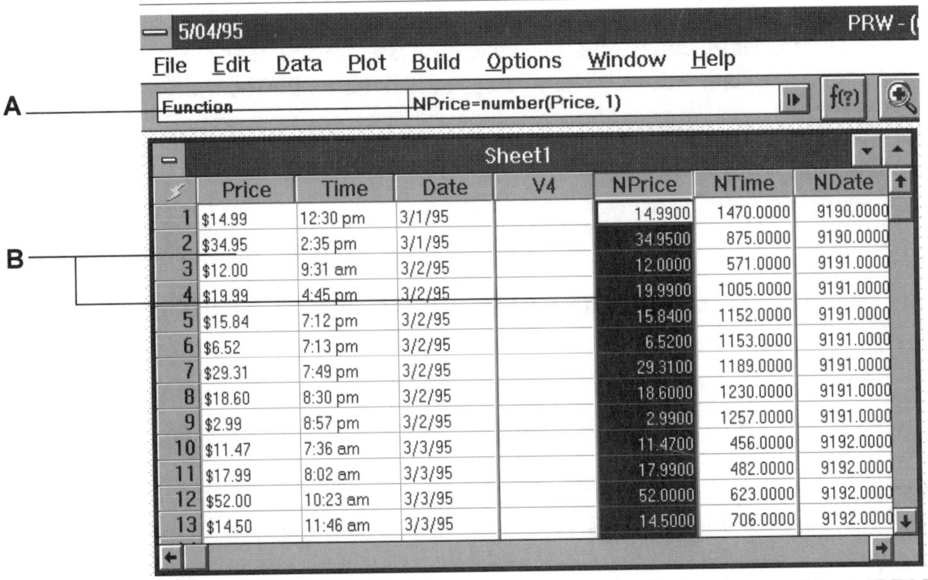

A. This simple macro function converts the first column of text (PRICE) into numerical equivalents.
B. This is the first (PRICE) column containing text strings. The highlighted column shows the converted numerical values.

The NUMBER macro function also can convert the first five characters of any text string into unique numerical values. This is very useful for converting classification labels. It does not matter what numerical value a class is transformed into, as long as every example of that "class" gets converted into the same value. This is exactly what the NUMBER macro function does.

For example, referring to the omelette example with the "male" and "female" inputs, we can map these to any two unique numbers as follows:

```
NGENDER = NUMBER(GENDER, 0)
```

Solving Data Mining Problems through Pattern Recognition

where GENDER is the column containing the text strings and NGENDER is the newly created column containing the numerical transformation. The second argument to NUMBER says to generate unique numerical values for each different text string.

> ☞ **NOTE:** Since NUMBER only considers the first five characters of a text string in this mode (*conversion_keyword* = 0), this will only work if each class label is uniquely identified with the first five characters. If this is not the case, you will need to use other string manipulation functions to make the text strings unique before applying the NUMBER macro function.

Manual Text Substitution Using IF

You may often encounter text-valued input variables with sequential relationships. In these cases, they can be converted using the IF macro function. Referring to the omelette example with the "small," "medium," and "large" inputs, we can map these to the number of eggs used in the omelette (2, 3, and 4 respectively) as follows:

```
NSIZE = IF(SIZE = "small", 2,
          IF(SIZE = "medium", 3, 4))
```

> ☞ **NOTE:** In this example, the "else" clause is used to assign the value "4" to any omelette that is not "small" or "medium" (i.e., "large").

If you have many different text values to convert, you may want to resort to a different method for conversion (e.g., a program or search and replace with a word processor).

Using SUBSTITUTE

Similarly, we can perform the same transformation using the SUBSTITUTE macro function. This is accomplished in several steps in the spreadsheet.

1. Use the COUNT_DIFF macro function to generate a listing of the unique values (this should give us the values small, medium, large).

```
UNIQUE = COUNT_DIFF(SIZE)
```

2. Create a column of numbers corresponding to the replacement values. For example, if the strings appeared in the previously specified order:

```
REPLACE = 2 TO 4
```

If the values were jumbled (say large, small, medium), then:

```
REPLACE = 4, 2, 3
```

3. Use the substitution table you just created to replace the string values with numbers:

```
NSIZE = SUBSTITUTE(SIZE, UNIQUE, REPLACE)
```

A.3   Handling Inconsistent Data or Outliers

PRW provides all of the basic tools required for identifying and filtering out inconsistent data or outliers. The techniques described in Section 8.1 are addressed here.

Scatter Graphs of Classification Data

If you have a classification problem, you can view any two input variables at a time in a scatter plot, using different colors to indicate the output classes. You may then be able to identify clearly inconsistent data points (i.e., a point lying in a midst of different colored points). While this approach may work well for low-dimensional problems, it may be more difficult to visualize any clear classification regions for higher-dimensional problems.

To plot a scatter graph using an output class variable, you must use the full graphing method. This means no data in the spreadsheet can be selected when you invoke the **Plot➔Scatter Graph** command. This will bring up the **Scatter Graph** window shown in Figure 8-5.

Figure 8-5   Identifying Outliers in a Classification Scatter Graph

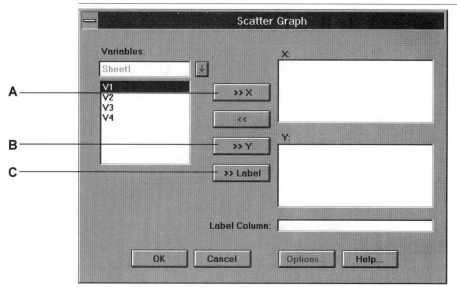

A. Click here to move the selected variable into the X list box.
B. Click here to move another variable into the Y list box.
C. Click here to move the output class variable into the Label Column box.

If we had a simple classification problem where we were trying to classify inputs V1–V3 into one of the classes defined in column V4, we might plot V1 vs. V2 with V4 as the label column. A simple vowel recognition classification problem is shown in Figure 8-6.

Figure 8-6 Vowel Classification Scatter Graph

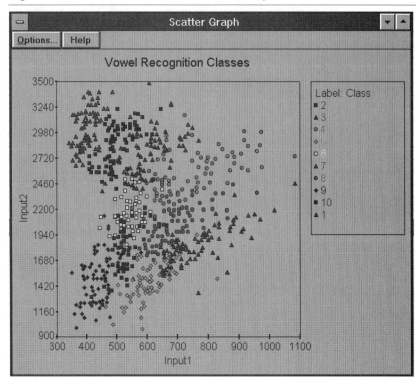

Using a Histogram to Identify Outliers

You can easily plot a histogram of each of the input variables to look at the distribution of data values and see if there are any outliers. To plot the histogram of a column, simply select the column and invoke the **Plot➔Histogram** command. Once the **Histogram** window appears, you can increase the number of bins interactively to view the histogram in more detail.

Solving Data Mining Problems through Pattern Recognition

Figure 8-7   Using a Histogram to Discover Outliers

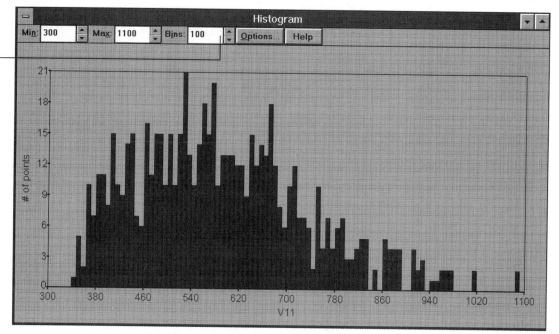

A. Click the up and down arrows here to interactively change the number of bins in the histogram. You also can enter a value directly in the Bins text box.

In the histogram example in Figure 8-7, you can see there are a small number of points with values greater than 1,000. You could decide to filter out and examine these particular points and potentially discard them as outliers or set them to the value of 1,000.

Calculating a Mean and Standard Deviation to Identify Outliers

Another method to identify outliers is to calculate the mean and standard deviation of an input column. You might then decide any data points further than three standard deviations from the mean will be considered outliers as shown in the following function definition program:

```
V2:
ColMean = AVG(V1)
ColStd = STDV(V1)
Thresh = ColMean + 3*ColStd
V2 = IF(ABS(V1) < Thresh, 1, 0)
```

This simple program creates a column V2 containing a 1 for valid values and a 0 for outliers. You can then use the EXTRACT macro function (as described below) to extract the desired example patterns.

Filtering and Extracting Example Patterns

You can determine a threshold value for filtering in any number of ways (e.g., by viewing a histogram of the input variable, using a mean and standard deviation, using a percentage of the min/max range, etc.). Once you have selected a threshold value, it is easy to identify patterns exceeding the threshold using the IF macro function:

```
V2 = IF(V1 > threshold, 0, 1)
```

You can replace threshold in the above equation with a value, or you can define a column called threshold in the spreadsheet containing a single constant value, the threshold to use. Column V2 now contains a 1 for each value within the specified threshold.

To extract the "valid" patterns (i.e., those falling under the threshold), you can use the EXTRACT macro function:

```
V3 = EXTRACT(V2, V1)
```

Similarly, you can easily extract the outliers:

```
V3 = EXTRACT(!V2, V1)
```

Once you have extracted the "outliers," you can perform analysis on them, view them in graphs, and decide whether they should be discarded or not. You might also decide to tweak the threshold value used for filtering after viewing the identified outliers.

Solving Data Mining Problems through Pattern Recognition

**Winzorizing
Outlier Values**

Alternatively, you can use a similar macro function to winzorize or thresh-old outliers:

```
V2 = IF(V1 > upper_bound, upper_bound,
        IF(V1 < lower_bound, lower_bound, V1))
```

This macro function replaces values in V1 greater than upper_bound with the upper_bound value and the values less than lower_bound with lower_bound. All other values remain the same.

Chapter 9

Data Preprocessing

The fourth step of the development process is data preprocessing. Though this step is often critical to the success of a model, it is often overlooked. The goal of preprocessing your data is to simplify the pattern recognition problem *without* throwing away any important information. This chapter covers the following topics:

❏ Why should you preprocess your data?
❏ Reducing noise
❏ Enhancing the signal
❏ Reducing the input space
❏ Normalizing data
❏ Modifying prior probabilities
❏ Other Considerations

9.1 WHY SHOULD YOU PREPROCESS YOUR DATA?

Reducing Noise

One of the primary reasons for preprocessing data is to reduce noise and inconsistent data. Noisy data can obscure the underlying signal and cause confusion, especially if a key input variable is noisy. Preprocessing can often reduce noise and enhance the signal.

Reducing the Input Space

The input space consists of all possible input patterns and is typically huge. The size of the input space increases *exponentially* with respect to the input dimension (i.e., the number of input variables). If the input space is very large compared to the amount of available data, the amount of data in any local region of the space will be insufficient for accurate modeling. This typically means the model will do poorly on future patterns. Preprocessing can help to reduce the input space, improving the mapping of the model.

By identifying the most important input variables and eliminating correlated variables that offer little or no independent information, you can significantly reduce the number of input variables. One often effective way to do this is to combine one or more input variables as a single input (e.g., taking a ratio of two variables).

Reducing the input space can result in significantly improved results if you have limited amounts of data.Unless there is a very large number of patterns so the model can discriminate the useful features from noise, it will inevitably mistake some noise as valuable. This is because if you present a large number of unimportant inputs to the model, probability dictates that some of them will randomly correlate with the outputs to the point that the model assigns weight to them. Accumulating more data will expose these untrue inputs, but that is not always possible. Preprocessing serves as a method of reducing the number of inputs and the input variances, which reduces noise.

Feature Extraction

In many problems, extracting "features" from the raw data will result in significantly improved pattern recognition. Features capture characteristics of the inputs that are most relevant for the estimation or classification problem at hand. Typically, domain-specific knowledge is used to develop good features.

One example where feature extraction is employed is in character recognition. The raw data might be a bitmap of values. While this bitmap could be used as input to a model for classification, it is a very complex problem requiring a very long time and a large number of examples. Features such as the presence of horizontal and vertical lines or circles could be used instead to simplify the problem. These characteristics are insensitive to scaling or rotation and thus incorporate some of our prior knowledge concerning character recognition. Other less obvious "features" might include a histogram projection along various axes. These combined features often can result in a more intelligent characterization of the problem.

Feature extraction is a very problem-specific topic and the commonly used techniques vary for different problem domains. Although this topic is not further addressed in this book, research literature often can provide good leads and suggestions for preprocessing data for your problem.

Normalizing Data

Normalization (i.e., scaling) of the input data can be critical for many training algorithms. Inputs with large numerical values can dominate the effects of inputs and adversely affect model accuracy of many training algorithms. Renormalizing all input data to the same range of values is essential in this context. How you should normalize the data will depend on the distribution of your data.

Modifying Prior Probabilities

Typically for classification problems, you will want the probability of the example patterns in your training and test sets to represent the actual probabilities you will encounter in real life. Preserving these probabilities allows the classifier to optimize the solution to minimize overall expected error. Another frequently employed tactic is to set the prior probability[1] of all output classes to be equal. This ensures that a classifier's resources are devoted equally to minimizing error for each class.

Caveat

While preprocessing is very important and it often holds the key for successful or unsuccessful data modeling, you want to be careful of the amount of preprocessing. Preprocessing can help in many ways, but if you

---

1. The prior probability of an output class is the expected frequency of occurrence of a given class, given no previous assumptions.

throw out too much data or information in an attempt to simplify the problem, you may be inadvertently throwing away important features. Sometimes it is better to not "overprocess" the data, but instead allow a nonparametric method sort out what are important distinctions and what are not.

A good approach to preprocessing is to start with minimal preprocessing and then incrementally add more preprocessing while evaluating the results. Since the development process is one of iterative refinement and experimentation, you should not expect to achieve "perfect" preprocessing the first time. You will very likely return to the preprocessing step and experiment with and compare different approaches.

9.2 AVERAGING DATA VALUES

If you have a noisy system with time-series data (i.e., data for a single input variable collected over time), one good method for reducing noise is to average several data points to produce new example patterns. Averaging makes the values of each input variable less sensitive to small fluctuations. Moving averages can work especially well in time-series modeling problems, where oversampling gives the luxury to be able to do so.

Averaging to reduce noise has a good theoretical basis. If a noisy measurement has a standard deviation of σ, the expected RMS error between an average and the true mean (expectation) decreases at a rate of $1/\sqrt{N}$. Figure 9-1 shows an example of how noise can be reduced by averaging.

Figure 9-1   Example of Noise Reduction by Averaging

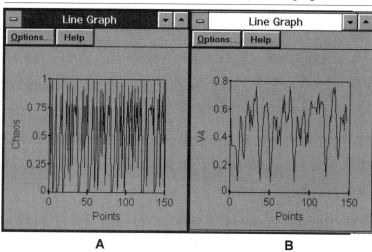

A. Original noisy time-series data
B. Time-series data averaged over a window of 5 data points

9.3   THRESHOLDING DATA

Once data is in a numeric format, it may benefit from simple signal
enhancement techniques such as thresholding.

**Thresholding
in Image Data**

For example, when dealing with gray-scale, bitmap images for a handwriting recognition problem, we really only care if a particular bitmap pixel is
"on" (black) or "off" (white). A camera capturing the input may capture
the data in grayscale values between 0–255, where 0 represents a purely
white pixel and increasing values indicate darker shades of gray until 255,
which represents black. A simple threshold of the bitmap data could
change all pixel values of less than 200 to zero and all values greater than
200 to 255. This simple technique converts the gray-scale image into a

monotone image, eliminating most gray smudges and other noisy effects that might be confusing.[2]

9.4 REDUCING THE INPUT SPACE

You may want to consider reducing the input space if you do not have much available data in comparison to the size of the input space. To give you an idea of how fast input spaces grow with respect to the number of inputs, let's consider some quick examples.

Exponential Input Space Size

If we define a classification problem to have 10 input features, each of which can have only 2 possible values (0 or 1) indicating the presence or absence of a particular feature, there are a total of $2^{10} = 1024$ possible different inputs. Increasing this by 50% to 15 input variables increases the input space to $2^{15} = 32768$, a 32-fold increase!

As another example, if you have a problem with 10 inputs and each input can have 10 possible values (which is actually very little, since many input variables can have an infinite number of input values),[3] you have an explosion of $10^{10} = 10,000,000,000$ possible different values in the input space. Suddenly, you will need one million patterns to cover just 0.01% of the 10 billion possible inputs.

Luckily, in most problems, the inputs cluster in a tiny region of the total input space, so problems can be solved using only thousands or tens of thousands of example patterns. However, you do need to consider that the more input variables you have and the more values those inputs independently assume, generally the more example patterns you need to generate an accurate mapping of the inputs to the outputs.

---

2. In imaging, low-pass filters are commonly used to reduce noise in pictures and high-pass filters are used to detect edges.

3. Having only 10 possible values is equivalent to preprocessing all input values into 10 different bins. For example, 1 might represent all values less than 0, 2 might represent all values between 0 and 100, 3 might represent all values between 100 and 200, etc.

Solving Data Mining Problems through Pattern Recognition

Reducing the Input Space

Unless you have an exceedingly large number of input variables compared to the amount of available data, you may want to try a few preliminary models using all of your input variables. You can then try reducing the number of input variables and compare the performance. Some methods for reducing the input space are discussed below.

Principal Component Analysis

Principal component analysis (PCA) is one method of factor analysis for reducing the number of input variables. Intuitively, PCA attempts to identify an m-dimensional subspace of the n-dimensional input space that seems most "significant," and then project the data onto this subspace. In doing so, the number of input variables is reduced from n to m.

To describe the process in greater detail, PCA begins by computing n orthonormal vectors, known as the principal components, which provide a basis for the input space. These principal components are ordered in sequence from most to least significant. Since these unit vectors each point in a direction perpendicular to the others, they can be viewed as a new set of axes for the input space. Due to the computation performed by PCA, this new set of axes possesses useful properties that are lacking in the original set of axes (i.e., the original input variables). In particular, when the input data is viewed using this new set of axes, the variance of the data is maximal along the first axis, next highest along the second axis, etc. Figure 9-2 illustrates an example of two-dimensional data transformed using PCA. The input data set is viewed using alternative sets of axes: the original axes and the principal components.

Because of the way PCA operates, it is essential all input variables are normalized within the same range of data values before application. Otherwise, a dimension of data with large numerical values will dominate and determine one of the principal axes when it may not be ideal.

If PCA is performed subsequent to normalizing the original input variables, it seems reasonable to suspect that the first principal components, i.e., those along which the data exhibits highest variance, are the most significant. Hence, the size of the input space may be reduced in a sensible and systematic way by eliminating the latter principal components. When performing this reduction, it is important to examine the difference in variance between the variables maintained and those eliminated. Only the variables of relatively low variance should be eliminated. We refer the reader to [Jolliffe, 1986] for a detailed description and analysis of PCA.

Figure 9-2 Principal Component Analysis Example

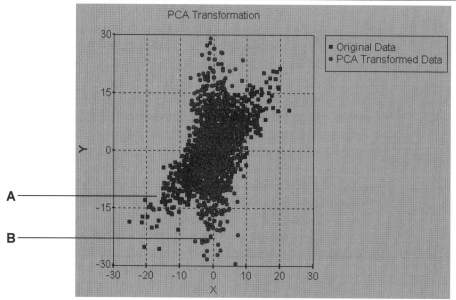

A. The input data viewed on original axes (diagonal data)
B. The input data viewed on principal components (vertical data)

Eliminating Correlated Input Variables

Another method for reducing the input space is to remove highly correlated input variables. You can determine if two or more input variables are correlated by

- Performing statistical correlation tests (e.g., s-test, t-test, etc.)
- Visual inspection of graphed data variables
- Seeing if a data variable can be modeled using one or more others

Once you have identified highly correlated variables, you can eliminate all but one of them as input variables. Some other methods for eliminating unimportant input variables include the following:

- Use linear regression to rank each input variable's importance. Then use the best n input variables.

- Experiment by picking different subsets of the available input variables and compare the modeling performance of each subset.

- Perform feature searches forwards or backwards. In a forward feature search, if you have n input variables, you start by creating n one-input models and select the best one. Then create n-1 two-input models using the best single input combined with each of the remaining n-1 inputs and select the best one. You can continue this way, adding another input variable each time, until you have reached the desired number of input variables.

  In a backwards feature search, you begin with n models, each with a different set of n-1 inputs (each model eliminates a different input variable) and select the best one. You can then proceed to a model with n-2 inputs by constructing the n-1 different variations and picking the best one, and so on. Though this method often works well in practice, it can lead to potential dangers. In particular, it is possible that two features independently demonstrate no predictive power, but when used together generate excellent predictions.

Combining Non-Correlated Input Variables

For independent variables, you can combine two or more into a single input variable to reduce the input space. For example, in a manufacturing process, you might use temperature divided by pressure instead of temperature and pressure as two independent inputs.[4] This is another area where you can incorporate your knowledge of the problem behavior to help construct more meaningful features by combining them. By providing such

---

4. You also could provide a new variable (ratio of temperature over pressure) in *addition* to the input variables temperature and pressure. Sometimes, this provides new information (the ratio) more readily to the model, yet retains important input variables so that the model is not forced to decompose the individual components from the ratio.

combinations of input variables, you can not only potentially reduce the size of the input space, but you can provide your insight into the problem and simplify the modeling problem.

Sensitivity Analysis

An additional method for reducing the input space involves using sensitivity analysis to rank input variables in order of significance. We discuss this approach in the context of a single-output estimation model, though this discussion naturally extends to estimation models with multiple outputs, as well as classification models employing estimates of posterior probabilities.

Sensitivity analysis is the study of how changes in input variables affect the output variable. This typically involves the use of a gradient model. A gradient model can usually be generated from an underlying estimation model, and for an estimation model with n inputs and one output, the corresponding gradient model takes n inputs and generates n outputs. Each of the outputs is the derivative of the estimation model output with respect to the corresponding input variable, evaluated at the current set of inputs. Figure 9-1 illustrates this relationship between the input/output structure of an estimation model and its gradient model.

Figure 9-3 Input/Output Structure Gradient Model vs. Estimation Model

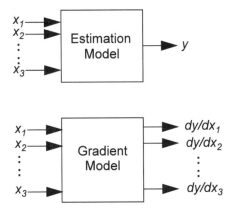

Solving Data Mining Problems through Pattern Recognition

In general, if variations of a particular input variable cause large changes in the estimation model output, the variable is very significant. On the other hand, a variable is insignificant when its value has little or no effect on the value of the output variable. Hence, the significance of a particular input variable x_i is related to the average size of the output gradient dy/dx_i over typical input values.

Given this reasoning, one way to get a rough approximation of the significance of an input variable is to construct a simple estimation model using a data set, generate a gradient model based on the estimation model, and then measure the average of squared output values of the gradient model over another data set. Input variables for which the average squared gradient is small may be discarded when a more accurate estimation model is to be produced.

Note there is an important fundamental difference between the use of sensitivity analysis to reduce the input space and the other approaches we have discussed. That is, sensitivity analysis prunes input variables based on information provided by both input and output data. Other methods we have discussed rely only on the structure of the example data over the input space. The use of information provided by output data often makes sensitivity analysis a more powerful approach to dimensionality reduction. However, with this extra power comes many complications in the process of getting sensitivity analysis to work well.

9.5 NORMALIZING DATA

Data normalization is one of the most commonly used preprocessing techniques.

9.5.1 Why Normalize Data?

Models that Perform Better

Many nonparametric algorithms implicitly assume distances in different directions in the input space carry the same weight. For example, the K-nearest neighbor classifier using a Euclidean distance measure depends on all input dimensions being scaled equally. In this case, it is important to normalize the data along every input dimension. Otherwise, a single dimension can vastly dominate the distance measure.

Similarly, the backpropagation (BP)/multi-layered perceptron (MLP) model often performs better if all of the inputs and outputs are normalized. Since BP performs gradient descent to minimize error, scaling the outputs prevents traversing long valleys in a dimension with much larger magnitude than the others. Since large values can affect a weight change significantly, unscaled inputs can slow down the error minimization process. In addition, always scaling inputs to a known range (e.g., 0–1)[5] gives you a good idea of what learning parameters to use (e.g., step size).

Avoiding Numerical Problems

Some kind of data normalization also may be necessary to avoid numerical problems such as precision loss from arithmetic overflows. If you are working with very large numbers, you should consider either subtracting a constant (such as the minimum of the input variable) from each value or normalizing the data range.

9.5.2   Types of Normalization

There are many ways to normalize or scale data. We will discuss several types and the advantages of each.

Min-Max Normalization

Min-max normalization performs a linear transformation of the original input range into a newly specified data range (typically 0–1). The old minimum, $min1$, is mapped to the new minimum, $min2$. Similarly, the old maximum, $max1$, is mapped to the new maximum, $max2$. All points inbetween are linearly mapped to the new scale. For example, the points 100, 110, 150, 200 normalized into the range of 0–1.0 would be 0, 0.1, 0.5, and 1.0. The mathematical formula for min-max normalization is shown in Eq. 1:

---

5. The range into which the data should be scaled depends on the transfer function being used. Data should be normalized between 0–1 for a sigmoid transfer function or -1–1 for a hyperbolic tangent transfer function, etc.

$$y' = \left(\frac{y - min1}{max1 - min1}\right)(max2 - min2) + min2 \qquad \textbf{(EQ 1)}$$

where y is the original value, y' is the new value, *min1* and *max1* are the minimum and maximum of the original data range, and *min2* and *max2* are the minimum and maximum of the new data range.

One of the advantages of min-max normalization is that it preserves all relationships of the data values exactly. It does not introduce any potential biases into the data (the shape of the histogram is preserved). This normalization method is very commonly used and is a good method to benchmark other methods against. Figure 9-4 shows an example of data normalized using min-max normalization. Notice that the data looks the same; only the values on the y-axis have changed.

Figure 9-4   Example of Min-Max Normalization

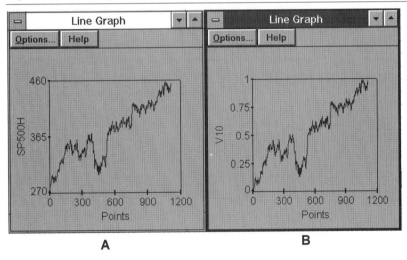

A

B

A. Original unnormalized data
B. Data normalized using min-max normalization

Zscore Normalization

Zscore normalization (sometimes referred to as zero-mean, unit-variant normalization) translates the input variable data so the mean is zero and the variance is one. It computes the mean and standard deviation of the input data. Then it transforms each input value by subtracting the mean and dividing by the standard deviation. The formula is shown in Eq. 2:

$$y' = \frac{y - mean}{std}$$

(EQ 2)

where y is the original value, y' is the new value, and *mean* and *std* are the mean and standard deviation of the original data range, respectively.

Zscore normalization works well in cases where you do not know the actual minimums and maximums of your input variables or when you have outlier values that dominate a min-max normalization. For example, if the majority of your data values fall between 50 and 100, yet you have a few data points with a value of 10,000, normalizing the data using min-max will compress the majority of your values into a tiny range of values. Zscore normalization bases the normalization on the standard deviation of the example population. Figure 9-5 shows an example of data normalized using zscore normalization.

Figure 9-5   Example of Zscore Normalization

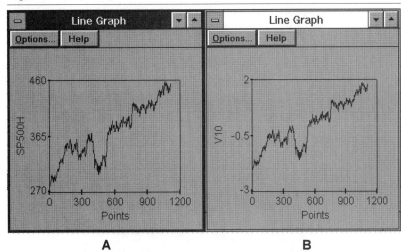

A. Original unnormalized data
B. Data normalized using Zscore normalization

Sigmoidal Normalization

Sigmoidal normalization transforms the input data nonlinearly into the range -1 to 1, using a sigmoid function. It calculates the mean and standard deviation of the input data. Data points within a standard deviation of the mean are mapped to the almost linear region of the sigmoid. Outlier points are compressed along the tails of the sigmoidal function. The formula is shown in Eqs. 3 and 4:

$$y' = \frac{1 - e^{-\alpha}}{1 + e^{-\alpha}} \qquad \text{(EQ 3)}$$

where

$$\alpha = \frac{y - mean}{std} \qquad \text{(EQ 4)}$$

Sigmoidal normalization is especially appropriate when you have outlier data points you wish to include in the data set. It prevents the most commonly occurring values from being compressed into essentially the same values without losing the ability to represent very large outlier values.

To show the advantage of using sigmoidal normalization, we have added two outlier points to the original signal (see Figure 9-6). While both min-max and zscore normalization tend to compress the real signal data, sigmoidal normalization captures the very large outlier values without overly compressing the real range of data values.

Figure 9-6   Example of Sigmoidal Normalization

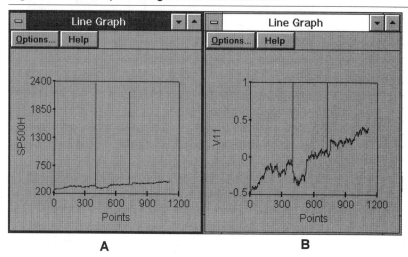

A

B

A. Original unnormalized data
B. Data normalized using sigmoidal normalization

9.6 MODIFYING PRIOR PROBABILITIES

☞ **NOTE:** This section applies only to classification problems.

Matching Expected Probabilities

In classification problems, each output class will have a certain number of examples in the data set. This allows you to easily compute a prior probability for each output class. Generally, you want this probability to match the future expected frequency of occurrences as closely as possible to minimize total classification error (Bayesian classification theory). However, by sampling and presenting patterns from each class with different frequencies, you can, in effect, modify the apparent probability of each output class.

If you know what the expected probabilities of each class should be, you can simulate that probability by presenting the available data to the classifier in the "right" frequency. For example, if you had two output classes, A and B, each occurring 50% of the time in the training set, but you have reason to believe they actually occur in a 2:1 ratio, you could present each pattern of class A twice for each time you present a pattern from class B. This increases the probability of class A to 67% and lowers the probability of class B to 33%.

Another way to look at this is to consider each output class as having a "weight" or a "cost" association. This allows you to essentially stipulate that making a mistake in one class may be more costly than making a mistake in the other. This "cost" can result in the classifier modeling one class better than the others.

Other Probabilities

While matching expected probabilities is the most common approach, sometimes you may want a model that treats all output classes as equally important, even if they do not occur with equal probability in real life (e.g., manufacturing defect detection). By sampling classes equally, the classifier will dedicate its resources to the correct modeling of each output class equally.

9.7   OTHER CONSIDERATIONS

This section discusses some other issues you may want to consider. Some of these preprocessing suggestions have been shown to work over a large class of problems; others are algorithm specific.

Classifier Characteristics

You must consider the characteristics of the specific classifier being used for modeling when contemplating preprocessing issues. For example, some classifiers like CHAID use categorical inputs directly, which may reduce the amount of preprocessing required on categorical variables. CHAID does, however, require that continuous variables be preprocessed into bins.

Another potentially important factor in choosing preprocessing methods is the level of understanding you want to achieve from the final results. More complicated systems (e.g., neural networks) are more difficult to interpret than simpler systems (e.g., decision trees).

In general, you want to reduce the input space while minimizing the loss of information content. You also want to keep the input space smooth by combining similar variables/values. Following these two heuristics results in models with better generalization capabilities as well as being easier to understand.

Uniform and Gaussian Histograms

One generally applicable heuristic is that input variables produce the best modeling accuracy when exhibiting a histogram that is uniform or Gaussian in shape. Uniform distributions contain evenly distributed numbers of examples across the input range of interest. A Gaussian distribution has fewer examples along the tails of the histogram, which will result in a model that is less constrained on the boundaries. However, since there are fewer points along the tails, the overall error will still likely be low.

To evaluate your input variables, plot the histogram of each. Use various functions (e.g., ln, exp, pow, $1/x$) to transform the histogram into a more Gaussian or more uniform shape. Figure 9-7 shows a histogram of a sample signal that is made more Gaussian by taking its log.

Figure 9-7   Making a Histogram More Gaussian

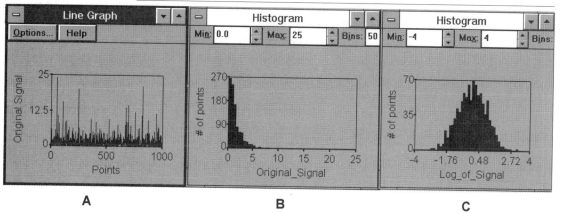

A. The original values of the input variable.
B. A histogram of the input variable.
C. A histogram of the log of the input variable.

Independent Inputs

Some classifiers work better if their inputs are independent for each class (e.g., decision tree, unimodal Gaussian, Gaussian mixture). The Gaussian classifiers can use a diagonal-covariance matrix instead of a full-covariance matrix if the inputs are independent for each class, resulting in faster training and a smaller model size. The decision tree classifier creates boundaries parallel to the input dimensions, and as a result, independent input variables often provide better results.

Some classifiers (e.g., linear regression, logistic regression) gain other benefits from independent input variables. For linear regression and logistic regression, the trained weights of the classifier indicate the exact importance of each input variable when the inputs are independent. This type of information can provide insights into the problem solving process and help determine what inputs can be safely eliminated from the problem definition.

Incorporating Domain-Specific Knowledge

There are probably many ways in which you can enhance the signals or features in your data. Your expert knowledge of your problem and domain can be used during the preprocessing stage to add knowledge to the problem and/or simplify the problem. While we have discussed some common examples and rules of thumb, preprocessing data can involve extensive experimentation to reach superior results.

APPENDIX: PREPROCESSING IN PRW

PRW provides a wealth of preprocessing tools from automated procedures like normalization and prior probabilities modification to a full-function spreadsheet where you can manipulate the data any way you want. Virtually every preprocessing method discussed in this chapter is supported by PRW and is discussed below.

Preprocessing is a very problem-dependent activity. This is the opportunity for you to incorporate what you know about the problem or behavior of the system to simplify the problem. PRW's spreadsheet and library of built-in macro functions provide great flexibility in manipulating data. Being able to wrap any function definition into a user function (which can be saved, exported, and shared) makes it easy to develop your favorite preprocessing tools for easy re-use.

A.1   Averaging Time-Series Data

Time-series data are common in many problems. When collecting time-series data, there is always a question of sampling frequency. As discussed previously, sampling at too high of a rate can introduce small fluctuations which can be ameliorated by averaging together a number of consecutive time-series values.

Averaging multiple data examples to reduce noise can be done simply in a PRW spreadsheet using macro functions. Recall that a time-series variable appears as a single column of data in the spreadsheet. Let's say we would like to produce a new input, a moving average AVGTIME, which averages three adjoining values from the input variable TIME (see Figure 9-8).

Figure 9-8 How Time-Series Data Is Averaged Using SLIDE_WINDOW

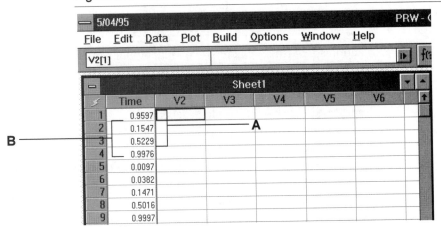

A. The first three values here are averaged to create one new value.

B. The next three values are averaged to create the second new value, and so on. The "window" of three values slides down the column of data vertically to generate the new column of averaged data.

We could then define a function definition program for AVGTIME as follows:

```
AVGTIME:
;First create a window covering three values and
;slide it over the TIME column data. Slide3 will
;contain 3 columns.
Slide3 = (3, TIME)

;Then take the average of each row of Slide3.
AVGTIME = AVG(Slide3, ROW)
```

You also could define this as a single line function definition:

```
AVGTIME = AVG(SLIDE_WINDOW(3, TIME), ROW)
```

To average together more or less values, you simply change the size of the sliding window (i.e., change the value 3 to however many values should be averaged together).

A.2   Thresholding and Replacing Input Values

The simple technique of converting multivalued inputs into binary inputs is easy to implement in the PRW spreadsheet. For the 255 gray-scale imaging problem, we might have:

```
V2 = IF(V1 < 200, 0, V1)
```

This reduces all pixel values less than 200 to white space (0), hopefully eliminating noise and other distractions. To intensify the signal in the remaining pixels, you can make all other values pure black (255) with:

```
V3 = IF(V2 > 0, 255, 0)
```

These can be performed together as follows:

```
V2 = IF(V1 < 200, 0, 255)
```

A.3   Reducing the Input Space

PRW provides both automatic and manual methods for reducing the input space. Both of these are accessed through the **Reduce Input Space** option on the **Experiment Parameters** tab of the **Configuration** window (see Figure 9-9).

Figure 9-9   Reducing the Input Space

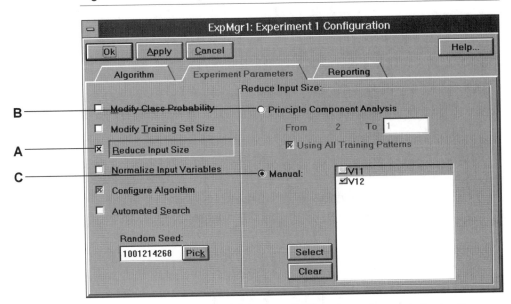

A. Click here to enable the Reduce Input Size option and display the parameters on the right side of the screen.
B. Click here to use PCA to transform the input space.
C. Click here to manually select which input variables to use.

Using Principal Component Analysis

If you select principal component analysis (PCA) to reduce the input space, you simply select the number of input variables you wish to use. The **Using All Training Patterns** option allows you to use all training patterns specified in the train/test screen of the experiment manager, as opposed to the potentially reduced set of patterns specified in the **Modify Training Set Size** preprocessing option.

☞   **TIP:** If you use the **Reduce Input Size** option to perform PCA, you can view any of the **Input Patterns** reports and export the data to a spreadsheet to see the preprocessed data values.

You also can use PCA directly in the spreadsheet using the PCA and PCA_FEATURES macro functions. The PCA macro function generates the eigenvalues and eigenvectors of the specified data range. The PCA_FEATURES macro function generates the transformed variables and is exactly the same as using the **Reduce Input Size** option to perform PCA preprocessing. For example, to reduce the input variables V1–V10 to five variables, you can define:

```
V11 = PCA_FEATURES(5, V1:V10)
```

This function definition generates five output columns spanning V11–V15.

Using Manual Reduction

Using your knowledge of the problem or by performing data analysis in the spreadsheet, you can manually identify which variables you want to use as inputs to your problem. Of course, you can simply define your problem to use your selected inputs, but PRW provides an easy method to change the inputs on a per experiment basis without having to change them on the I/O screen of the experiment manager.

Simply enable the **Manual** option of the **Reduce Input Size** parameters and select the variables you wish to use (only the variables listed on the I/O screen are listed, so you need to include all variables you might want to use on that screen to access them later). This provides an easy way to configure multiple experiments, each using different input variables for comparison.

Sensitivity Analysis

One of the methods for decreasing the number of input variables is to use linear regression (or some other model) to rank the importance of each input variable. This allows you to select the top *n* variables for building your model.

In PRW, you can train a linear regression, logistic regression, MLP, or RBF model and use the **Build Derivative Function** option of the **Build Function From Experiment** window to perform sensitivity analyses on the input variables. The steps are as follows:

1. **Using an experiment manager, define the problem using all available input variables.**

2. **Configure a linear regression, logistic regression, MLP, or RBF experiment and train it.**

   This may be an iterative process to achieve good results. (You may need to normalize your input variables.)

3. **Wrap the trained experiment into a user function with the Build Derivative Function option enabled.**

   Use the **Build→Function...** command to display the **Build Function From Experiment** window. Enable the **Build Derivative Function** option. Fill in the the other parameters in the window and click the **OK** button.

4. **Apply the user function on the data in the spreadsheet.**

   Create a function definition using the new user function. For example, if the user function name is USER1 and the inputs are V1–V10, you might have the function definition:

   ```
   V11 = USER1(V1:V10)
   ```

   This will generate a set of output columns for each input variable. If we had one output, this would generate 10 columns (2 outputs would generate 20 columns, etc.). Each column shows the "sensitivity" of that output to the input.

5. **Sum the absolute value of the derivative function values for each input variable.**

   With 10 output columns, you can use the SUM macro function as follows:

   ```
   V21 = SUM(ABS(V11:V20), COL)
   ```

If you had more than one output, you would need to sum each set of columns corresponding to a single input separately. For example, with two outputs, you might have:

```
V31 = SUM(ABS(V11:V12))
V32 = SUM(ABS(V13:V14))
:
:
V40 = SUM(ABS(V29:V30))
```

6. Normalize the values.

Before comparing the sums, you must normalize them by computing the average and multiplying by the data range spanned by the input variable.

```
V31:
;Compute the average of each column
Col_avgs = AVG(V21:V30, COL)

;Compute the range of each input variable
Mins = MIN(V1:V10, COL)
Maxs = MAX(V1:V10, COL)
Ranges = Maxes - Mins

;Multiply each value by the range
V31 = Col_avgs * Ranges
```

7. Select the input variables with the highest values.

The input variables with the highest computed values have the most impact on the output variables. You can try discarding the input variables with the lowest computed values.

Feature Searches

PRW's experiment manager allows you to easily configure the experiments necessary to perform forward or backwards feature searches. As an example, say we have 10 input variables which we want to reduce to the best 5. To perform a feature search, you will create one experiment manager for each initial input variable. For a forward search, each experiment manager will have a different single input variable (for a backwards search, each experiment manager will have 9 of the 10 input variables, each one missing a different input variable).

After running a similarly configured experiment in each experiment manager (which can be run in parallel), you would view the report summaries of each and select the best performing model. To continue to find the next best input variable, add the top input variable to each of the other 9 experiment managers and run another set of experiments (in a backwards search, you would find the worst performing input variable and eliminate it from each of the experiment managers). You can continue in this way (either forward or backwards) until you reach the desired number of input variables.

A.4   Normalizing Data

Normalization in the Spreadsheet

Normalizing data in PRW can be as simple as turning on the **Normalize Input Variables** option and selecting the type of normalization to use. However, you can always perform your own normalization in the PRW spreadsheet. The built-in macro functions, NORM_MINMAX, NORM_ZSCORE, and NORM_SIGMOID implement min-max, zscore, and sigmoidal normalization respectively. Using the other built-in macro functions, you can write your own custom normalization functions as well. You would then define the normalized variables as inputs to the problem in the I/O screen of the experiment manager.

Normalize Input Variables Option

Automated normalization can easily be performed by enabling the **Normalize Input Variables** option on the **Experiment Parameters** tab of the **Configuration** window (see Figure 9-10). You can choose to normalize all input variables using zscore, min-max, or sigmoidal normalization, or you can choose different normalization methods for different input variables. Simply select the **All Variables** or the **Selected Var.** option and then choose one of the listed methods (including no normalization).

The **Selected Var.** option provides great flexibility allowing you to leave some variables unnormalized or to normalize different input variables using different methods. To view or change the normalization for an input variable, enable the **Selected Var.** option and use the up and down arrows to the right of the text box to list the desired input variable.

Figure 9-10   Normalizing Input Variables

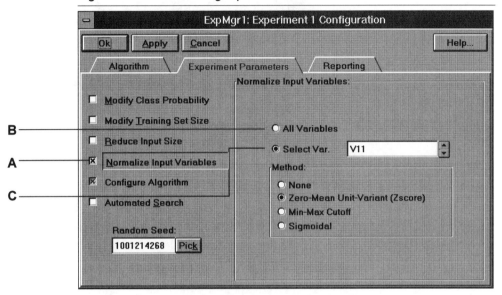

A. Click here to enable the Normalize Input Variables option and display the parameters on the right side of the screen.
B. Click here to normalize all input variables using the method specified below.
C. Click here to choose a different normalization method for each input variable.

A.5   Modifying Prior Input Probabilities

For classification problems, PRW automates control of the class probabilities in the training set. Simply enable the **Modify Class Probability** option on the **Experiment Parameters** tab of the **Configuration** window (see Figure 9-11).

Figure 9-11 Modifying the Class Probabilities

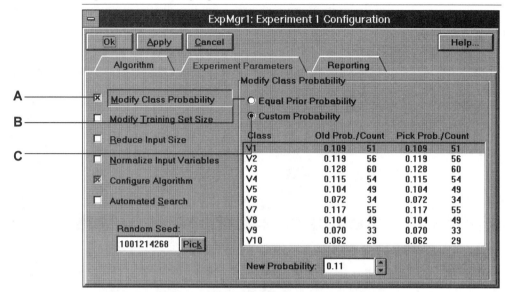

A. Click here to enable the Modify Class Probability option and display the parameters on the right side of the screen.

B. Click here to set all output classes to equal prior probabilities.

C. Click here to specify the probability on a class by class basis.

To make the apriori probabilities for all classes equal, simply enable the **Equal Prior Probability** option. To view or set the probabilities for each output class, enable the **Custom Probability** option. Each of the output classes are listed in the list box. The **Old Prob./Count** columns show the original probability for the class as represented in the training set and the number of actual patterns in that class. The next columns, **New Prob./Count** show the modified class probabilities. To change the probability for a class, select the class and enter a new probability value in the **New Probability** text box at the bottom of the screen. The probabilities of the other classes are all automatically adjusted so that the sum of the probabilities always equals one.

Using the **Custom Probability** option, you can set the class probabilities to their expected or known values (even though these probabilities may not be reflected in your training set). You also can increase the probability of one or more classes that are not performing well. Once you run the experiment, PRW automatically samples patterns from the various output classes to match the prior probabilities you have specified.

Chapter 10

Selecting Architectures and Training Parameters

Architectures and Algorithms

The fifth step of the development process is to select architectures, algorithms, and appropriate training parameters. An architecture is the basic structure of a pattern recognition model. A learning algorithm (referred to simply as "algorithm" for short) tunes free parameters of the architecture according to some objective function (e.g., minimizing RMS error). For example, multilayered perceptron (MLP) is an architecture and backpropagation is one way of tuning the MLP weights (free parameters).

Different algorithms can be used with the same architecture to perform pattern recognition. However, for simplification, since each architecture described in this chapter has only one associated algorithm, we refer to both the architecture and algorithm together simply as an "algorithm."

This chapter discusses some of the most widely used data-driven methods and their practical characteristics.

Algorithms	The following algorithms are considered in this chapter:

- ❏ Linear regression
- ❏ Logistic regression
- ❏ Unimodal Gaussian
- ❏ Multilayer perceptron (MLP)/Backpropagation
- ❏ Radial basis functions (RBF)
- ❏ K nearest neighbors
- ❏ Gaussian mixture
- ❏ Nearest cluster
- ❏ K means clustering
- ❏ Binary decision trees
- ❏ Linear decision trees
- ❏ Projection pursuit
- ❏ Estimate-Maximize (EM) clustering
- ❏ Multivariate Adaptive Regression Splines (MARS)
- ❏ Group Method of Data Handling (GMDH)
- ❏ Parzen's windows
- ❏ Hypersphere classifiers
- ❏ Learning Vector Quantization (LVQ)

10.1 TYPES OF ALGORITHMS

There are many ways of categorizing algorithms. In this section, we will discuss three different perspectives—parametric vs. nonparametric, classification vs. estimation, and the kernel functions of the algorithms.

Parametric vs. Nonparametric

Parametric algorithms assume that the data to be modeled takes on a structure that can be described by a known mathematical expression with a few free parameters (e.g., linear or Gaussian). It then tunes the parameters to best fit the data. If the underlying data is consistent with the parametric model, then good modeling results can be achieved. However, if the form of the data is unknown or does not fit the assumed structure well, then results may be poor. The parametric algorithms discussed in this chapter include linear regression, logistic regression, and unimodal Gaussian.

Nonparametric algorithms do not assume that the data to be modeled follows any particular form. These algorithms have the ability to model any data distribution with high accuracy, though certain nonparametric algorithms are still better suited for particular types of problems. All of the remaining algorithms discussed in this chapter can be considered nonparametric. These are summarized in Table 10-1.

Table 10-1 Parametric and Nonparametric Algorithms

Parametric Algorithms	**Nonparametric Algorithms**
Linear regression	MLP/Backpropagation
Logistic regression	Radial basis functions
Unimodal Gaussian	K nearest neighbors
	Gaussian mixture
	Nearest cluster
	K means clustering
	Binary decision tree
	Linear decision tree
	Projection pursuit
	Estimate-Maximize clustering
	MARS
	GMDH
	Parzen's window
	Hypersphere classifier
	Learning vector quantization

Classification vs. Estimation

Another way to look at these algorithms is to distinguish them by which ones can be used to solve classification problems and which ones can be used for estimation. For a review of "classification" and "estimation" problems, see Section 1.5 and Section 1.6.

☞ **NOTE:** Any estimation algorithm can be used to solve classification problems. The output(s) can either be thresholded into the various classes (e.g., the weight of shrimp can be used to classify the shrimp as "small," "medium," or "large") or each output can be used to estimate the posterior probability of a class.

The algorithms which can be used for classification vs. estimation are shown in Table 10-2.

Table 10-2 Classification vs. Estimation Algorithms

Classification Algorithms	Estimation Algorithms
Unimodal Gaussian	Linear regression
Gaussian mixture	Logistic regression
Nearest cluster	MLP/Backpropagation
Binary decision trees	Radial basis functions
Linear regression	K nearest neighbors
Logistic regression	K means
Backpropagation	Projection pursuit
Radial basis functions	Estimate-Maximize clustering
K nearest neighbors	MARS
K means	Parzen's window
Projection pursuit	Linear decision tree
Estimate-Maximize clustering	GMDH
MARS	
GMDH	
Parzen's window	
Linear decision tree	
Hypersphere classifier	
Learning vector quantization	

Solving Data Mining Problems through Pattern Recognition

Kernel Functions

Another way to look at different algorithms is based on the kernel function used by each algorithm. Understanding the type of kernel function employed by each algorithm helps you understand how the decision region or mapping of the input space is created [Lippmann, 1989]. Algorithms sharing the same type of kernel functions also often share similar characteristics which will be described below.

Table 10-3 shows how the algorithms are divided by their kernel functions (i.e., computing elements).

Table 10-3 Kernel Functions and Decision-Regions Boundaries of Algorithms (Part 1 of 2)

Algorithms	Kernel Function	Boundaries (for classification)	Mapping (for estimation)
Linear regression	Line	Hyperplanes	Best fit line
Projection pursuit	Line	Hyperplanes	Linear inner product
K nearest neighbors Nearest cluster E-M clustering *K* means clustering	Euclidean Norm	Piece-wise linear	Linear combination of weighted Euclidean distances
MLP/Backpropagation Logistic regression	Sigmoid	Hyperplanes	Weighted sum of inputs passed through a sigmoid nonlinearity
Radial basis functions Unimodal Gaussian Gaussian Mixture Parzen's window	Gaussian	Overlapping radial (receptive) fields	Weighted sum of Gaussian outputs
Binary decision tree Linear decision tree	Decision tree	Hyperplanes parallel to input axes	N/A

Table 10-3 Kernel Functions and Decision-Regions Boundaries of Algorithms (Part 2 of 2)

Algorithms	Kernel Function	Boundaries (for classification)	Mapping (for estimation)
MARS	Polynomial decision tree	Piece-wise polynomial	Piece-wise polynomial
GMDH	Polynomial	Piece-wise polynomial	Nonlinear spline
Hypersphere	Hypersphere	Overlapping hyperspheres	N/A

Clearly, the better the fit of the underlying kernel function to the region of interest being modeled, the higher the accuracy the algorithm should achieve. Although nonparametric algorithms are theoretically able to model any data distribution, it is obvious that some algorithms will perform better in specific situations. For example, data that is radially centered around their classifications might be more easily learned by an algorithm using a Gaussian kernel function than one using splines. Another algorithm may require greater complexity, and thus more data to generate a model of comparable accuracy.

General Characteristics

Algorithms using a Euclidean norm often train quickly, but can require large amounts of memory and have slow classification times. Algorithms using a sigmoidal kernel function tend to have low memory requirements and are fast in classification times. However, they typically require long training times. Algorithms with Gaussian kernels tend to train quickly[1] and have medium memory requirements. These practical constraints are discussed in more detail in Section 10.3, "Practical Constraints."

---

1. This of course depends on the actual algorithm used to train an architecture based on Gaussian kernels. The matrix inversion method described in this chapter provides quick training. However, a gradient descent algorithm could be used instead, which would result in much slower training times.

Solving Data Mining Problems through Pattern Recognition

10.2 HOW TO PICK AN ALGORITHM

This section provides some guidelines on finding the best algorithms for your particular pattern recognition problem. While some algorithms will perform better on a class of problems with particular characteristics, most algorithms can achieve statistically equivalent error rates. In many cases, choosing a particular algorithm will be based more on other practical constraints, such as training times, testing times, memory requirements, etc.

Hard Constraints

You may have some hard constraints on selecting an algorithm. For example, if you have an estimation problem, only some of the algorithms described in this book are appropriate. You also may have performance constraints. For example, in a quality control problem for a cookie manufacturing plant, you may need to operate on conveyor belt samples passing by at one per second. One of your solution requirements might then be that all feature extraction, preprocessing, and classification of the input vector must be performed in less than one second.

Other Considerations

Although you may have some hard constraints, most other considerations are probably less restrictive. For example, you may have a dynamic situation where retraining needs to occur frequently, in which case training times may be an issue.

In selecting an algorithm that will balance your problem constraints of accuracy, performance, retraining, etc., you will need to ask yourself the following questions:

- How fast does the model need to be?
- How long can the model take to train?
- What memory requirements are there for the trained model?
- How often will the model need to be retrained?

Prior Knowledge

The more you know about a problem, the less "parameters" must be fit using the data. If you know the form of the underlying relationships, then you can use a parametric algorithm which assumes that form. In this case, a parametric model is not only faster to train due to fewer free parameters, but may provide better accuracy as well (especially on a test set if the training set is not truly representative). Prior knowledge also can bias you towards one algorithm or another (e.g., whether a parametric algorithm is appropriate or not).

If you do not know the underlying form of the data, then it is usually best to use nonparametric algorithms. You can either try a number of them, or you can select one based on algorithm characteristics. Here are some general guidelines that may help you select an appropriate algorithm:

- Parametric algorithms should be used where their form is known to fit the data well (i.e., linear regression for linear systems, logistic regression for sigmoidal distributions, and unimodal Gaussian for Gaussian distributions).

- Binary decision trees are well suited for conjunctive problems (e.g., an object is in class A if it has property x, property y, but not property z). Decision trees divide the input space into regions by defining boundaries that are parallel to the input axes.

- Gaussian mixture estimates probability density functions from data. This can be used to determine when to trust a model's output or for classification.

- In classification problems, methods based on estimating posterior probabilities can be useful for generating confidence measures as well as classifications [Lippmann, 1993].

An alternative strategy is to evaluate linear regression, a more complicated parametric model, and then proceed to nonparametric models. This approach provides good baseline measurements and tackles the easiest algorithms first.

10.3 PRACTICAL CONSTRAINTS

Research [Lee, 1989; Ng, 1990] has shown that often times, many modeling methods can achieve statistically equivalent error rates on the same pattern recognition problem, but may differ by orders of magnitude in other characteristics, such as memory requirements, training time, classification time, training program complexity, and ability to adapt to new data. This section summarizes some of the practical constraints with respect to each algorithm.

10.3.1 Memory Usage

Memory usage refers to the amount of memory required by a model to store the decision regions or mapping of inputs to outputs. While memory usage is heavily dependent on the complexity of the pattern recognition problem (e.g., the number of input variables and the degree of regularity), models vary in the amount of memory required to solve the same problem.

Table 10-4 shows relative memory requirements of each of the different models.

Table 10-4 Memory Usage Comparison

Algorithm	Relative Memory Requirement
Linear regression	Very low
Logistic regression	Very low
Unimodal Gaussian	Very low
Backpropagation	Low
Radial basis functions	Medium
K nearest neighbors	High
Gaussian mixture	Medium
Nearest cluster	Medium
K means	Medium–High
Binary decision tree	Low
Linear decision tree	Low
Project pursuit	Low
Estimate-Maximize clustering	Medium
MARS	Low
GMDH	Low
Parzen's window	High
Hypersphere classifier	Medium
Learning vector quantization	Medium

10.3.2 Training Times

Training time refers to the amount of time (typically measured in CPU seconds) required for a particular algorithm to reach the statistically equivalent error rate. These times vary significantly among the different models and may be an issue if frequent retraining is required.

Table 10-5 shows the relative training time requirements for the different algorithms.

Table 10-5 Training Times Comparison

Algorithm	Relative Training Times
Linear regression	Fast
Logistic regression	Medium
Unimodal Gaussian	Medium–Fast
Backpropagation	Slow
Radial basis functions	Medium
K nearest neighbors	Very fast
Gaussian mixture	Slow–Medium
Nearest cluster	Medium
K means	Medium
Binary decision tree	Fast
Linear decision tree	Fast
Project pursuit	Medium
Estimate-Maximize clustering	Medium
MARS	Medium
Parzen's window	Very fast
GMDH	Medium–Fast
Hypersphere classifier	Medium
Learning vector quantization	Slow

10.3.3 Classification/Estimation Times

Classification/estimation time refers to the amount of time it takes to generate an output when presented with an input pattern (i.e., the testing time). This speed may be very important for real-time and high-throughput applications.

Table 10-6 shows the relative classification times for the different algorithms.

Table 10-6 Classification Times Comparison

Algorithm	Relative Classification Times
Linear regression	Very fast
Logistic regression	Very fast
Unimodal Gaussian	Fast
Backpropagation	Very fast
Radial basis functions	Medium
K nearest neighbors	Slow
Gaussian mixture	Medium
Nearest cluster	Medium–Fast
K means	Medium–Fast
Binary decision tree	Very fast
Linear decision tree	Very fast
Project pursuit	Fast
Estimate-Maximize clustering	Medium
MARS	Fast
GMDH	Fast
Parzen's window	Slow
Hypersphere classifier	Medium
Learning vector quantization	Medium

10.4 ALGORITHM DESCRIPTIONS

This section describes each of the algorithms, their training parameters, and how to select appropriate training parameter values.[2] This section is provided more as a reference than for reading straight through. This section can be skipped without any loss of continuity.

10.4.1 Linear Regression

Linear regression generates a linear mapping between the input variables and each output variable. A multivariate linear relationship between variable y and variables $x_1, x_2, ..., x_N$ can be expressed as:

$$y = w_0 + w_1 x_1 + ... + w_N x_N \qquad \text{(EQ 1)}$$

where the w_i's are the free parameters. In this case, $X = [x_1, x_2, ..., x_N]$ is the input vector and y is an output scalar. Note that the output can be generalized from a scalar to an output vector by producing as many linear models as there are outputs.

If an exact linear relationship exists between y and the x_i's, then a set of w_i's satisfying Eq. 1 can be found using a number of numerical techniques. If the relationship is not exactly linear, then w_i's will satisfy:

$$y = w_0 + w_1 x_1 + ... + w_N x_N + error \qquad \text{(EQ 2)}$$

such that the sum of the squared error terms is minimized over the data set. This is the common least-squares minimization procedure.

The w_i's are found by the solution to the least-squares problem as follows:

---

2. The "free parameters" specified here are the *architecture* parameters (e.g., weights of an MLP network) that must be adjusted to fit the data. The "training parameters" are parameters of the *algorithm* used to tune the architecture parameters (e.g., in backpropagation, training parameters might include the learning rate and momentum).

$$W^* = (X^T X)^{-1} (X^T D) \qquad \textbf{(EQ 3)}$$

where, written in matrix notation, W^* is a column vector containing the weights, and

$$X = \begin{bmatrix} 1 & X_1 \\ 1 & X_2 \\ \dots & \dots \\ 1 & X_N \end{bmatrix}, \qquad D = \begin{bmatrix} d_1 \\ d_2 \\ \dots \\ d_N \end{bmatrix} \qquad \textbf{(EQ 4)}$$

where X_i is the i-th input pattern, recorded as an N-dimensional row vector, and d_i is the desired output for pattern i of the training set.

Linear Regression Typical Settings

Globally optimal parameters are computed without any iterative cycling through the data. Linear regression is parametric since it makes a strong assumption that the underlying relationship between y and the x_i's is linear. Therefore, if the true relationship is nonlinear, linear regression can generate a very poor model.

Linear regression can be used as a baseline algorithm to compare against all other estimation and classification algorithms.

Some implementations of linear regression may allow the selection of different objective functions (e.g., weighted least-squares, cross-entropy).

10.4.2 Logistic Regression

Logistic regression generates a mapping between the input variables and an output according to the logistic function expressed by Eqs. 5 and 6:

$$y = \frac{1}{(1 + e^{-\Sigma})} \qquad \textbf{(EQ 5)}$$

$$\Sigma = w_0 + \sum_{i=1}^{N_{inputs}} w_i x_i \qquad \text{(EQ 6)}$$

where y is the output of the logistic function, the x_i's are the inputs, and the w_i's are the free parameters. To produce multi-output models, logistic regression constructs one model per output.

The cross-entropy cost function is commonly used to fit the logistic function to a data set:

$$E_k = d_k \cdot \ln(1/y_k) + (1 - d_k) \cdot \ln(1/(1 - y_k)) \qquad \text{(EQ 7)}$$

where E_k is the error from the i-th example pattern, y_k is the output produced with the input vector of the k-th example pattern (x_k), d_k is the desired output for the k-th example pattern, and "ln" is the natural log operator. The cross-entropy error for the whole training set is:

$$E = \sum_{k=1}^{N_{train}} E_k \qquad \text{(EQ 8)}$$

This error can be minimized over the entire training set using a fixed-step gradient-descent procedure. Extra smoothing constraints can be incorporated by stopping the procedure before convergence.

The training flow chart for logistic regression is shown in Figure 10-1. The test flow chart is shown in Figure 10-2.

Figure 10-1 Logistic Regression Training Flow Chart

Until the stopping criteria are reached, for each pattern x_k in the training set, compute the logistic output y_k:

$$y_k = \frac{1}{(1 + e^{-\Sigma})}$$

where

$$\Sigma_k = w_o + \sum_{i=1}^{N_{inputs}} w_i x_{ki}$$

Note that $w_{N_{inputs}+1}$ and $x_{N_{inputs}+1}$ are both constants for a compact representation of the bias term c.

Compute the gradient of the entropy error with respect to each weight w_i due to x_{ki}:

$$E_k = d_k \cdot \ln(1/y_k) + (1 - d_k) \cdot \ln(1/(1 - y_k))$$

$$\frac{\partial E_k}{\partial w_i} = \frac{\partial \Sigma}{\partial w_i} \cdot \frac{\partial y_k}{\partial \Sigma} \cdot \frac{\partial E_k}{\partial y_k}$$

$$= x_{ki} y_k (1 - y_k) \left(\frac{y_k - d_k}{y_k(1 - y_k)} \right)$$

$$= x_{ki}(y_k - d_k)$$

Compute the change in weights:

$$\Delta w_i = (-\eta)\frac{\partial E_k}{\partial w_i} = \eta x_{ki}(d_k - y_k)$$

If updating weights on a per pattern basis, then update the weight. If updating weights once per epoch, then accumulate the weight and update at the end of the epoch.

Solving Data Mining Problems through Pattern Recognition

Figure 10-2 Logistic Regression Test Flow Chart

For each pattern in the test set, compute:

$$y_k = \frac{1}{1 + e^{-\Sigma_k}}$$

where

$$\Sigma_k = w_0 + \sum_{i=1}^{N_{input}} w_i x_{ki}$$

Training Parameters

Training parameters for logistic regression include the following:

- **Learning Rate** — The learning rate affects how much weights in the logistic regression network are changed on each update.[3]

- **Update Frequency** — The logistic regression algorithm typically updates the weights of the network either once after the presentation of every pattern, or once after the presentation of all patterns in the training set (i.e., once per epoch).

- **Stop Conditions** — Stop condition(s) determine when the logistic regression algorithm will terminate training. Typical stop conditions are a maximum time, number of epochs of training, or until a specific error (RMS or classification error) reaches a specified value.

There are other variations of logistic regression algorithms. In particular, there is a multipass method using matrix inversion for computing parameters that optimizes the cross-entropy cost function. Also, there are iterative

---

3. This is the step size used in the gradient descent algorithm.

methods for optimizing alternative cost functions such as mean-squared-error.

Logistic Regression Typical Settings

A typical step size for logistic regression minimizing the cross-entropy function is 0.001. Too large of a step size can cause huge random fluctuations of parameters. Too small of a value can result in slow training.

Interactively monitoring the convergence progress is the best way to determine the number of epochs needed for good convergence. Typical values are on the order of 20 to 100 epochs.

Other Notes

Logistic regression using the cross-entropy cost function allows the interpretation of the output variable y as a probabilistic binary value. That is, if y takes on the values of 0 and 1, and the underlying probability of y=1 is generated from a Bernoulli (or point-binomial) variable with probability p, then the logistic regression has a nice theoretical interpretation of the weights w_i's. The exponent of each weight, e^{w_i}, can be interpreted as the odds ratio of the probability that y is associated with input variable x_{ki} [Kleinbaum et al., 1988].

10.4.3 Unimodal Gaussian

The unimodal Gaussian algorithm is a relatively simple parametric model for pattern classification. The basis for this model relies on the assumption that the probability distribution for input vectors of each class is Gaussian. By using Bayes' Rule, the probability of a particular class C_j given an input pattern X is:

$$P(C_j|X) = P(X|C_j)\frac{P(C_j)}{P(X)} \qquad \text{(EQ 9)}$$

where $P(C_j|X)$ is the probability that an input vector X belongs to class C_j; $P(X|C_j)$ is the probability density function (PDF) of an input vector X if the class was known to be j, $P(C_j)$ is the prior probability for class j, and $P(X)$ is the overall PDF of X. A pattern X is classified as the class associated with the largest $P(C_j|X)$ (i.e., the most probable class).

The unimodal Gaussian method generates an estimate of $P(X|C_j)$. It is a parametric method that assumes a Gaussian form:

$$P(X|C_j) = \frac{1}{(2\pi)^{n/2}|V_j|^{1/2}} \cdot e^{[-1/2(X-M_j)^T V_j^{-1}(X-M_j)]} \qquad \textbf{(EQ 10)}$$

Free parameters include the mean M_j of input vectors of each class and the covariance matrix V_j of each class j. Sometimes there is insufficient data for a good estimate of all of these parameters (e.g., the full-covariance matrix for all classes). Therefore, more restrictive forms of the covariance matrix with fewer free parameters are often used. In addition, covariance matrices can be shared among classes to further reduce the number of free parameters.

Figure 10-3 summarizes the Gaussian model training algorithm and Figure 10-4 shows the testing algorithm.

Figure 10-3 Unimodal Gaussian Algorithm Training Flow Chart

For all classes

Compute the Gaussian means M_j:

$$M_j = \frac{1}{N_j} \cdot \sum_{i=1}^{N_j} X_i$$

where M_j is the mean of the distribution for inputs of class j, N_j is the number of patterns in the training set belong to class j, and X_i is the i-th pattern belong to class j.

Compute the covariance matrixes V_j:

For a full-covariance matrix, for each class j with example inputs $X_1, ..., X_{j}$,

For a diagonal-covariance matrix, compute the full-covariance matrix and then zero out the off-diagonal elements of V_j.

$$V_j = \frac{1}{N_j} \cdot \sum_{i=1}^{N_j} (X_i - M_j)(X_i - M_j)^T$$

If the covariance matrix is to be shared among all classes, replace N_j by N, the number of patterns in the whole training set.

Estimate the prior probability $P(C_j)$:

$$P(C_j) = \frac{N_j}{\displaystyle\sum N_{j'}}$$

where N_j is the number of patterns in class j, and N_c is the number of classes.

Corrections

- On page 10–20, the correct equation for $P(C_j)$ is:

$$P(C_j) = \frac{N_j}{\displaystyle\sum_{j'}^{N_c} N_{j'}}$$

- On page 10–21, the correct equation for $L_j(X)$ is:

$$L_j(X) = P(X|C_j) \cdot P(C_j)$$
$$= P(X|C_j) \cdot N_j \bigg/ \left(\sum_{j'}^{N_c} N_{j'} \right)$$

- On page 10–22, the correct equation for $P(C_j|X)$ is:

$$P(C_j|X) = \frac{L_j(X)}{\displaystyle\sum_{k'} L_k(X)}$$

- On page 10–28, the correct equation for $\dfrac{\partial E_i}{\partial y_{jk}}$ is:

$$\frac{\partial E_i}{\partial y_{jk}} = \sum_{m=1}^{N_{k+1}} \frac{\partial net_{mk+1}}{\partial y_{jk}} \cdot \frac{\partial y_{mk+1}}{\partial net_{mk+1}} \cdot \frac{\partial E_i}{\partial y_{mk+1}}$$

$$= \sum_{m=1}^{N_{k+1}} w_{jm} y_{mk+1} (1 - y_{mk+1}) \cdot \frac{\partial E_i}{\partial y_{jk+1}}$$

- On page 10–43, the correct equation for τ_{ip} is:

$$\tau_{ip} \equiv P(G_i|X_p) = \frac{\pi_i p(X_p|\theta_i, C_i)}{p(X_p)} = \frac{\pi_i p(X_p|\theta_i, C_i)}{\displaystyle\sum_{j=1}^{G} \pi_j p(X_p|\theta_j, C_i)}$$

- On page 10–47, the correct equation for $P(C_j|X)$ is:

$$P(C_j|X) = \frac{L_j(X)}{\displaystyle\sum_{j'} L_{j'}(X)}$$

- On page 10–48, the correct equation for distance is:

$$Dist(X, Y) = \sqrt{\sum_{i=1}^{m} (X_i - Y_i)^2}$$

Figure 10-4   Unimodal Gaussian Algorithm Testing Flow Chart

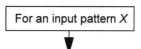
For an input pattern X

Compute the Gaussian of X for all classes:

$$P(X|C_j) = \frac{1}{(2\pi)^{\frac{n}{2}} |V_j|^{\frac{1}{2}}} e^{\left[-\frac{1}{2}(X-M_j)^T (V_j^{-1})(X-M_j)\right]}$$

Compute the estimated likelihood for all classes:

$$L_j(X) = P(X|C_j) \cdot P(C_j)$$

$$= P(X|C_j) \cdot N_j / \left(\sum^{N_c} N_{j'}\right)$$

where N_c is the number of classes.

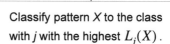
Classify pattern X to the class
with j with the highest $L_j(X)$.

☞ **NOTE:** This classifier is parametric since it is limited to modeling
data with Gaussian distributions. This method will perform worse than
nonparametric methods when the underlying data distribution is not
Gaussian. However, the Gaussian model should always be used to benchmark against other more complicated models so the benefit of the more
complex nonparametric models can be gauged.

**Gaussian
Typical
Settings**

The Gaussian algorithm trains and tests quickly. A good technique for
selecting the best combination of training parameters is to experiment with
combinations of covariance matrix settings:

- Full-covariance matrix, not shared among classes
- Diagonal covariance matrix, not shared among classes
- Full-covariance matrix, shared among classes
- Diagonal-covariance matrix, shared among classes

In addition, the following are useful rules-of-thumb:

- If input variables for each class are known to be linearly independent (i.e., uncorrelated), then a diagonal covariance matrix will be sufficient. Otherwise, use a full-covariance matrix to capture the correlations between input variables.

- Unless the number of training samples per class is very low (as a rule of thumb, if the number of patterns is less than the square of the number of input dimensions), a full-covariance matrix should be used.

- If the input dimension is high (e.g., greater than 10) and the number of input patterns is low with respect to the number of classes (in particular, if the number of patterns is less than the square of the number of input dimensions times the number of classes), then the covariance matrix should be shared among the classes. Otherwise, each class should have its own covariance matrix.

Other Notes

The Gaussian model returns the likelihood of each class $L_j(X)$, as opposed to the posterior probability $P(C_j|X)$. This is useful for more general cases of multitarget-class classification (i.e., a pattern X belonging to more than one class) and empty classes (i.e., the pattern X does not belong to any of the classes). To obtain the posterior probability for a single-target class classification, simply normalize the likelihood of the output classes:

$$P(C_j|X) = \frac{L_j(X)}{\sum_k L_k(X)} \qquad \textbf{(EQ 11)}$$

10.4.4 Multilayered Perceptron/Backpropagation

Multi-layered perceptron (MLP) is a nonparametric architecture. Used with the backpropagation algorithm it is capable of generating smooth nonlinear mappings between input and output variables. The multi-layered perceptron is considered a type of neural network. Both of these terms come from the fact that this architecture was originally proposed as a model for neurobiological processes. However, we ignore this vantage point, viewing MLP simply as a useful architecture for nonparametric modeling.

As shown in Figure 10-5, an MLP can be viewed as an interconnected network made up of nodes that can be thought of as simple computational elements. The nodes are arranged into one or more layers. The first layer is the input layer, the final layer is the output layer, and other layers inbetween are called hidden layers. The output of a node in a hidden layer is used as an input to the nodes of the next layer. Each hidden node outputs the value obtained from applying a sigmoidal function to a weighted sum of its inputs. In classification, the output nodes also apply a sigmoidal function. In estimation, output nodes simply output weighted sums of their inputs.

Figure 10-5 MLP Network Architecture Example (1 Hidden Layer)

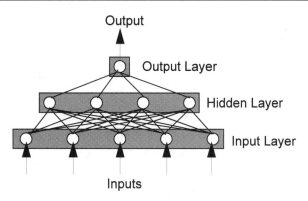

A separate weight exists for each connection in the network (i.e., between each pair of nodes in adjoining layers). These are the weights used by nodes to weigh the inputs they are summing, and they constitute the free parameters to be tuned by data. Backpropagation is one of many error-minimizing functions which tunes these weights to generate the desired mapping. The error function used is usually the mean-squared error (MSE) over a data set.

The hyperbolic tangent function is often used as the transfer function to calculate the output y for each node (Eq. 12):

$$y = \frac{(1 - e^{-net})}{(1 + e^{-net})} \qquad \text{(EQ 12)}$$

where

$$net = w_0 + \sum_i w_i x_i \qquad \text{(EQ 13)}$$

where w_0 is the bias of the node, each w_i is a weight for the connection from the i-th node of the previous layer, and x_i is the input from the i-th node of the previous layer.

When used for estimation purposes, it is standard to use only linear transfer functions in the nodes of the output layer.

$$y(x) = w_0 + \sum_i w_i x_i \qquad \text{(EQ 14)}$$

For classification, the output layer consists of nodes with a sigmoidal nonlinear function assuming the same shape, but different scaling and orientation from the hyperbolic tangent (Eq. 15):

$$y(x) = \frac{1}{(1 + e^{-net})} \qquad \text{(EQ 15)}$$

where *net* is defined as in Eq. 13.

The hyperbolic tangent function (Eq. 12) is used instead of the more common sigmoidal node (Eq. 15) because its zero-centered transformation tends to improve the training time. The linear output nodes in Eq. 14 are necessary to generate a mapping of arbitrary range in function estimation, while sigmoidal output nodes are natural for modeling posterior probabilities of classes [Richard and Lippmann, 1990].

As weights to each node change, the nonlinear transformation performed by each node is modified. If given a sufficient number of hidden nodes, a network with one or more hidden layers can approximate arbitrary mappings over a bounded region of the input space [Cybenko, 1989]. Also, this architecture has some desirable properties for approximating high-dimensional mappings [Jones, 1994; Barron, 1994].

Backpropagation is an algorithm for modifying the weights of an MLP based on incremental gradient descent of mean-squared error. The basis of backpropagation is as follows:

1. Backpropagation aims at minimizing the squared error cost function over a training set (Eq. 16):

$$E = \sum_{i=1}^{N_{train}} \left\{ \frac{1}{2} \sum_{j=1}^{J} (d_{ij} - y_{ij})^2 \right\} \qquad \text{(EQ 16)}$$

where i indexes each pattern in the training set and j indexes each output variable (N_{train} patterns in the training set; each pattern has J outputs); d_{ij} is the desired value of output j as given by example pattern i, and y_{ij} is the actual output value from the model.

2. The algorithm tunes weights by means of gradient descent. The two standard versions of the backpropagation algorithm perform gradient descent using the *fixed-step steepest descent* procedure or an incremental variant [Bertsekas, 1995]. Each step of the first version, often called the batch version, is in the negative gradient direction of MSE.

The incremental version takes steps that minimize the squared error on a single example pattern, but cycles through all the example patterns one at a time. Each cycle through the training set is called an epoch.

The flow chart in Figure 10-6 illustrates the backpropagation training algorithm. The test algorithm, which is the same as the feed-forward part of the training algorithm, is shown in Figure 10-8.

Figure 10-6   MLP/Backpropagation Training Flow Chart (Part 1 of 2)

```
┌─────────────────────────────────────────┐
│    For each pattern in the training set   │
└─────────────────────────────────────────┘
```

For each node j of layer k (except the output layer), compute its output, starting from the lowest layer first:

$$y_{jk} = \frac{1 - e^{-net_{jk}}}{1 + e^{-net_{jk}}} \quad \text{where} \quad net_{jk} = \sum_{l=1}^{N_{k-1}+1} w_{lj}x_l$$

w_{lj} is the weight of the connection between node l of layer k-1 to node j of layer k; x_l is the output of the connection from node l of layer k-1; N_{k-1} is the number of nodes in layer k-1 (the bias node is the reason why the number of inputs is plus one in the calculation of net_{jk}).

For the output layer, compute:

$$y_{jk} = \sum_{l=1}^{N_{k-1}+1} w_{lj}x_l \quad \text{for linear output nodes } or$$

$$y_{jk} = \frac{1}{1 + e^{-net_{jk}}} \quad \text{where} \quad net_{jk} = \sum_{l=1}^{N_{k-1}+1} w_{lk}x_l \quad \text{for sigmoidal output nodes}$$

Compute and accumulate the average root-mean square error:

$$E_i = \frac{1}{2}\sum_{j=1}^{J} (d_{ij} - y_{ij})^2$$

Figure 10-7 MLP/Backpropagation Training Flow Chart (Part 2 of 2)

Change the weight (w_{jl}) between node j and its input node l as follows:

$$\Delta w_{jl} = -\eta \frac{\partial E_i}{\partial w_{jl}} + \alpha (\Delta w'_{jl} - \Delta w''_{jl})$$

where $\dfrac{\partial E_i}{\partial w_{jl}}$ is the partial derivative of the error with respect to the weight w_{jl};

η is the step size of the steepest descent;

α is a momentum term to which the minimization is "smoothed" over successive descents.

$\dfrac{\partial E_i}{\partial w_{jl}}$ must be computed from the output layer down to the input layer since the computation of suc-

cessively lower layers depend on the computation of upper layers. Using the chain rule, we have:

$$\frac{\partial E_i}{\partial w_{jl}} = \frac{\partial net_{jk}}{\partial w_{jl}} \cdot \frac{\partial y_{jk}}{\partial net_{jk}} \cdot \frac{\partial E_i}{\partial y_{jk}}$$

$$\text{where} \quad \frac{\partial net_{jk}}{\partial w_{jl}} = x_l \text{ and } \frac{\partial y_{jk}}{\partial net_{jk}} = y_{jk}(1 - y_{jk})$$

The $\dfrac{\partial y_{jk}}{\partial net_{jk}}$ term simplifies as follows. For $y = \dfrac{1 - e^{-net}}{1 + e^{-net}}$, it becomes $\dfrac{1}{2}(1 + y)(1 - y)$; for

$y = \dfrac{1}{1 + e^{-net}}$, it becomes $y(1 - y)$; for a linear y, it is one.

For nodes y_{jk} in the output layers $\dfrac{\partial E_i}{\partial y_{jk}} = (d_{ij} - y_{ij})$;

and for nodes in layers other than the output layer

$$\frac{\partial E_i}{\partial y_{jk}} = \sum_{m=1}^{N_{k+1}} \frac{\partial net_{mk+1}}{\partial y_{jk}} \cdot \frac{\partial y_{mk+1}}{\partial net_{mk+1}} \cdot \frac{\partial E_i}{\partial y_{mk+1}}$$

$$= \sum_{m=1}^{N_{k+1}} w_{jm} y_{mk+1}(1 - y_{mk+1}) \cdot \frac{\partial E_i}{\partial y_{jk+1}}$$

Figure 10-8 MLP/Backpropagation Algorithm Testing Flow Chart

For each pattern in the test set

For each node j of layer k (except the output layer), compute its output, starting from the input (lowest) layer first:

$$y_{jk} = \frac{1 - e^{-net_{jk}}}{1 + e^{-net_{jk}}} \text{ where } net_{jk} = \sum_{l=1}^{N_{k-1}+1} w_{lk} x_l$$

w_{lj} is the weight of the connection between node l of layer k-1 to node j of layer k; x_l is the output of the connection from node l of from layer k-1; N_{k-1} is the number of nodes in layer k-1 (the bias node is the reason why the number of inputs is plus one in the calculation of net_{jk}.

For the output layer, compute:

$$y_{jk} = \sum_{l=1}^{N_{k-1}+1} w_{lj} x_l \quad \text{for function estimation } or$$

$$y_{jk} = \frac{1}{1 + e^{-net_{jk}}} \text{ where } net_{jk} = \sum_{l=1}^{N_{k-1}+1} w_{lk} x_l \quad \text{for classification.}$$

**Training
Parameters**

Common training parameters for MLP include:

- **Network Topology** — This is the structure of the backpropagation model, including the number of hidden layers and the number of nodes in each hidden layer. The number of input and output nodes are determined by the problem definition (and sometimes the preprocessing).

- **Learning Rate** — The learning rate affects how much weights in the backpropagation network are changed on each update.[4]

- **Momentum** — The momentum affects how quickly learning accelerates or decelerates depending on the differences between the desired pattern and the estimated pattern. Using momentum can often decrease training times by moving weights faster in the direction of prior changes. A value of zero uses no momentum.

- **Update Frequency** — The backpropagation algorithm typically updates the weights of the network either once after the presentation of every pattern (i.e., the iterative version), or once after the presentation of all patterns in the training set (i.e., the batch version).

- **Stop Conditions** — Stop condition(s) determine when the MLP algorithm will terminate training. Typical stop conditions are a maximum time, number of epochs of training, or until a specific error (RMS or classification error) reaches a specified value.

**Typical
Settings for an
MLP Model**

The following section provides some reasonable ranges for the training parameters of the MLP/ backpropagation model. Although these settings are highly problem dependent, the list below, nevertheless, provides novice users some basis for beginning experiments:

---

4. This is the step size used in the gradient descent algorithm.

Solving Data Mining Problems through Pattern Recognition

- **# of Layers** — Typical values for the number of hidden layers are one or two. There are a number of theoretical proofs that a single hidden layer is sufficient to generate any arbitrary mapping. However, certain mappings have been found to be difficult for single-hidden-layer MLP to generate without large amounts of data.

- **# of Hidden Nodes** — Typical values depend on the size of the training set and the complexity of the problem involved. A good rule of thumb is to use a number of hidden nodes on the order of the square root of the number of training patterns or lower.

- **Learning Rate** — The learning rate or step size (η) of the backpropagation gradient descent typically has values between 0.01 and 0.5 when input ranges are between -1 and 1 and output ranges are between 0–1. Increase this rate during training if you find the training error rates descend very slowly. Decrease this rate during training if the training error rates oscillate up and down excessively.

- **Momentum** — The momentum or α (coefficient to the momentum term) tends to dampen oscillation during training. Typical values are between 0.0 and 0.5.

- **Update Interval** — Updating weights once per epoch induces a gradient descent of the error function. Updating weights after each example pattern corresponds to an incremental gradient descent. Theory and practice suggest that this approach offers faster convergence when the weights are far from the local minimum and slower when close to a local minimum [Bertsekas, 1995]. Empirical studies suggest that the incremental gradient method should be used over the batch method for most practical problems.

- **Stop Conditions** — Using several stop conditions together (first stop condition that is satisfied terminates training) can be used to help bound how long the algorithm will train. A good strategy for setting the stop condition is to stick with one type of stop condition (e.g., the number of epochs). By monitoring the training error, find a value for which the training error seems to converge. Then use a number of different values around the original value to experiment with other settings.

**Typical
Preprocessing
for MLP**

MLP is capable of generating smooth mappings in both low and high dimensions. Typical preprocessing steps used with the MLP model include the following [Lippmann, 1992; Rumelhart and McClelland, 1986]:

- Normalizing each input variable to have zero mean and unit variance.

- For estimation, normalize the output variables similarly.

10.4.5 Radial Basis Functions

The Radial Basis Functions (RBF) architecture generates a mapping between inputs and outputs using a weighted sum of basis functions. The basis functions are radial Gaussians (i.e., the basis functions are invariant to rotations about their centers). Free parameters include the Gaussian center locations, the spread (standard deviation) of each Gaussian, and the weights which determine the degree to which each Gaussian contributes to each output. An output y of the RBF architecture takes on the form:

$$y = \sum_{i=1}^{N} w_i e^{\left(-\frac{1}{2\sigma_i^2 h} \cdot (X - Mean_i)^T (X - Mean_i)\right)}$$

(EQ 17)

where N is the number of basis functions, X is the input vector, $Mean_i$ and σ_i are the center location and spread of the i-th basis function, h is the overlap parameter, w_0 is the bias, and the other w_i's are weights given to each basis function. Figure 10-9 illustrates the structure of the RBF architecture.

Figure 10-9   Radial Basis Functions Architecture Example

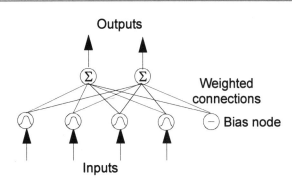

An RBF model can be trained by an iterative gradient descent method similar to the Backpropagation algorithm used for training the MLP. However, empirical results have shown that RBF can be trained much faster using a two-step process, without much degradation in performance. The two steps are:

1. Determine the centers and spreads of the Gaussians by minimizing the average variation of all training patterns to Gaussian centers using *K* Means clustering (see Section 10.4.9, "K Means Clustering").

2. Adjust the weights from each Gaussian to the outputs by minimizing the mean square error. Since the weighted-sum relationship between an output variable and the Gaussian is linear, the global optimum can be computed quickly (via the use of pseudo-matrix inversion to solve a standard least-squares problem).

Figure 10-10 shows the training flow chart and Figure 10-11 shows the test flow chart.

**Training
Parameters**

Common training parameters for RBF include the following:

- **Number of Basis Function** — The number of basis functions used.

- **Spread Computation** — You can choose the initial basis function variances based on the nearest N clusters or based on the variances from the clustering algorithm (e.g., K Means).

- **Overlap Factor** — An overlap factor (h) controls the degree of overlap between basis functions. Too large of an overlap factor will blur the basis functions, causing poor discrimination among input patterns (all basis functions will respond with a large value). Too small of an overlap factor will cause many input patterns to respond with near zero values, providing poor generalization capabilities. The value of h is often critical in the final performance of the RBF model.

**Typical RBF
Settings**

The number of basis functions to use is highly problem dependent and should be limited by compute time and memory. A typical setting is one cluster per 10–100 input patterns for each class.

One must experiment with the way in which spread is computed. Empirical results have shown that using the distance of the nearest cluster works well. Another typical setting is to use the standard deviation calculated from the K Means clustering algorithm.

In the K means stage, the stop condition for each binary split (i.e., when to split cluster centers) is less important than the stop condition for the overall clustering (i.e., when to stop moving cluster centers). Therefore, if the training set is large, pick a faster binary-split stopping condition (e.g., 3 epochs per split) and use a slower stopping condition (e.g., 20 epochs) for the overall clustering.

The performance of RBF is very sensitive to the overlap factor (h). A typical setting for the overlap factor is one, but different values should be tried for optimal results.

Solving Data Mining Problems through Pattern Recognition

Typical Preprocessing for RBF

Both the K means clustering and the radial nature of the Gaussian basis functions in RBF rely on the standard Euclidean distance measure. Therefore, inputs should be normalized to the same scale for best results.

Figure 10-10 Radial Basis Functions Training Flow Chart

Calculate the center location and spread of the Gaussians using K means clustering. Initialize the spread of each Gaussian to either the standard deviation calculated by the K means clustering algorithm or the distance between each cluster to the n nearest clusters.

Solve one linear least-squares problem per output to compute basis functions weights. For a particular output, the error to be minimized is

$$E = \sum_{j=1}^{N_{train}} (d_j - y_j)^2$$

where d_j is the desired value for the output, from the j-th example pattern, and y_j is the output generated by the mapping, given the input of the j-th example pattern. The solution for the optimal set of weights, for this output, is then:

$$W^* = (G^T G)^{-1} (G^T D)$$

where W^* is a column vector containing the weights (including the bias), and:

$$G = \begin{bmatrix} 1 & G_1 \\ 1 & G_2 \\ \dots & \dots \\ 1 & G_N \end{bmatrix}, \quad D = \begin{bmatrix} d_1 \\ d_2 \\ \dots \\ d_N \end{bmatrix}$$

where G_i is a row vector of the Gaussian outputs for the input pattern i,

$G_i = [g_1(X_i), g_2(X_i), \dots, g_{N_g}(X_i)]$; and d_i is the desired output for pattern i.

Solving Data Mining Problems through Pattern Recognition

Figure 10-11   Radial Basis Functions Test Flow Chart

For each cluster, compute the Gaussian outputs:

$$g'_k(X) = e^{\left(-\frac{1}{2\sigma^2 h} \cdot (X - Mean_k)^T (X - Mean_k)\right)}$$

$$g_k(X) = \frac{g'_k(X)}{\displaystyle\sum_{k=1}^{N_g} g'_k(X)}$$

Compute the outputs:

$$y_j = w_{j0} + \sum_{k=1}^{N_g} w_{jk} g_k(X)$$

where w_{jk} is the weight between the j-th output and the k-th normalized

Gaussian, and c_j is a constant bias for the j-th output.

10.4.6 *K* Nearest Neighbors

The *K* Nearest Neighbor (KNN) architecture is a classical nonparametric architecture that is simple, yet powerful. The basic idea behind the KNN is very straight-forward. For training, all input-to-output pairs in the training set are stored into a database. When an estimation or a classification is needed on a new input pattern, the answer is based on the *K* nearest training patterns in the database (see Figure 10-12).

KNN requires no training time other than the time required to preprocess and store the entire training set. It is very memory intensive since the entire training set is stored. Classification/estimation is slow since the distance between input pattern and all patterns in the training set must be computed. KNN typically performs better for lower dimensional problems (less than 10), as theoretical and empirical results suggest that the amount of training

Figure 10-12 *K* Nearest Neighbor (KNN) Example

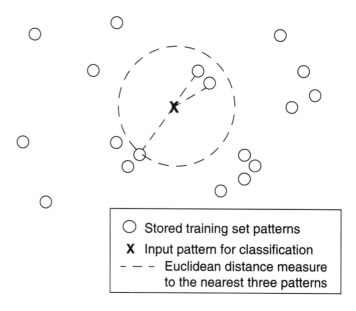

○ Stored training set patterns

X Input pattern for classification

– – – Euclidean distance measure
  to the nearest three patterns

data needed in higher dimensions is greater than that required in other models.

The key issues involved in training this model includes setting the variable *K* and the type of "distance metric" to use. The best setting of *K* is typically determined empirically using validation techniques such as cross validation over the fitted model. In estimation, larger values of *K* lead to smoother mappings. In classification, regularity also increases with *K*.

The distance metric determines the meaning of "nearest neighbor." The most widely used distance metric is the Euclidean measure shown in Eq. 18.

$$Dist(X, Y) = \sqrt{\sum_{i=1}^{D} (x_i - y_i)^2} \qquad \textbf{(EQ 18)}$$

where $Dist(X, Y)$ is the distance between two D-dimensional vectors X and Y. A flow chart of the KNN algorithm implementation is shown in Figure 10-13.

Figure 10-13 *K* Nearest Neighbor (KNN) Algorithm Flow Chart

Training

> Store all input/output pairs in the training set.

Testing

> For each pattern in the test set

> Search for the *K* nearest patterns to the input pattern using a Euclidean distance measure.

> For classification, compute the confidence for each class as C_i / K, where C_i is the number of patterns among the *K* nearest patterns belonging to class *i*. The classification for the input pattern is the class with the highest confidence.
>
> For estimation, the output value is based on the average of the output values of the *K* nearest patterns:
>
> $$y = \sum_{i=1}^{K} \frac{y_i}{K}$$

Training Parameters

Common training parameters for KNN include the following:

- **Number of Nearest Neighbors** — This is the number of nearest neighbors (K) used to classify the input patterns.

- **Input Compression** — Since KNN is very storage intensive, you may want to compress data patterns as a preprocessing step before classification. Compression calculates the minimum and maximum data range for each input variable and linearly compresses the data into a specified number of bytes. Typically, using input compression will result in slightly worse performance (as resolution in the input data is lost). However, sometimes using compression will improve performance because it performs automatic normalization of the data which can equalize the effects of each input in the Euclidean distance measure.

Other training parameters include:

- Distance metric (e.g., Euclidean, Manhattan, absolute dimension)
- How to combine the k neighbors for estimation (e.g., equal or weighted average)

KNN Typical Settings

The following section provides some reasonable ranges for the parameters of the KNN model. Although these settings are highly problem dependent, the list below nevertheless provides novice users some basis for beginning experiments:

- **# of Nearest Neighbors** — The number of nearest neighbors (K) should be based on cross validation over a number of K settings. $K=1$ is a good baseline model to benchmark against. A good rule-of-thumb number is K should be less than the square root of the total number of training patterns.

- **Input Compression** — Since KNN is a memory/storage intensive model, you can choose to represent the data with limited precision (i.e., use data compression). Although empirical results have shown that high precision is usually not needed in KNN, you should use the KNN algorithm without any compression unless there is a memory problem.

Typical Preprocessing for KNN

Common preprocessing methods used with KNN include:

- Input normalization (zero mean, unit variance), which ensures the variance in all input dimensions are equal.

- Since KNN is better at lower dimensional problems, principle component analysis (PCA) can be used to map higher dimensional inputs into lower dimensional inputs.

10.4.7 Gaussian Mixture

Similar to the Gaussian model, the Gaussian mixture architecture estimates probability density functions (PDF) for each class, and then performs classification based on Bayes' rule:

$$P(C_i|X) = P(X|C_j) \cdot \frac{P(C_j)}{P(X)} \qquad \text{(EQ 19)}$$

where $P(X|C_j)$ is the PDF of class j, evaluated at X, $P(C_j)$ is the prior probability for class j, and $P(X)$ is the overall PDF, evaluated at X.

Unlike the unimodal Gaussian architecture, which assumes $P(X|C_j)$ to be in the form of a Gaussian, the Gaussian mixture model estimates $P(X|C_j)$ as a weighted average of multiple Gaussians. Given enough Gaussian components, this architecture can approximate arbitrarily complex distributions.

In the Gaussian mixture architecture, the estimate of the PDF for each class j takes on the form:

$$P(X|C_j) = \sum_{k=1}^{N_c} w_k G_k \qquad \text{(EQ 20)}$$

where w_k is the weight of the k-th Gaussian G_k and the weights sum to one. One such PDF model is produced for each class.

Each Gaussian component is defined as:

$$G_k = \frac{1}{(2\pi)^{n/2}|V_k|^{1/2}} \cdot e^{[-1/2(X-M_k)^T V_k^{-1}(X-M_k)]} \qquad \text{(EQ 21)}$$

where M_k is the mean of the Gaussian and V_k is the covariance matrix of the Gaussian.

Free parameters of the Gaussian mixture model consist of the means and covariance matrices of the Gaussian components and the weights indicating the contribution of each Gaussian to the approximation of $P(X|C_j)$.

These parameters are tuned using a complex iterative procedure called the estimate-maximize (EM) algorithm [Ng, 1990], that aims at maximizing the likelihood of the training set generated by the estimated PDF. The likelihood function L for each class j can be defined as:

$$L_j = \prod_{i=0}^{N_{train}} P(X_i|C_j) \qquad \text{(EQ 22)}$$

The log likelihood of Eq. 22 is a numerically easier cost function to maximize, while maintaining the desired effect of the likelihood function:

$$\ln(L_j) = \sum_{i=0}^{N_{train}} \ln(P(X_i|C_j)) \qquad \text{(EQ 23)}$$

The flow chart in Figure 10-14 and Figure 10-15 summarize the training algorithm. The test algorithm is shown in Figure 10-16.

Figure 10-14 Gaussian Mixture Training Flow Chart (Part 1 of 2)

Initialize the initial Gaussian means μ_i, $i = 1, ..., G$ using the K means clustering algorithm (either one set of G Gaussians for all classes, or one set for each class).

Initialize the covariance matrices, V_i, to the distance to the nearest cluster (either one set of G covariance matrices for all classes, or one set for each class).

Initialize the weights $\pi_i = 1/G$ so that all Gaussians are equally likely.

Present each pattern X of the training set and model each of the classes K as a weighted sum of Gaussians:

$$p(X|\theta_s, K) = \sum_{i=1}^{G} \pi_i p(X|\theta_i, K)$$

where $\theta_i = \{\mu_i, K\}$, G is the number of Gaussians, the π_i's are the weights, and

$$p(X|\theta_i, K) = \frac{1}{(2\pi)^{d/2}|V_i|^{1/2}} \cdot e^{[-1/2(X-\mu_i)^T V_i^{-1}(X-\mu_i)]}$$

where V_i is the covariance matrix.

Compute:

$$\tau_{ip} \equiv P(G_i|X_p) = \frac{\pi_i p(X_p|\theta_i, C_i)}{p(X_p)} = \frac{\pi_i p(X_p|\theta_i, C_i)}{\sum_{i=1}^{G} \pi_j p(X_p|\theta_j, C_i)}$$

Figure 10-15 Gaussian Mixture Training Flow Chart (Part 2 of 2)

Iteratively update the weights, means, and covariances:

$$\pi_i(t+1) = \frac{1}{N_c} \sum_{p=1}^{N_c} \tau_{ip}(t)$$

$$\mu_i(t+1) = \frac{1}{N_c \pi_i(t)} \sum_{p=1}^{N_c} \tau_{ip}(t) X_p$$

$$C_i(t+1) = \frac{1}{N_c \pi_i(t)} \sum_{p=1}^{N_c} \tau_{ip}(t)((X_p - \mu_i(t))(X_p - \mu_i(t))^T)$$

Recompute τ_{ip} using the new weights, means, and covariances. Stop training if

$$\Delta \tau_{ip} \equiv \tau_{ip}(t+1) - \tau_{ip}(t) \leq threshold$$

or the number of epochs reach the specified value. Otherwise, continue the iterative updates.

Figure 10-16   Gaussian Mixture Test Flow Chart

Present each input pattern X and compute the confidence for each class j:

$$P(C_j)P(X|\theta_x, C_j)$$

where $P(C_j) = \dfrac{N_{c_j}}{N}$ is the prior probability of class C_j estimated by counting the number of training patterns. Classify pattern X as the class with the highest confidence.

Training Parameters

Common training parameters for Gaussian mixture include the following:

- **Number of Components** — The number of Gaussian components to use to approximate the PDF of each class.

- **Same Gaussians for Each Output Class?** — You can choose whether the PDF model for each class should be constrained so that the means and covariances of the Gaussian components should be equal. (The PDF's should still be different if the weights used by each class are different.)

- **Covariance Matrix Type** — You can choose to use either full- or diagonal-covariance matrices. If there are any possible correlations between the input variables, use the full-covariance matrix. If you know the input variables are independent, you may use a diagonal-covariance matrix.

- **Covariance Matrix Computation Method** — This determines how the covariance matrix is computed. Typical choices are to generate a covariance matrix for each Gaussian (which allows the multiple Gaussians representing a single class to each have different shapes), to generate a single covariance matrix per output class (which means that all

Gaussians representing a class will have the same shape), or to generate one covariance matrix that is used for all Gaussians for all classes (i.e., all Gaussians for all classes will have the same shape).

If you know the covariance matrix for all classes are similar, you can use the one covariance matrix for all Gaussians to save space. In cases with limited data, it may improve performance to link all the Gaussians in this manner.

- **Stop Conditions** — The stop condition(s) determine when the Gaussian mixture algorithm will terminate training. Typical stop conditions are a maximum number of epochs of training, or until the percentage log likelihood change is less than a specified value.

Gaussian Mixture Typical Settings

The following rules-of-thumb should be followed:

- The number of Gaussians should be on the order of the square-root of the number of patterns in the training set.

- If input variables are known to be mutually independent (i.e., not correlated), then a diagonal covariance matrix is sufficient. Otherwise, use a full-covariance matrix to capture the correlations between input variables.

- Unless the number of training samples per class is very low (as a rule of thumb, if the number of patterns is less than the square of the number of input dimensions), the full-covariance matrix should be used.

- If the input dimension is high (e.g., greater than 10) and the number of input patterns is low with respect to the number of classes (as a rule of thumb, if the number of patterns is less than the square of the number of input dimensions times the number of classes), then the covariance matrix should be shared among the classes. Otherwise, each class should have its own covariance matrix.

Other Notes

The likelihood of each class $L_j(X)$ is returned by the Gaussian mixture model as opposed to the posterior probability $P(C_j|X)$. This is useful for gauging confidence in classification. To obtain the posterior probability for a single-target class classification, simply normalize the likelihood of the output classes:

$$P(C_j|X) = \frac{L_j(X)}{\sum_{i'} L_{j'}(X)}$$

(EQ 24)

10.4.8 Nearest Cluster

The nearest-cluster architecture can be viewed as a condensed version of the K nearest neighbor architecture. This architecture can often deliver performance close to that of KNN, while reducing computation time and memory requirements. Though it is feasible to develop a similar scheme for estimation, the nearest-cluster architecture is widely used only for classification.

The nearest-cluster architecture involves a partitioning of the training set into a few clusters. Each cluster is associated with a set of numerical values. For a given cluster, these values estimate the posterior probabilities of all possible classes for the region of the input space in the vicinity of the cluster. During classification, an input is associated with the nearest cluster, and the posterior probability estimates for that cluster are used to classify the input. Figure 10-17 shows the nearest cluster training algorithm, and Figure 10-18 shows the test algorithm.

Figure 10-17 Nearest Cluster Training Flow Chart

Perform *K* means clustering on the data set.

For each cluster, generate a probability for each class according to:

$$P_{jk} = \frac{N_{jk}}{N_k}$$

where P_{jk} is the probability for class *j* within cluster *k*, N_{jk} is the number of class-*j* patterns belonging to cluster *k*, and N_k is the total number of patterns belonging to cluster *k*.

Figure 10-18 Nearest Cluster Test Flow Chart

For each input pattern, *X*, find the nearest cluster C_{k^*} using the Euclidean distance measure:

$$Dist(X, Y) = \sqrt{\sum_{i=1}^{m} (X_i - Y_i)^2}$$

where *Y* is a cluster center and *m* is the number of dimensions in the input patterns.

Use the probabilities P_{jk} for all classes *j* stored with C_{k^*}, and classify pattern *X* into the class *j* with the highest probability.

Nearest Cluster Typical Settings

See "Typical K Means Settings" on page 10-53 for settings for the *K* means algorithm. The number of cluster centers should be limited by compute time and available memory. A typical setting is one cluster center for each 10–100 input patterns for each class.

Typical Preprocessing for Nearest Cluster

A common implementation of the nearest cluster model uses the basic Euclidean distance metric. A common preprocessing step is to normalize input variables (to zero mean, unit variance) to ensure the variances in all input dimensions are equal.

Similar to KNN, the nearest cluster model works better for lower dimensional problems. Another common preprocessing method used in conjunction with nearest model is principle component analysis (PCA).

10.4.9 *K* Means Clustering

Clustering algorithms are used to find groups of "similar" data points among the input patterns. *K* means clustering is an effective algorithm to extract a given number of clusters of patterns from a training set. Once done, the cluster locations can be used to classify patterns into distinct classes. In this section, we describe the *K* means clustering algorithm, which is used by algorithms we have described for training RBF, Gaussian mixture, and nearest-cluster architectures.

Solving Data Mining Problems through Pattern Recognition

Figure 10-19 *K* Means Training Flow Chart

Initialize the number of cluster centers selected by the user by randomly selecting them from the training set.

Classify the entire training set. For each pattern X_i in the training set, find the nearest cluster center C^* and classify X_i as a member of C^*.

Loop until the change in cluster means is less the amount specified by the user

For each cluster, recompute its center by finding the mean of the cluster:

$$M_k = \frac{1}{N_k} \cdot \sum_{j=1}^{N_k} X_{jk}$$

where M_k is the new mean, N_k is the number of training patterns in cluster *k*, and X_{jk} is the *j*-th pattern belonging to cluster *k*.

If the number of cluster centers is less than the number specified, split each cluster center into two clusters by finding the input dimension with the highest deviation:

$$\sigma_i = \sum_{j=1}^{N_k} (X_{ij} - M_{ij})^2$$

where X_{ij} is the *i*-th dimension of the *j*-th pattern in cluster *k*, M_{ij} is the *i*-th dimension of the cluster center, and N_k is the number of training patterns in cluster *k*. (If splitting all cluster centers will exceed the number of desired cluster centers, a random subset of cluster centers are chosen for splitting.)

Store the *k* cluster centers.

The K means clustering algorithm places clusters among similar patterns in a training set by minimizing the overall average distance of member points to each cluster. Like a number of other algorithms, a distance measure is needed to quantify the meaning of "similarity." Since the meaning of similarity is highly problem dependent, the input patterns must be properly preprocessed and scaled. A commonly used metric is the Euclidean distance in Eq. 25.

$$Dist(X, Y) = \sqrt{\sum_{i=1}^{m} (X_i - Y_i)^2}$$ (EQ 25)

A binary-split procedure is commonly used to generate successive clusters. This method is efficient and has worked well in practice. The flow chart in Figure 10-19 summarizes the K means clustering algorithm. Figure 10-20 shows the K means test flow chart.

Figure 10-20   *K* Means Test Flow Chart

For each pattern X, associate X with the cluster Y closest to X using the Euclidean distance:

$$Dist(X, Y) = \sqrt{\sum_{i=1}^{m} (X_i - Y_i)^2}$$

Solving Data Mining Problems through Pattern Recognition

**Tunable
Parameters**

Commonly tunable parameters for K means include the following:

- **Number of Initial Clusters** — The number of cluster centers to begin with, randomly chosen from the training set.

- **Number of Cluster Centers** — This value specifies the number of clusters created by the K Means algorithm to represent the training data. Training will begin with the number of initial clusters and will proceed until there are the number of clusters specified.

- **Criteria for Splitting Cluster Centers** — Cluster centers can be split when a specified number of epochs have been reached or when the standard deviation change is less than a specified value (i.e., the minimum amount of change in the standard deviation of any cluster in order to continue moving; if all the standard deviation of all clusters are less than this value, then the movement of clusters stop).

- **Stop Conditions** — The stop condition(s) determine when the K means algorithm will terminate training. Typical stop conditions are a maximum number of epochs of training or a percent standard deviation change threshold.

**Typical *K*
Means
Settings**

The number of clusters to use is highly problem dependent. Typical values can range anywhere from 2 to 10 in data analysis applications upwards to hundreds of cluster centers in classification applications.

The stop condition for each binary split (i.e., when to split cluster centers) is less important than the stop condition for the overall clustering (i.e., when to stop moving cluster centers). Therefore, if the training set is large, pick a faster binary-split stopping condition (e.g., 3 epochs per split) and use a slower stopping condition (e.g. 20 epochs) for the overall clustering.

10.4.10 Decision Trees

Decision trees are popular for pattern recognition because the models they produce are easier to understand. Decision-tree based models have a simple top-down tree structure where decisions are made at each node. The nodes at the bottom of the resulting tree provide the final classification. This general structure is depicted in Figure 10-21.

Figure 10-21   Basic Structure of Decision Trees

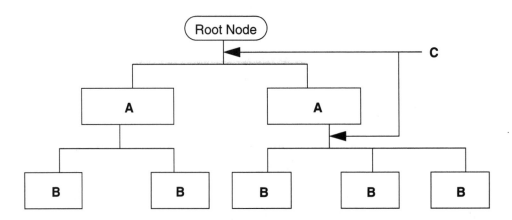

A. Nodes of the tree
B. Leaves (terminal nodes) of the tree
C. Branches (decision points) of the tree

The connections in the tree never form closed-loops. Each node with branches below it is a *parent* node. The nodes immediately below it are *children* or *offspring*. A node with no offspring is a *terminal* node or *leaf*. A *splitting rule* at a node forms the branches beneath it. In binary decision trees, each splitting rule results in a binary answer (e.g., yes/no). In other trees, multiple branches may be formed.

The final decisions made at the leaves of the decision tree can be easily "read off" the preceding branches of the tree as "rules." Because of this characteristic, it is easy to understand why patterns are classified into the different "bins" or leaves of the tree.

Key Issues

The key issues for any decision tree are the following:

- The criteria used to build the tree (i.e., for determining which variables to use and what splits to use at each point in the tree)

- The criteria for stopping growth of the tree (i.e., when does branching at a given node stop?)

- How to prune the tree for maximum classification effectiveness (i.e., which branches of the tree should be removed?)

Two of the most commonly used decision trees, CART and CHAID, are discussed individually after an overview of binary and linear decision trees.

Binary Decision Trees

Binary decision trees are architectures for classification that draw decision region boundaries through constructing a binary tree. Classification of an input vector is done by traversing the tree beginning at the root node, and ending at a leaf. Each node of the tree computes an inequality based on a single input variable. If the inequality is satisfied, the left child is the next node traversed, otherwise the right node is the next. Each leaf is assigned to a particular class, and input vectors are classified as the class associated with the leaf at which the trajectory ends. Since each inequality that is used to split the input space is only based on one input variable, each node draws a boundary that can be geometrically interpreted as a hyperplane perpendicular to the axis that corresponds to the variable of its inequality. Hence, the final decision regions are made up of hyper-rectangles.

There are a variety of algorithms (e.g., CART) used to construct binary decision trees based on training data. The gist of most of these is to first construct a (possibly complex) tree that performs perfectly on the test set, and then to prune the tree using heuristic approaches to achieve a desired degree of regularization. Breimann, et al. (1984) presents some representative algorithms.

Linear Decision Trees

Linear decision trees are similar to binary decision trees, except that the inequality computed at each node takes on an arbitrary linear form that may depend on multiple variables. Hence, while the decision region boundaries produced by binary decision trees are composed of hyperplanes perpendicular to axes of the input space, linear decision trees draw boundaries composed of hyper-planes in the input space with arbitrary orientation.

The training algorithms used for linear decision trees are similar to those employed by binary decision trees in that trees are built up to perform perfectly on a data set and then pruned. The only difference is that methods for choosing inequalities to be computed at each node are more complicated and rely heavily on heuristics. A training algorithm for linear decision trees is presented in Breimann, et al. (1984).

Classification and Regression Trees (CART)

Classification and Regression Trees (CART) are binary decision trees, which split a single variable at each node. In the tree-building process, the CART algorithm recursively goes through an exhaustive search of all variables and split values to find the optimal splitting rule for each node. The form of a rule at each node is:

```
if Variable < Split_value then left branch,
    else right branch
```

The optimal splitting criteria at a specific node can be found as follows:

$$\Phi(s'/t) = Max_i(\Phi(s_i/t)) \tag{EQ 26}$$

$$\Phi(s/t) = 2P_L P_R \sum_{j=1}^{classes} |P(j/t_L) - P(j/t_R)|$$

Equation 26 says that the optimal splitting rule s' for a node t is found by maximizing the $\Phi(s/t)$, the "goodness" of the split.

$$t_L = \text{left offspring of node } t \tag{EQ 27}$$

$$t_R = \text{right offspring of node } t$$

$$P_L = \frac{\text{total number of patterns at } t_L}{\text{total number of patterns in the training set}}$$

$$P_R = \frac{\text{total number of patterns at } t_R}{\text{total number of patterns in the training set}}$$

$$P(j/t_L) = \frac{\text{total number of class j patterns at } t_L}{\text{total number of patterns at } t}$$

$$P(j/t_R) = \frac{\text{total number of class j patterns at } t_R}{\text{total number of patterns at } t}$$

The use of this splitting rule always picks a split that is perpendicular to the input axis of the selected variable. After the full tree is grown, a pruning rule is used to cut off branches of the tree that reduce the overall classification accuracy. This is accomplished by computing a strength $g(t)$ for each non-terminal node t. The strength takes into account the misclassification rate and the population (or statistical significance) of a node. The sub-tree with the smallest $g(t)$ can then be pruned from the tree.

$$g(t) = \frac{R(t) - R(T_t)}{|T'_T| - 1} \tag{EQ 28}$$

$$R(t) = r(t)p(t) \tag{EQ 29}$$

$$r(t) = 1 - Max_i \left[\frac{\text{number of class j patterns at } t}{\text{total number of patterns at } t} \right] \tag{EQ 30}$$

$$p(t) = \frac{\text{number of patterns at } t}{\text{total number of patterns in the training set}} \tag{EQ 31}$$

$$R(T_t) = \sum_{t' \in T'_t} R(t') \tag{EQ 32}$$

$|T'_t|$ is the number of terminal nodes in the sub-tree headed by t. $r(t)$ is the misclassification at a node t. The strength of a node is highest when the appropriately scaled misclassification rate of a node is much greater than that of its sub-tree. The strength measurement takes into account the magnitude of $|T'_t|$ to incorporate the cost of maintaining nodes.

Chi-Squared Automatic Interaction Detector (CHAID)

Chi-Squared Automatic Interaction Detector (CHAID) is a non-binary decision tree. The decision or split made at each node is still based on a single variable, but can result in multiple branches. The decision of which variable and what split values to use is based on a Chi^2 analysis of the output and input variable.

CHAID is designed specifically to deal with categorical variables. Continuous variables must be grouped into a finite number of bins to create categories. A reasonable number of "equal population bins" (e.g., 10–20) can be created for use with CHAID.[5]

The form of the rule at each node is (for continuous variables):

```
if Variable < Split_Value1, then branch #1
    else if Variable < Split_Value2, then branch #2
    . . .
```

For categorical variables, the splitting rule must encompass all values and each value must fall uniquely into one branch (several values may share the same branch).

A Chi-square value is computed for each variable and used to determine the best variable to split on. CHAID sorts categorical values based on the binary output variable. Neighboring bins with insignificant differences are combined together.

---

5. "Equal population bins" are groups, each with the same number of samples. For example, if there are 1,000 samples, creating 10 equal population bins would result in 10 bins, each containing 100 samples. Continuous variables are typically sorted and then divided into equal population bins.

Solving Data Mining Problems through Pattern Recognition

For any node of the tree, the calculations are as follows. Let:

t_0 = total number of zeros
t_1 = total number of ones
$N = t_0 + t_1$
$t[i]$ = total count in category i
$e_0[i]$ = expected number of zeros in category i
  $= (t_0 + t_1) * t_0 / N$
$e_1[i]$ = expected number of ones in category i
  $= (t_0 + t_1) * t_1 / N$

then the Chi-squared value χ^2 is computed in Equation 33:

$$\chi^2 = \sum_{i \,\in\, \text{categories}} \frac{(t_0[i] - e_0[i])^2}{e_0[i]} + \frac{(t_1[i] - e_1[i])^2}{e_1[i]} \qquad \text{(EQ 33)}$$

If d is the number of degrees of freedom and n is the number of different categories, the significance is defined as follows:

$$\frac{1}{\Gamma\left(\dfrac{d}{n}\right)} \int_x^\infty e^{-t} t^{a-1} dt \qquad \text{(EQ 34)}$$

$$\Gamma(z) = \int_0^\infty t^{z-1} e^{-t} dt \qquad \text{(EQ 35)}$$

Begin with d equal to two times the number of categories minus one. If either $e_0[i]$ or $e_1[i]$ equal zero in Equation 33, decrease d by one and set χ^2 equal to zero.

A simple stop condition can be used that stops building the tree when all variables at a node have significance values below a specified threshold. The threshold levels used in conjunction with CHAID can typically be tuned through trial and error. Pruning also can be implemented for CHAID trees based on miscalculation and population rates.

10.4.11 Other Nonparametric Architectures

The nonparametric architectures we have discussed so far constitute some of the most widely used ones. However, the list has by no means been exhausted. In this section, we give brief descriptions of some other popular architectures in current use, and references where more details can be found. The hope is that this will help the reader place other architectures in context.

Projection Pursuit

Projection pursuit regression [Friedman and Stuetzle, 1981] aims at decomposing the development of a high dimensional model into a sequence of low-dimensional modeling tasks. During each iteration of projection pursuit regression, the input data is projected onto a one-dimensional space, such that the projected data are highly correlated with the corresponding output data. A smooth mapping from the projected space to the output space is produced in a way geared to minimize error on the training set. This results in a two-step model relating input to output. The first step involves the projection, and the second involves the one-dimensional mapping. The subsequent iteration recursively projects and models the residual error resulting from this two-step model.

Multivariate Adaptive Regression Splines

Multivariate adaptive regressive splines (MARS) [Friedman, 1991] is an architecture involving a partitioning of the state space and approximation of the portion of the mapping in each partition using a multivariate low order polynomial. In particular, the algorithm begins by partitioning the input space into a lattice of hypercubes. The number of partitions here is exponential in the number of dimensions, and thus intractable for problems with high (> 10) dimensional inputs. However, the algorithm proceeds by using the data set as a guide in concatenating groups of partitions to end up with a reasonable number of partitions. The grouping is done in a heuristic fashion aimed at drastically reducing the number of partitions without significant detriment to the final model. Once the partitioning is done, one low-order polynomial is fit to the data within each partition. These polynomials are constrained so that the mapping over the entire input space transitions smoothly across partition boundaries.

Group Method of Data Handling

The group method of data handling (GMDH) is an architecture that uses high-order polynomial functions to produce input-output mappings for estimation. Instead of using all terms of a high order polynomial, which would result in intractability for high-dimensional problems, GMDH employs a heuristic method that selectively prunes out terms that do not contribute much to the model. The modeling process begins with a low order polynomial, and then combines terms to produce a higher order polynomial. All but a few of the resulting terms that seem to be highly related to the desired outputs are pruned out. The few terms left are then recombined to generate even higher order terms. This process is iterated until the added complexity of higher order terms do not contribute to modeling accuracy on the test set.

Parzen's Windows

Parzen's windows is a classical nonparametric architecture for PDF modeling [Duda and Hart, 1973]. By generating one PDF per class, the architecture can be used for classification, similar to the way in which unimodal Gaussian and Gaussian mixture architectures are used.

Parzen windows approximate PDFs using weighted averages of radial Gaussians (though the method will also work with some other types of basis functions). There is one Gaussian element per example pattern in the training set, and each Gaussian is centered at the point in the input space corresponding to one input vector in the training set. Equal weighting is assigned to each component in computing the weighted average. The key training parameter is the spread that is assigned to all the Gaussians. In general, the smaller the spread, the greater the degree of complexity allowed in the modeling.

Unlike other algorithms of similar architectures, Unimodal Gaussian, which tune free parameters so that the first two moments of the PDF match those of the data, and Gaussian mixture, which maximizes likelihood, the way in which parameters for Parzen windows are chosen makes no immediate promises. In particular, the accuracy of approximations produced by Parzen windows with few example patterns is questionable. However, as the number of example patterns grows to infinity and the spread of the Gaussian elements is made smaller and smaller, the approximations are guaranteed to converge to the desired PDF.

Hypersphere Classifier

The hypersphere classifier [Batchelor, 1974] is a classification architecture that constructs decision regions composed of unions of component hyperspheres. A set of hyperspheres is associated with each class, and any input vector in one of these hyperspheres is assigned to the class. If an input vector falls in more than one hypersphere, it is assigned to the one whose center is closest. By using large numbers of small hyperspheres, arbitrarily complex decision regions can be formed. Free parameters in the hypersphere classifier include hypersphere centers and radii, and these parameters are tuned by heuristic techniques that aim at minimizing the number of misclassifications on a training set.

Learning Vector Quantization

Learning vector quantization (LVQ) [Kohonen, 1988] refers to an architecture identical to the nearest cluster architecture we have discussed, but involves a different training procedure. In particular, the algorithm involves finding cluster centers using the K-means clustering algorithm, just as with the nearest cluster method. However, after this is done, the centers are incrementally adapted in order to reduce the number of misclassification on example patterns in the training set. There is often a large margin of improvement enabled in this second step, since the initial clustering performed by the K-means approach pays no attention to the classes associated with example patterns.

10.5 ALGORITHM COMPARISON SUMMARY

Picking the right algorithm may involve some experimentation and trial and error. Table 10-7 shows a summary of each of the algorithms discussed in this chapter.

Table 10-7 Algorithm Summary Comparison (Part 1 of 2)

Algorithm	Non-para-met-ric?	Estima-tion?	Kernel Function	Practical Characteristics		
				Memory	Train-ing Time	Test Time
Linear regression	N	Y	Hyper-plane	Very low	Fast	Very fast
Logistic regression	N	Y	Sigmoid	Very low	Medium	Very fast
Unimodal Gaussian	N	N	Gaussian	Very low	Med–fast	Fast
Backpropagation	Y	Y	Sigmoid	Low	Slow	Very fast
Radial basis functions	Y	Y	Gaussian	Medium	Medium	Medium
K nearest neighbors	Y	Y	Euclidean	High	Very fast	Slow
Gaussian mixture	Y	N	Gaussian	Medium	Slow–Med	Medium
Nearest cluster	Y	N	Euclidean	Medium	Medium	Med–Fast
K means	Y	Y	Euclidean	Med–Hi	Medium	Med–Fast
Binary decision tree (e.g., CART)	Y	N	Perpendic-ular Hyper-plane	Low	Fast	Very fast
Linear decision tree	Y	Y	Hyper-plane	Low	Fast	Very fast
Projection pursuit	Y	Y	Hyper-plane	Low	Medium	Fast
Estimate-Maxi-mize clustering	Y	Y	Euclidean	Medium	Medium	Medium

Table 10-7 Algorithm Summary Comparison (Part 2 of 2)

Algorithm	Non-para-met-ric?	Estima-tion?	Kernel Function	Practical Characteristics		
				Memory	Train-ing Time	Test Time
MARS	Y	Y	Polynomi-als	Low	Medium	Very fast
GMDH	Y	Y	Polynomi-als	Low	Med-Fast	Fast
Parzen's windows	Y	N	Gaussian	High	Very fast	Slow
Hypersphere classifiers	Y	N	Hyper-spheres	Medium	Medium	Medium
Learning vector quantization	Y	N	Euclidean	Medium	Slow	Medium

Solving Data Mining Problems through Pattern Recognition

APPENDIX: SELECTING ALGORITHMS AND TRAINING PARAMETERS IN PRW

The following algorithms are provided in PRW:[1]

- Linear regression
- Logistic regression
- Unimodal Gaussian

- Backpropagation/MLP
- Radial basis functions
- K nearest neighbors
- Gaussian mixture
- Nearest cluster
- K means clustering

The implementation of each of these algorithms is as described earlier in this chapter. All of the commonly available parameters can be specified and tuned in PRW. The remainder of this appendix describes how algorithms and parameters are selected.

A.1 Selecting an Algorithm in PRW

PRW makes it easy to configure experiments using different algorithms. Within a single (or multiple) experiment manager, each individual experiment appears as an icon. Multiple experiments can be configured at one time and then scheduled to run in either batch or interactive modes.

Experiment Configuration Window

To examine or configure the experiment parameters for a particular experiment, double-click on the experiment icon to display its **Experiment Configuration** window. This window can contain the following four tabs:

---

1. PRW also supports the use of external programs (i.e., your own algorithms can be incorporated into the PRW environment).

- Algorithm
- Experiment Parameters
- Reporting
- Other Info

Figure 10-22   Algorithm Tab of the Experiment Configuration Window

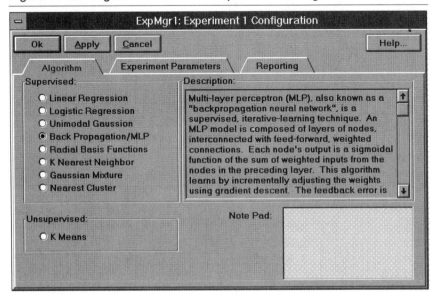

The **Algorithm** tab is shown in Figure 10-22. The available algorithms are listed on the left side. A description for the currently selected algorithm is displayed on the right. Any algorithms which are not available for the mode (classification or function estimation) selected on the setup screen of the experiment manager will be grayed out.

Selecting an Algorithm

To select an algorithm for the current experiment:

1. Click on the desired algorithm.

An algorithm is selected when the small white circle to its left contains a black dot.

2. Click on the Apply button.

You must click on either the **OK** or the **Apply** button for the changes on the **Algorithm** tab to take effect. Clicking **Apply** leaves the window open for further changes. Clicking **OK** closes the **Experiment Configuration** window.

A.2   Setting Algorithm Parameters

Defaults

When an algorithm is initially selected, it is configured with default parameters (an initial "guess" for appropriate training parameters). You may choose to run with the default configuration and/or run other experiment configurations.[2]

Displaying Algorithm Parameters

To view or modify the algorithm parameters:

1. Click on the Experiment Parameter tab to bring it forward.

2. Click on the Configure Algorithm option.

This will display the algorithm parameters (for the algorithm selected on the **Algorithm** tab) on the right side of the screen.

The following sections display the **Configure Algorithm** options available for each of the PRW-provided algorithms.

A.3   Linear Regression

Linear regression does not have any algorithm-specific parameters. To run linear regression on a data set, simply select the **Linear Regression** algorithm on the **Algorithm** tab, select any desired reporting parameters on the **Reporting** tab, and run the experiment.

---

2. Multiple variations of an experiment can be easily configured by using the **Copy** command to copy an experiment.

A.4 Logistic Regression

The logistic regression algorithm parameters are shown in Figure 10-23.

Figure 10-23 Logistic Regression Options

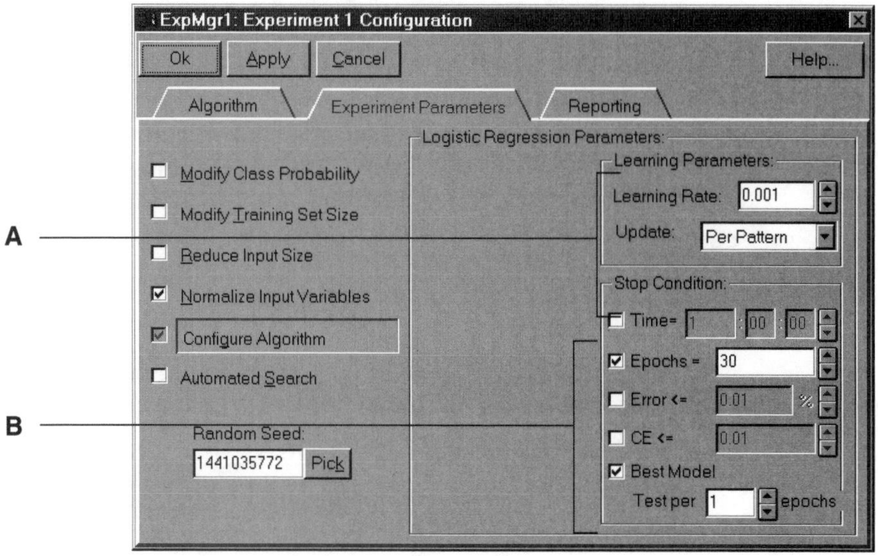

A. Select learning parameters here.
B. Select the training stop conditions here.

A.5   Unimodal Gaussian

The Unimodal Gaussian algorithm parameters are shown in Figure 10-24.

Figure 10-24   Unimodal Gaussian Options

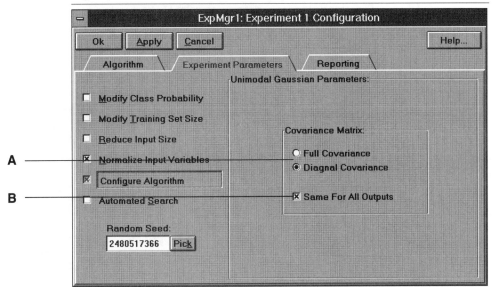

A. Select full or diagonal covariance matrix here.
B. Choose whether to use the same covariance matrix for all classes here.

A.6   Backpropagation/MLP

The backpropagation/MLP algorithm parameters are shown in Figure 10-25.

Figure 10-25   Backpropagation/MLP Configure Algorithm Options

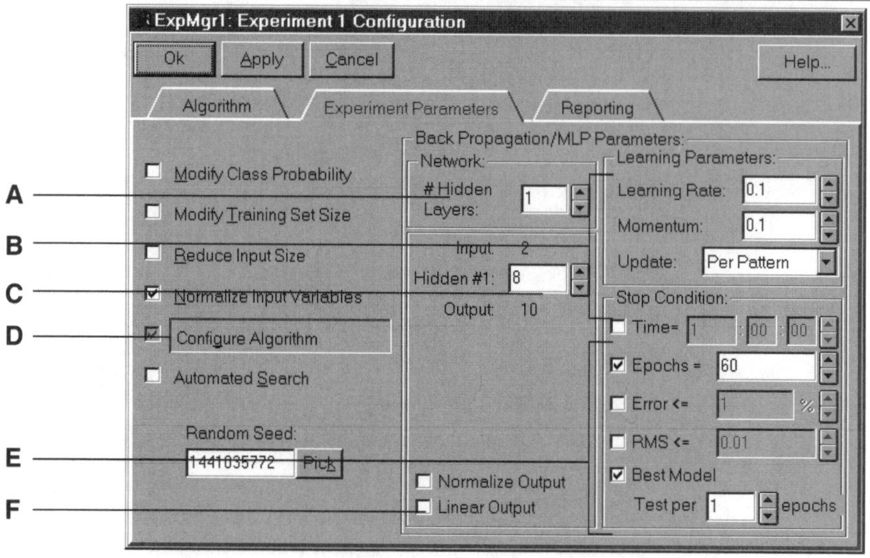

A. Select the number of hidden layers here.
B. Set the learning parameters for backpropagation here.
C. Set the number of nodes in each hidden layer here.
D. Click here to display the classifier-specific parameters.
E. Set the stop conditions for training here.
F. Enable or disable normalization of the outputs here.

Solving Data Mining Problems through Pattern Recognition

A.7 Radial Basis Functions

The radial basis function algorithm parameters are shown in Figure 10-26.

Figure 10-26 Radial Basis Functions Options

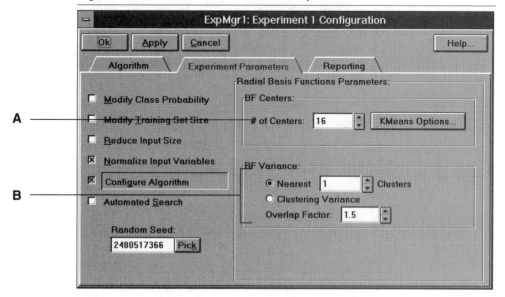

A. Enter the number of basis function centers to use here.
B. Select basis function variance parameters here.

A.8 *K* Nearest Neighbors

The *K* nearest neighbors algorithm parameters are shown in Figure 10-27.

Figure 10-27 *K* Nearest Neighbor Options

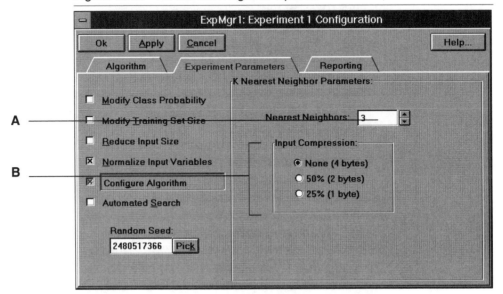

A. Enter the number of nearest neighbors to use for classification.
B. Select the amount of input compression to use.

A.9 Gaussian Mixture

The Gaussian mixture algorithm parameters are shown in Figure 10-28.

Figure 10-28 Gaussian Mixture Options

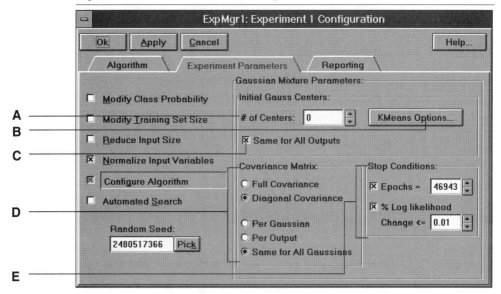

A. Select a clustering algorithm for creating Gaussian centers.
B. Click here to set the *K* means clustering options.
C. Click here to use the same Gaussian centers for all outputs.
D. Select covariance matrix parameters here.
E. Select the training stop conditions here.

A.10   Nearest Cluster

The nearest cluster algorithm parameters are shown in Figure 10-29.

Figure 10-29   Nearest Cluster Options

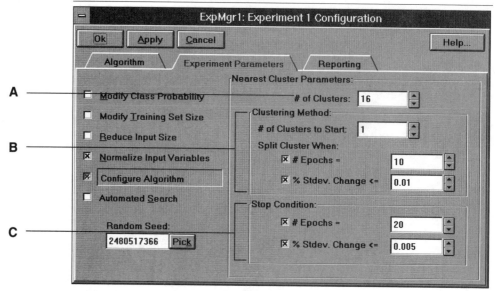

A. Select learning parameters here.
B. Select clustering parameters here.
C. Select the training stop conditions here.

A.11 *K* Means Clustering

The K means clustering algorithm parameters are shown in Figure 10-30.

Figure 10-30 *K* Means Options

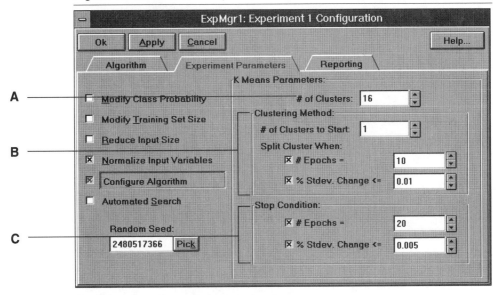

A. Select learning parameters here.
B. Select clustering method parameters here.
C. Select the training stop conditions here.

Chapter 11

Training and Testing

After you have defined your problem, collected, prepared, and preprocessed your data, selected an algorithm and training parameters, you are ready to train and test your algorithm(s). The train and test stage is an iterative one which allows you to tune the architecture free parameters, tune the training parameters, and test resulting models.

11.1 TRAIN, TEST, AND EVALUATION SETS

Because there are often two sets of parameters requiring tuning (the architecture's free parameters which are modified to minimize error in the training set, and the training parameters which specify how to modify the free parameters), the available data should be divided into three disjoint sets—a training set, a test set, and an evaluation set. The use of these three data sets is shown in Figure 11-1.

Figure 11-1 Using Train, Test, and Evaluation Sets

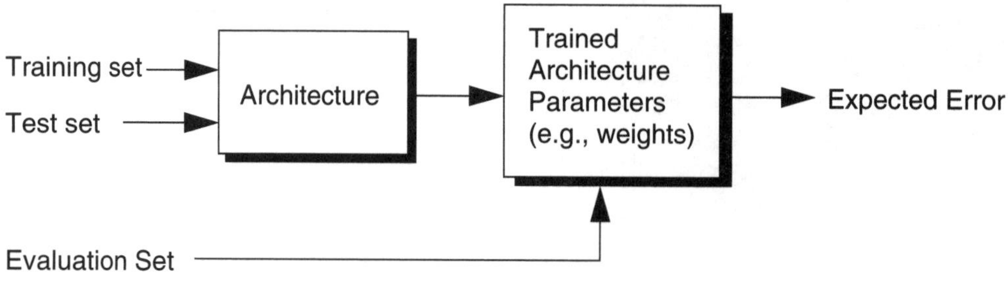

Architecture Free Parameters

A training set is used to select the architecture parameter settings (i.e., tune its free parameters). The result is a "trained" architecture, or a set of parameters that minimize the error on the training set.

Out-of-Sample Testing

To test a model, it is critical to use test data that was not used for training the model. This is called out-of-sample testing. By using out-of-sample testing, you are evaluating how well the model generalizes to new data versus how well the model learned (or memorized) the particular set of training data. Most models will achieve higher accuracy on the training set than on a separate test set.

Choosing the Training Parameters

Once you have a trained architecture, you will want to evaluate it using the test set. The test set will allow you to evaluate different experiments:

- Different architectures (i.e., different architecture parameters like the number of hidden nodes or layers in MLP *or* different architectures like MLP vs. RBF)

- Different training parameters (i.e., different values for the learning rate for backpropagation)

After training a number of different experiments, you can select the best trained experiment (i.e., combination of architecture and training parameters) using the test set.

For iterative training algorithms (e.g., backpropagation), you will need to decide when to stop training (oftentimes, it may be desirable to stop training early). In these cases, the test set also can be used to decide when the training should be stopped.

Final Evaluation of Expected Error

Finally, once you have selected the best architecture and training parameters, you are ready to test the final model to obtain an "expected error." This is done using the evaluation set.

The reason you need a separate evaluation set is to eliminate biases which may have been introduced by the test set. Since the test set is used to select the "best" architecture and training parameters, you may have selected a model that happens to perform particularly well on the test set. Using the training set to evaluate the model is even more misleading, since the model is tuned specifically to minimize error in the training set (some models always achieve 0% error on the training set, e.g., K nearest neighbors with $k = 1$). Therefore, using a separate evaluation set gives an unbiased value for expected error.

> After assessing the final model using the evaluation set, you must not further tune the model unless additional data is obtained. In this case, you should define a new training, test, and evaluation set. Otherwise, you risk biasing your accuracy results. See also the discussion on evaluation sets in "Assessing the Final Model" on page 2-24.

☞ **NOTE:** For algorithms that have no training parameters (e.g., linear regression), a separate test set may not be needed.

These steps are summarized as follows:

1. **Divide the available data into a training, test, and evaluation set.**

2. **Select an architecture and training parameters.**

3. **Train the model using the training set.**

4. **Test the model using the test set.**

5. **Repeat steps 2 through 4 using different architectures and training parameters.**

   Try different training parameter settings for the same architecture until you achieve the best possible results with that architecture. Then try different architectures.

6. **Select the best model and train it using data from the training and test set.**

   After selecting the best architecture and training parameters, use all data other than the evaluation set to train the model.

7. **Assess this final model using the evaluation set.**

   Generate an expected error by testing the model using the evaluation set.

11.2 VALIDATION TECHNIQUES

Using this technique of three separate data sets obviously requires more data than a simpler (but potentially biased) approach of only using two data sets (one for training and one for testing), or the unsubstantiated approach of using only a single data set (for training and testing).

Solving Data Mining Problems through Pattern Recognition

In cases where there is insufficient data to divide the available data into three disjoint sets, validation techniques can play a major role. These techniques provide statistically sound results using a minimal data set. In many cases, cross validation is the preferred method for obtaining statistically valid results. Cross validation can be used to select the architecture and training parameters instead of the train and test method described in Section 11.1. A separate evaluation set, however, is still required to assess the final model.

11.2.1 Cross Validation

Cross-Validation Basics

Cross validation is a heuristic that works as follows. Begin by randomly dividing the available data set into *n folds*, each with approximately the same number of data patterns. Then, create n models using the same architecture and training parameters, each model is trained with n-1 folds of data and tested on the remaining fold. Thus, every pattern in the available data set is evaluated as a test pattern as well as used for training. If n equals the number of patterns in the data set, this is also known as "leave-one-out" or "jack-knifing" cross validation.

Cross validation can be used to find the best architecture and its optimal training parameters. The model with the best cross-validation error is the best candidate solution. The basic steps are summarized below:

1. **Divide the available data into a training set and an evaluation set.**

2. **Split the training data into *n* folds.**

   Each fold should contain approximately the same number of patterns. For classification, example patterns from each output class should be evenly divided among the folds.

3. **Select an architecture and training parameters.**

4. **Train and test the n models.**

   Each model will use n-1 folds for training and a different fold for testing.

5. **Repeat steps 2 through 4 using different architectures and training parameters.**

   Try different training parameter settings for the same architecture until you achieve the best possible results with that architecture. Then try different architectures.

6. **Select the best model and train it using data from the training and test set.**

   After selecting the best architecture and training parameters, use all the training data to train the model.

7. **Assess this final model using the evaluation set.**

   Generate an expected error by testing the model using the evaluation set. Do not go back to further tune the model. Once you have run your evaluation set, you must not continue tuning the model, as this will bias your evaluation results.

Why Use Cross Validation?

The strongest reason for using cross validation is to avoid misleading results. Table 11-1 shows a 5-fold cross-validation run on a vowel recognition (classification) problem. The data set is relatively small (671 total available patterns).

Table 11-1 Five-Fold Cross Validation Classification Example

Fold	RMS Error	% Wrong
1	0.157	20.70%
2	0.152	19.34%
3	0.152	18.79%
4	0.155	18.55%
5	0.153	19.88%

Table 11-1 shows that the first fold had a test error of 20.70%, but the fourth fold only had an error 18.55% (a difference of 2.15%). If you only run a single experiment using 80% of your data for training and 20% for testing, you would have obtained different results depending on how the data happened to be randomly split among the training and test sets. Cross validation is the best way to select your architecture and training parameters when you have a limited amount of available data. The trade-off is that cross validation is more time consuming.

Estimating Error

You can think of the goal of training and testing a model as trying to estimate the true error E. Given a single model, you would generate a single estimate E'. Depending on the particular division of the training and test set, the E' value could vary significantly. In cross validation, by using a large value of n, you get to use more patterns in your training set (up to n-1 patterns in leave-one-out cross validation), yet you still get to evaluate each pattern in a disjoint test set.

Cross validation gives a much more accurate estimate of E by averaging the results from each of the n models produced using a particular architecture and set of training parameters:

$$E^* = \frac{1}{n} \cdot \sum_{1=1}^{n} E'_i \qquad \textbf{(EQ 1)}$$

It also is useful to calculate a standard deviation of error:

$$\sigma^* = \sqrt{\sum_{i=1}^{n} (E'_i - E^*)^2} \qquad \text{(EQ 2)}$$

Statistically, most of the individual classification errors E'_i will fall within one standard deviation of the mean E^*; almost all of your samples will fall within two standard deviations of the mean. In the example given in Table 11-1, the average error across the five folds is 19.45% with a standard deviation of 0.87%.

☞ **NOTE:** A separate evaluation set is still required to assess the final trained model.

How Many Folds?

A common question is how many folds are needed? The answer is dependent on the amount of data you have available and the degree of variation in your data. The trade-off for using a large number of folds is the computational requirements to train n models. You should be able to determine with a small number of cross validation experiments, the optimal value for your problem. You can use the smallest number of folds producing a stable estimate of E.

11.2.2 Bootstrap Validation

Bootstrap validation randomly selects (with replacement) n patterns from the data set of n patterns for each fold. When randomly sampling, duplicates are allowed. The test set contains all remaining patterns that were not selected for training (this value is likely to change from fold to fold).[1] This process is repeated for the specified number of folds (each time uses a different random seed).

---

1. If the number of remaining patterns for the test set is zero, the fold is discarded and is not counted.

Compared to basic cross validation, the bootstrap validation method increases the variance that can occur in each fold [Efron and Tibshirani, 1993]. This method is thought to be more realistic though, because it models real-life scenarios more accurately. The a prior probability of picking a data sample from the available data is held constant each time a pattern is selected.

In cross validation, in a data set of n patterns, let's say there are c example of a particular class C. The a priori probability of selecting a pattern from class C is then c/n. If we do select one of the patterns from class c, if we do not replace it for the next selection, then the probability of selecting another pattern from class c has changed to $(c-1)/(n-1)$. Sampling with replacement preserves the original a priori probability. This increases the variance across folds since we could (with extremely low probability) pick the same pattern each time from the n data patterns (resulting with a training set of one and a test set of n-1 patterns). This cannot occur in cross validation sampling, but it might occur (again with low probability) in real life.

The typical parameters for bootstrap validation are the number of folds n and a random seed used for selecting the patterns belonging to each fold.

Using Bootstrap Validation for Confidence Measures

You can use bootstrap validation to produce multiple models whose combined answers can provide more robust solutions as well as a *confidence measure*. That is, assume the distribution of model outputs is Gaussian, the take the mean of all models' output as the "answer" and use the standard deviation as the confidence bounds. A confidence measure is a value that indicates the reliability of a model's output. A value indicating high confidence means that the input is similar to patterns represented in the training set and that the model's output is reliable. A low confidence value means that the input is different from patterns present during training and that the model has extrapolated to an answer that may not be reliable.

To use bootstrap validation to generate a confidence value, generate n models using the bootstrap method described above. For the answer, average the n model outputs. Use the standard deviation as a confidence measure (high standard deviation = low confidence and vice versa).

11.2.3 Sliding Window Validation

Sliding window validation is a train and test technique especially well suited for time-series data that is slow-varying or non-stationary. This method treats all of the available data as a continuous "stream." It then slides a window across the stream of data generating a training and test set for each fold as shown in Figure 11-2.

Figure 11-2   Sliding Window Cross Validation

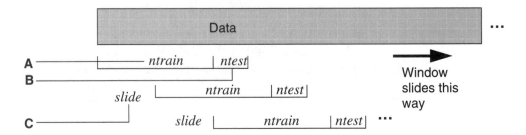

A. *ntrain* (the number of patterns to use in the training set)
B. *ntest* (the number of patterns to use in the test set)
C. *slide* (the number of patterns to skip between folds)

The parameters typically specified are:

- **# of Training Patterns** — The number of patterns, *ntrain*, used to train each model (i.e., the size of the sliding window).

- **# of Test Patterns** — The number of patterns, *ntest*, immediately following the sliding window to use to test each model.

- **# to Slide By** — The number of patterns, *slide*, to slide the over before generating the next fold of data.

This concept is illustrated in Figure 11-2. For example, if 1,000 patterns are available, you can specify a training set size of *ntrain* = 500 patterns, a test set of *ntest* = 100 patterns, and to slide by *slide* = 100 patterns each time. This generates five folds of data as shown in Table 11-2.

Table 11-2 Sliding Window Validation Example Folds

Fold Number	Patterns Used for Training	Patterns Used for Testing
1	1–500	501–600
2	101–600	601–700
3	201–700	701–800
4	301–800	801–900
5	401–900	901–1000

This validation method uses the characteristic that data recency is important in time-series data (i.e., recent data is more representative of the future than past data). It uses the serial nature of the time-series data to create the training and test set for each fold. By using a small "slide by" size (e.g., *slide* = 1) and test size (e.g., *ntest* = 1), you can create up to (*n-ntrain*) models, where *n* is the number of available patterns and *ntrain* is the size of the training set. Each model trains on *ntrain* data patterns and tests on one data pattern.

To select your sliding window validation parameters (*ntrain*, *ntest*, and *slide*), you will want to consider some of these issues:

- How much recent data do you need to generate an accurate model (i.e., what should the minimum size of *ntrain* be)?

- Does past data become inaccurate and misleading after some time frame (i.e., what should the maximum size of *ntrain* be)?

- How far into the future can you reasonably expect to predict (i.e., what is a reasonable size for *ntest*)? This will depend on how dynamic your system is.

- How many folds do you wish to generate? This will help determine the size of *slide*.

APPENDIX: TRAINING, TESTING, AND REPORTING IN PRW

Training and testing is performed in the control experiments screen of the experiment manager. In this screen, experiment icons are created, enabled or disabled for scheduling, and run.

☞ **NOTE:** You must have selected the **Train and Test** option on the setup screen of the experiment manager. If you selected the **Training** option, then no testing will be run. If you selected the **Testing** option, no training will be performed.

A.1   The Experiment Manager

Figure 11-3 shows the control experiments screen of the experiment manager.

Figure 11-3 Control Experiments Screen

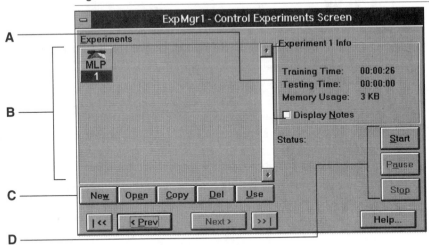

A. Experiment Info area (displays status for the current experiment)
B. Experiments area (contains experiment and report icons)
C. Experiment manager buttons
D. Experiment control buttons

A.2 Running Experiments

Running experiments is controlled by three buttons:

- **Start** — Begins running scheduled experiments
- **Pause** — Pauses the currently executing experiment
- **Stop** — Stops running all experiments immediately

To run experiments, you must:

1. **Configure one or more experiment icons and enable them.**

   Newly created experiments are enabled by default. Enabling and disabling icons is discussed in Section A.3.

2. Select the Start button to begin running experiments.

At any time when experiments are running, you can click the **Pause** button to temporarily pause all experiments in that experiment manager. After selecting **Pause**, you must click the **Start** button to restart the experiments or click the **Stop** button to stop the experiments.

☞ **NOTE:** Stopping experiments in the middle of execution may cause some or all training to be lost. For details, consult the *PRW User's Guide*.

A.3 Enabling and Disabling Experiments

Only enabled experiments will be scheduled and run in the experiment manager. Enabling and disabling experiments is controlled by the **Use** button. Clicking the **Use** button toggles the state (enabled or disabled) of the currently selected experiment(s). An enabled experiment icon is displayed in color; a disabled experiment icon is grayed out.

By default, when an experiment is created or copied in PRW, it is enabled and ready to run. When an experiment completes training, it becomes disabled (i.e., you must enable it again if you wish to continue training that experiment).

Enabling Experiments

To enable one or more disabled experiments:

1. Select the disabled experiment(s).

Click on an experiment to select it. To select multiple consecutive icons, shift-click the last icon.

☞ **NOTE:** Icons wrap in the **Experiments** area from top to bottom, left to right.

2. Select the Use button.

This will enable all of the selected disabled experiments.

☞ **NOTE:** If you selected both enabled and disabled experiments, all selected experiments are toggled to the opposite state of the first selected experiment. The first selected experiment is the topmost, leftmost experiment icon. Report icons are ignored by the **Use** button.

Continuing Training

The following algorithms are iterative and can continue training from their current state:

- Backpropagation/MLP
- Nearest cluster classifier
- Gaussian mixture
- K means
- Radial basis functions

To continue training an experiment:

1. **Enable the experiment icon.**

   Select the experiment icon and click the **Use** button as described above.

2. **Check the experiment stop conditions and modify as necessary.**

   a. **Open the Experiment Configuration window.**

      Double-click the experiment icon to open the **Experiment Configuration** window.

   b. **Bring the Experiment Parameter tab to the front (if necessary).**

   c. **Click on the Configure Algorithm option.**

d. Modify any stop conditions as necessary.

If an absolute stop condition triggered (e.g., a threshold was exceeded), you must change the threshold value in order for the experiment to continue training. Any **# Epochs** stop condition will continue training for another n epochs.

e. Click the Apply button to apply any changes (if necessary).

3. Click on the Start button in the experiment manager.

All enabled experiments will run in their scheduled execution order.

A.4   Scheduling Experiments

When the **Start** button is selected in the experiment manager, all enabled experiments are run in their scheduled execution order. The scheduled order is from the top to bottom, left-to-right in the **Experiments** area. To change the execution order, you simply drag-and-drop an experiment icon into a new location (existing icons will automatically move over to make room for the inserted icon).

☞   **NOTE:** Any changes to the scheduling order must be made *before* any experiments are started. Once experiments are started, dragging icons to new locations does *not* change their execution order.

A.5   Selecting Report Options

PRW allows you to specify what report data to capture after training and testing. Progress data during training is automatically captured.

To select reporting options, bring the **Reporting** tab to the front of the **Experiment Configuration** window by clicking on it. The default settings are shown in Figure 11-3.

Figure 11-3 Reporting Tab

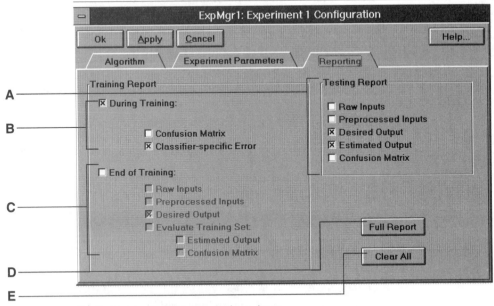

A. Select testing report options here.
B. Select training report options here.
C. Select end of training options here.
D. Click here to turn on all reporting options.
E. Click here to turn off all reporting options.

Report Parameters

The **Training Report** area on the left side of the **Reporting** tab contains the reporting options for evaluation of the training set. This is divided into two sections: **During Training** and **End of Training**. The **Testing Report** area on the right side contains the reporting options for the test set. Default values are initially shown.

Reporting During Training

During training, you can view training progress by enabling the **During Training** option. Results will be reported every *n* epochs, where *n* is specified in the **Epochs/Report** text box. Monitoring training results can help you decide when training should be stopped.

Solving Data Mining Problems through Pattern Recognition

The following reporting options also are available during training:

- **Confusion Matrix** — This option generates a confusion matrix (available only for classification). Each of the possible output classes are represented both along the x and the y-axis. Each cell of the matrix shows the number of patterns from the class on the y-axis that was mapped into the class on the x-axis. Diagonal entries represent patterns that were correctly classified and are shown in blue. If training were perfect, the confusion matrix would only have non-zero values along the diagonal. Misclassifications are displayed off the diagonal in red.

  The confusion matrix can help identify which classes are being learned well and which classes are being confused. This may identify additional features that can be added in order to help the classifier differentiate among the confused classes.

- **Classifier-specific Error** — This option displays training error(s) according to the specific classifier type. For iterative algorithms, these errors should decrease as training progresses.

To generate reports during training:

1. **Bring up the Reporting tab.**

   In the **Experiment Configuration** window, bring forward the **Reporting** tab by clicking on index tab labeled **Reporting**.

2. **Select the During Training option.**

   Click the small white box to the left of the **During Training** label. A black "X" will appear in the box when it is selected.

3. **Enter the number of epochs per report.**

   Each *epoch* is one pass through the training set. Enter the number of epochs to train before generating a report data point in the text box to the right of the **Epochs/Report** label. Click MB1 in the text box and enter a positive value.

☞ **TIP:** To report more often than once per epoch, enter a value less than one in the **Epoch/Report** text box. For example, to report twice per epoch, enter 0.5. To report ten times per epoch, enter 0.1. (In general, enter 1/*n* to generate *n* reports per epoch.)

---

4. Select the Confusion Matrix option if desired.

If you wish to generate a confusion matrix, click the small white box to the left of the **Confusion Matrix** label. A black "X" will appear in the box when it is selected.

5. Select the Classifier-specific Error option if desired.

If you wish to see the training set error, click the small white box to the left of the **Classifier-specific Error** label. A black "X" will appear in the box when it is selected.

6. Select Apply.

☞ **NOTE:** The actual inputs and outputs during training cannot be permanently captured (i.e., there is no option for them on the **Reporting** tab). However, the inputs and outputs can be viewed interactively during training through the **Reports...** window.

Evaluating the Training Set After Training

After training has completed (or anytime after a graduation hat appears on the experiment icon), you can evaluate the training set. This reporting is enabled with the **End of Training** option. The following report options are available:

- **Raw Inputs** — This option displays the inputs from the training pattern before preprocessing.

- **Preprocessed Inputs** — This option displays the actual inputs presented to the model. It includes any effects of the data preprocessing algorithms selected in the **Parameters** tab.

- **Desired Outputs** — This option displays the desired output values for each training pattern. This can be directly compared against the estimated output from the model to see if it was correctly classified or estimated.

- **Evaluate Training Set** — This options evaluates the results of the training set.[1] Select from:

  - **Estimated Outputs** — This option reports the outputs of the model for each training pattern.

  - **Confusion Matrix** — This option generates a confusion matrix of desired and estimated outputs (see description on page 11-19). This option is only available in classification mode.

To evaluate the training set after training has completed:

1. Bring up the Reporting tab.

In the **Experiment Configuration** window, bring forward the **Reporting** tab by clicking on index tab labeled **Reporting**.

2. Select the End of Training option.

3. Select the Raw Inputs option if desired.

If you wish to see the original raw inputs (as loaded into the spreadsheet) for each training pattern, click the **Raw Inputs** option.

4. Select the Preprocessed Inputs option if desired.

If you wish to see the preprocessed inputs (after manipulation by any selected preprocessing algorithms) for each training pattern, click the **Preprocessed Inputs** option.

---

1. The **Evaluate Training Set** option is separate from the **During Training** option because the suboptions under **During Training** can be captured without evaluating the training set. The suboptions under **Evaluate Training Set** require evaluation.

5. Select the Desired Output option if desired.

If you wish to see the desired class for each training pattern, click the **Desired Output** option.

6. Select the Evaluate Training Set option if desired.

a. Select the Confusion Matrix option if desired.

If you wish to generate a confusion matrix, click the **Confusion Matrix** option. (This option is only available in classification mode.)

b. Select the Estimated Output option if desired.

If you wish to see the model outputs for each pattern in the training set, click the **Estimated Output** option.

7. Select Apply.

Evaluating the Test Set

The same reporting options for evaluating the training set are available for evaluating the test set.

To evaluate the test set:

1. Select the End of Testing option.

2. Select the Confusion Matrix option if desired.

If you wish to generate a confusion matrix, click the **Confusion Matrix** option. (This option is only available in classification mode.)

3. Select the Report Also option if desired.

If you wish to include additional information about the training set patterns in the report, click the **Report Also** option.

a. Select the Raw Inputs option if desired.

If you wish to see the original raw inputs (as loaded into the spreadsheet) for each training pattern, click the **Raw Inputs** option.

b. Select the Preprocessed Inputs option if desired.

If you wish to see the preprocessed inputs (after manipulation by any selected preprocessing algorithms) for each training pattern, click the **Preprocessed Inputs** option.

c. Select the Desired Outputs option if desired.

If you wish to see the desired class for each training pattern, click the **Desired Output** option.

d. Select the Estimated Outputs option if desired.

If you wish to see the output class generated for each pattern in the training set, click the **Estimated Output** option.

4. Select Apply.

Reporting Buttons

At the bottom right corner of the **Reporting** tab are two buttons:

- **Full Report** — This button enables all possible reporting options.

☞ **NOTE:** Generating a full report, in particular the input and output reports, may consume a lot of disk space, depending on the size of your training set.

- **Clear All** — This button clears all reporting options.

☞ **TIP:** To save time, you can click on the **Full Report** button and *deselect* the reporting options you do not want, or you can click the **Clear All** button and select the reporting options you want.

A.6   Viewing Different Reports

While an experiment is running, you may view any of the training progress
reports. After an experiment has completed, you can view test reports on
the training set and/or the test set.

**Selecting the
Report Type**

On the top of the **Report** window is a **Report...** button. This button brings
up the **Report...** window which allows you to select different report types.
You can monitor any of the four report types available under the **Training
Progress** report option (i.e., confusion matrix, training error, input patterns
and output patterns).

To view a different report type:

1. **Select the Report... button to bring up the Report... window.**

   The **Report...** window is shown in Figure 11-4.

   Figure 11-4   The Report... Window

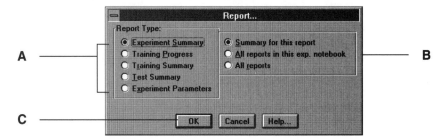

   A. Select a report type here.
   B. Select a report sub-type under the main report type.
   C. Click here to display the specified report.

2. **Select one of the available report types.**

3. **If sub-options appear, select a report sub-type.**

Solving Data Mining Problems through Pattern Recognition

4. Select the OK button.

As soon as the new report type has been selected, the **Report** window will update to display the new data.

A.7   Cross Validation

One useful feature in PRW is the ability to easily perform cross validation. Cross Validation creates a specified number of folds (n) and runs n tests, each with (n-1) folds for training and the remaining fold for testing.

Setup Screen

To run cross validation, you must select the **Validate** option in the setup screen of the experiment manager (see Figure 11-5).

Figure 11-5   Setup Screen

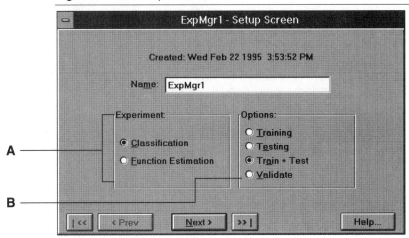

A. Select the experiment type here.
B. Click here to select the Validate option.

Once you have selected this option, the train/test screen appears as shown in Figure 11-6.

Figure 11-6   Train/Test Screen for Validation

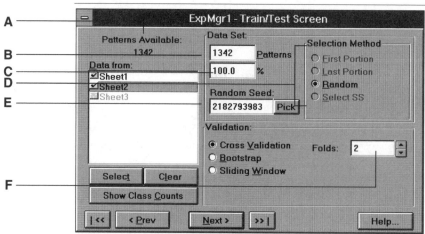

A. The total number of available data patterns is shown here.
B. Set the number of patterns to use for training here.
C. Or set the percentage of available patterns to use for training here.
D. Choose the data selection method here.
E. Enter a random seed for the experiment here or press the Pick button to automatically generate a new one.
F. Enter the number of folds of cross validation to perform here.

In this screen, you can select a validation method and specify parameters for them.

Reporting

Running cross-validation experiments is basically the same as running regular experiments. The multiple folds are automatically trained and tested. The cross-validation reports will report results for each fold as well as overall results. A sample experiment summary report is shown in Figure 11-7.

Figure 11-7 Experiment Summary Report with Cross Validation

```
┌─  Report 1A: Experiment Summary                              ▼ ─
│ Report...  Help...
│
│   Report: 1A
│   Created: 5/18/95 12:38:04
│
│   Experiment Completed: 5/18/95 12:42:19
│   Status: Normal completion.
│
│   Warnings:
│           none.
│
│   Experiment Result:
│   =====================
│   Training Set Error:
│           N/A
│
│   Test Set Error:
│         ┌─  Fold #1:          0.249062 RMS (46.27% Error)
│         │   Fold #2:          0.243044 RMS (35.07% Error)
│ A───────┤   Fold #3:          0.244995 RMS (38.06% Error)
│         │   Fold #4:          0.248312 RMS (39.55% Error)
│         └─  Fold #5:          0.24034 RMS (33.33% Error)
│
│         ┌─  Mean:             0.245151 RMS (38.46% Error)
│ B───────┴─  Stdev:            0.00363636 RMS (5.00% Error)
└─
```

A. The individual fold test set errors are reported here.
B. Summary data across all folds is reported here.

Classification and Cross Validation

Since heuristically, cross validation produces more accurate estimates when patterns from classes are divided equally among the folds, PRW automatically does this. When randomly dividing the available data patterns into the number of specified folds, every fold is guaranteed to have no more than one extra pattern from any particular class.

A.8   Sliding Window Validation

Using sliding window validation for time-series data in PRW is very similar to using cross-validation techniques described in Section A.7. The Sliding Window option treats all available data as a "stream" of data and slides a window along the stream to create various training and testing folds. Three parameters, **# Train**, **# Test**, and **Slide By**, are specified for this option.

The Train/Test screen for sliding window validation is shown in Figure 11-8.

Figure 11-8 Train/Test Screen for Sliding Window Validation

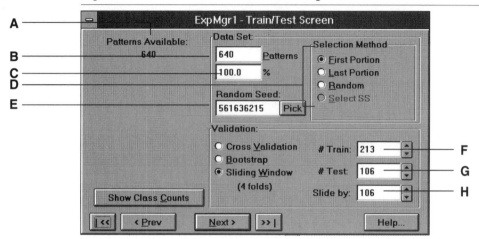

A. The total number of available data patterns is shown here.

B. Set the number of patterns to use for training here.

C. Or set the percentage of available patterns to use for training here.

D. Choose the data selection method here.

E. Enter a random seed for the experiment here or press the Pick button to automatically generate a new one.

F. Enter the number of patterns to use for each fold of training..

G. Enter the number of patterns to use for each fold of testing.

H. Enter the number of patterns to skip by inbetween folds.

Chapter 12

Iterating Steps and Trouble-Shooting

The next to last step of the development process, and often the most time-consuming, is iteration and fine-tuning. As every pattern recognition problem has its own complexities and uniqueness, solving one inherently involves iterating through the development process to try to improve the solution. This chapter describes the iteration process and then gives suggestions for trouble-shooting different algorithms. The last step, evaluating the final model using the evaluation step also is discussed briefly.

12.1 ITERATING TO IMPROVE YOUR SOLUTION

Ways to Iterate   Figure 12-1 again shows the overview of the steps in the development process. The following is a list of the different ways you can loop through the process:

Figure 12-1   Pattern Recognition Solution Process

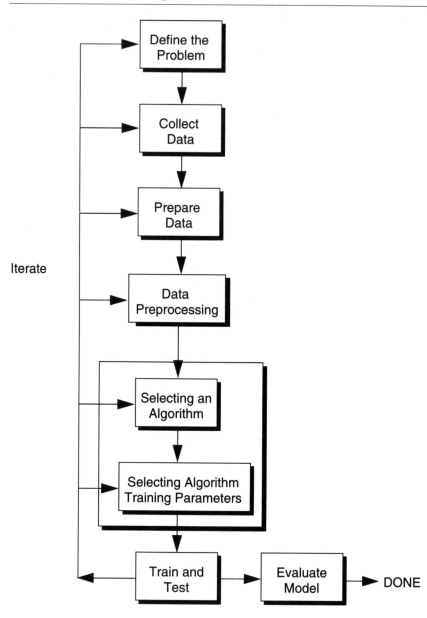

Solving Data Mining Problems through Pattern Recognition

- Select different algorithm training parameters
- Select different algorithms
- Select different data preprocessing
- Collect different data
- Redefine the problem

Typical Iteration Process

When trying to improve your solution, you typically begin with items at the top of the list. Each item further down in the list involves more changes and repeating more steps of the development process. A typical scenario is to proceed through the development steps (defining the problem, collecting data, preprocessing the data, selecting an architecture and training parameters, and training and testing that model) to generate a "baseline" solution. You would then configure additional experiments (e.g., using the same architecture with different training parameters, or different architectures altogether). By running each of these experiments and evaluating their results, you strive to continually improve on the solution. Your experiments may take you down several different paths, trying to optimize various parameters.

After thoroughly examining possibilities of different training parameters and architectures, you may have reached a satisfactory solution. If not, you would typically back up one more step in the development chain and look at different ways of preprocessing your data. By evaluating your test results from your previous experiments, you may discover additional insights that may help you "preprocess" your data to simplify the problem. In the course of this iteration, you may want to increase or decrease the number of input variables.

If you are still unable to achieve a good solution, you may want to consider iterating through the data collection step. In this scenario, you might examine particular problem patterns to try and identify areas of confusion. If you can identify another independent variable to help distinguish among those confused cases, you may be able to capture that data and incorporate it to improve your solution.

☞ **NOTE:** If you are not already overwhelmed with data, more data can often improve your results. To see if your solution is bounded by the amount of available data, you can run some several experiments using a different amount of training data for each. After plotting the number of training patterns vs. test accuracy, you should be able to judge if additional data might help.

If you have problems collecting additional data, you should consider using the cross-validation techniques discussed in Section 11.2, "Validation Techniques."

The last resort is to redefine your problem. Perhaps the input to output mapping you have selected is simply too complex for the data you have available. You might want to consider redefining your problem in a simpler form. For estimation problems, you might want to consider turning it into a classification problem with a small number of classes. For example, instead of trying to predict the Dow Jones Industrial Average (DJIA) each day, you might try predicting whether it will go up or down (a simpler two-class classification problem).

Automated Searches

To facilitate iteration and experimentation, you should use automate searches whenever possible. Automated searches can be very useful to optimize the set of input variables to use as well as the optimal algorithm parameter settings. For more information, see Section 12.2, "Automated Searches."

Flexible Iteration

The iteration process is not rigorous by any means. This section has outlined some of the ways you can think about iterating through the development process, but depending on the problem at hand, you may have better ideas. You may discover a missing key input variable right away, or come up with a brilliant way to preprocess your data before even running a handful of experiments. Each person must iterate through the process as they feel is best, based on the experiments and the results they have achieved so far. As you gain more experience with various algorithms, you will find yourself iterating much more quickly and in bigger leaps as you learn and recognize common problems and how to overcome them.

Solving Data Mining Problems through Pattern Recognition

Iteration and experimentation is a crucial part of the development process. This step of the process is where the analysis and evaluation of the results and the hard work often begins. Don't become discouraged when you seem to have hit a brick wall in your progress. Remember you are solving a hard problem—that you are trying to build a solution better than any existing solution! Most likely, this will involve a significant amount of work, but hopefully, your payoff will be great.

Evaluation   The last step of the development process is to evaluate the final model. After all iteration is completed and you have a final model, you generate an expected error for the model using the evaluation set. It is important that this final evaluation step take place after all iteration is completed. Otherwise, you allow the evaluation set to bias the results.

For more information on evaluating the final model, see Section 11.1, "Train, Test, and Evaluation Sets," and "Assessing the Final Model" on page 2-24.

12.2 AUTOMATED SEARCHES

Computer automated searches are an easy way to automate some portions of the iteration process. This section discusses some automated search methods for selecting the optimal set of input variables and for selecting the optimal set of algorithm parameters. If you use software that supports automated searches (e.g., Unica's Pattern Recognition Workbench), this feature can drastically simplify your fine-tuning and iteration process.

To use an automated search, you must specify a *cost function* or an *objective function* for evaluating different search permutations. Commonly used cost functions include out-of-sample minimum RMS error and maximum R^2 error. The cost function is typically based on a train-test split of experiments (see "Out-of-Sample Testing" on page 11-2) or on the more extensive cross validation of experiments (see Section 11.2, "Validation Techniques").

12.2.1 Input Variable Selection

Number of Inputs

The input variables specified for building a pattern recognition solution is often based on educated guesses when more concrete information is not available. You can typically identify a set of input variables that potentially have some degree of relevancy to the model. As a result, it may be tempting to throw all the variables that have any relevancy to the output variables into the modeling process and hope the classifier will be able to decipher which variables are salient and which are not.

Unfortunately, this approach will work only if the amount of data available is very large. Otherwise, the entire modeling process may be flawed, since with limited data, the classifier cannot distinguish the difference between random statistical correlations and salient correlations between inputs and outputs. A direct result of this problem is that one needs to choose inputs carefully, incorporating only inputs that add value within the limited-data modeling process.

Heuristics

A common heuristic that works well in selecting the right set of input variables is to first identify a set of all potentially relevant input variables. A subset of variables is then used to generate experiments of pattern recognition models (provided that good out-of-sample results are generated for each experiment). The best set of inputs is then determined based on the performance of the experiments.

This heuristic is essentially a search process in selecting the subset of input variables. The number of possible input combinations from n available inputs (call this the *input selection space*) is the sum of possible combinations of selecting one variable from n inputs to n variables from n inputs. Or expressed mathematically, the number of input select combinations is:

$$\binom{n}{1} + \binom{n}{2} + \dots + \binom{n}{n} \qquad \textbf{(EQ 1)}$$

where each $\binom{n}{m}$ is:

$$\binom{n}{m} = \frac{n!}{(m!)(n-m)!} \qquad \text{(EQ 2)}$$

The total size of the input selection space can be simplified to 2^n. It is clear that trying to find the absolute optimal combination of inputs in this space is exponentially difficult with respect to the number of possible inputs n. Therefore clever heuristics are often used to search through this space. Some of the most significant heuristics are presented below:

- **Forward Search** — In a forward search, you begin by creating one experiment for each input. If there are n inputs, create n experiments, each with a different input. The inputs from the best performing c experiments are used in all remaining configurations, where c is an increment value you specify. Then create $(n-c)$ experiments using the best c inputs determined already and each of the other remaining $(n-c)$ inputs (each experiment now has $c+1$ inputs). Add the next c best inputs for all remaining experiments (now a total of $2c$ inputs). The next round of $(n-2c)$ experiments each use $2c+1$ inputs. Continue adding inputs in this manner until all available inputs are used. The best performing experiment in this path of experiments is deemed to contain the optimal set of inputs.

  In the example shown in Figure 12-2, there are initially eight inputs ($n=8$) and the increment value is two ($c=2$). Each input is represented by a letter (A–H).

Figure 12-2 Forward Search Example with c=2

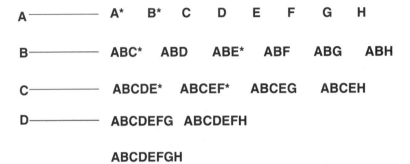

A. The first set of eight experiments, each with a single input.
B. Inputs A and B performed the best, so they are kept. The second round of experiments pair AB with each of the remaining six inputs.
C. In round two, ABC and ABE performed best, so inputs C and E are kept. The third round of experiments pair ABCE with the remaining four inputs.
D. In round three, experiments containing E and F performed best, so they are kept. The fourth round of experiments pair ABCDEF with the remaining two inputs. This continues until all inputs are used in round four.

- **Backward Search** — In a backward search, you begin by creating one experiment for each combination of *n*-1 inputs (i.e., create *n* experiments, each missing a different input). The missing inputs from the best performing *d* experiments are discarded (i.e., eliminated from all remaining configurations), where *d* is a decrement value you specify. Then create (*n*-*d*) experiments using combinations of the remaining (*n*-*d*) inputs (each experiment now has *n*-*d*-1 inputs). Discard the next *d* worst inputs for all remaining experiments. The next round of (*n*-2*d*) experiments each use *n*-2*d*-1 inputs. Continue removing inputs in this manner until only single inputs are used. The best performing experiment in this path of experiments is deemed to contain the optimal set of inputs.

In the example shown in Figure 12-3, there are initially five inputs ($n=5$) and the decrement value is one ($d=1$). Each input is represented by a letter (A–E).

Figure 12-3 Backwards Search Example

A————	ABCD	ABCE	ABDE	ACDE	BCDE*
B————	BCD	BCE	BDE	CDE*	
C————	CD	CE	DE*		
D————	D	E			

A. The first set of five experiments, each missing one input.
B. The experiment missing input A performed the best, so A is discarded. The second round of four experiments each remove one additional input.
C. In round two, the experiment missing input B performs the best, so B is discarded. The third round of three experiments each remove one additional input.
D. In round three, the experiment missing input C performs the best, so C is discarded. The last round of experiments look at the last two remaining inputs singly.

- **Forward/Backward Search** — A forward/backward search alternates between forward and backwards searches (see previous explanations for details). You specify both an increment value (c) and a decrement value (d), where $d < c$. You search forward for the c best inputs and then discard the d worst inputs from the previously selected c inputs. This leaves (c-d) inputs. Continue to add the next best c inputs and discarding the d worst inputs, until all available inputs are used. The best performing experiment in this path of experiments is deemed to contain the optimal set of inputs.

In the example shown in Figure 12-4, there are initially six inputs ($n=6$), the increment value is three ($c=3$), and the decrement value is one ($d=1$). Each input is represented by a letter (A–E).

Figure 12-4 Forward/Backward Search Example

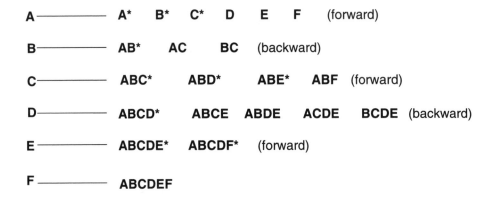

A ———	A*	B*	C*	D	E	F	(forward)
B ———	AB*	AC	BC	(backward)
C ———	ABC*	ABD*	ABE*	ABF	(forward)
D ———	ABCD*	ABCE	ABDE	ACDE	BCDE	(backward)
E ———	ABCDE*	ABCDF*	(forward)
F ———	ABCDEF

A. (Forward search) The first set of five experiments, each with a single input.
B. Inputs A, B, and C performed the best, so they are kept. (Backward search) The second round of experiments eliminate one input from the set of three inputs kept.
C. In round two, the experiment missing C performed the best, so C is discarded, leaving inputs A and B. (Forward search) The third round of experiments pair AB with the remaining three inputs.
D. In round three, C, D, and E perform the best, so they are kept. (Backward search) The fourth round of experiments eliminate one input from the set of five inputs kept.
E. In round four, the experiment missing E performs the best, so E is discarded. (Forward search) In the fifth round, the four inputs ABCD are paired with the two remaining inputs.
F. The last uses all available inputs.

- **PCA-Based** — Principal component analysis (PCA) can be used to determine the most significant input variables. See the discussion of "Principal Component Analysis" on page 9-7.

- **Sensitivity-Based** — Sensitivity analysis can be used to determine the optimal inputs by ordering the importance of all inputs. This is done by first performing an experiment using all input variables. Based on the experiment, create a derivative model that computes the partial derivative of the output with respect to the inputs. This partial derivative model can then be used to generate a sensitivity measure for each input variable (see "Sensitivity Analysis" on page 9-10 for more information). Once the inputs are ordered by their importance, n experiments are generated, each with a different number of inputs. The first experiment has the most significant input. The next experiment uses the first two most significant inputs, and so on. The best set of inputs is then determined by the experiment with the best out-of-sample error rate.

- **Genetic Search** — In a genetic search algorithm, you specify the number of samples (or genes) per generation (s), the number of generations (g), and the mutation rate (m). Create and evaluate $s \times g$ experiments. Begin by randomly creating s genes for the first generation (not necessarily unique). If there are n input variables, randomly generate n-bit binary numbers. An input is used if its corresponding bit is one. It is not used if its corresponding bit is zero. Each of these binary masks is considered a "gene." The pool of s genes is called a *gene pool*.

  Each gene determines the inputs to be used in an experiment which is run and ranked using the cost function you specify.

  To create each of the successive g generations, repeat the following steps s times:

  a. Randomly select two genes from the gene pool.

  These genes are the "mother" and "father" of the new gene.

b. For each bit of the new gene, randomly use the bit value from either the mother or father gene.

c. For each bit of the new gene, there is an *m* percent chance the bit may "mutate."

If a bit mutates, change the bit value from one to zero or zero to one as appropriate.

d. Replace the "worst" gene in the gene pool with the newly created gene.

As the genetic algorithm runs, the best genes remain in the gene pool. The worst genes are constantly replaced from variations from the current pool during an evolutionary process. Over time, the "optimal" genes satisfying the cost function remain. The best parameter combination is the experiment with the best out-of-sample test performance.

12.2.2 Algorithm Parameter Searches

If an algorithm has *n* parameters to tune and there are m_i possible settings for the *i*-th parameter, the number of possible combinations grows very quickly as shown in Eq. 3:

$$\text{parameter space size} = m_1 \cdot m_2 \cdot \ldots \cdot m_n \qquad \textbf{(EQ 3)}$$

where m_1 is the number of values to try for the first parameter, m_2 is the number of values to try for the second parameter, and so on.

While an exhaustive search may be possible in some circumstances, a more intelligent search is recommended when searching the entire search space is impractical. Some heuristics that intelligently search through the parameter space are described below.

- **Gradient Descent** — Uses gradient descent (minimizing error) to try to converge on the optimal set of parameter values. Gradient descent operates for the number of iterations you specify. Each iteration consists of changing the values of the n parameters, one at a time, in a direction that maximizes performance (or minimizes error). The "gradient" direction is kept based on past experiment information. The best performing experiment in this path of experiments is deemed to contain the optimal parameter setting.

- **Genetic Search** — For a genetic search, you specify the number of samples (or genes) per generation (s), the number of generations (g), and the mutation rate (m). Create and evaluate $s \times g$ experiments. Begin by randomly creating s genes for the first generation. If there are n different algorithm parameters, randomly generate n numbers to compose a gene. Each algorithm parameter is represented by a value in the gene (a number in a particular position in the gene). Randomly select one of the possible values for each algorithm parameter.

  Each gene generates an experiment which is run and ranked using the cost function you specify.

  To create the each of the successive g generations, repeat these steps s times:

  a. Randomly select two genes from the gene pool.

  These genes are the "mother" and "father" of the new gene.

  b. For each algorithm parameter in the new gene, randomly use the value from either the mother or father gene.

  c. For each algorithm parameter in the new gene, there is an m percent chance it may "mutate."

  If an algorithm parameter mutates, randomly select one of the other available values for the algorithm parameter.

  d. Replace the "worst" gene in the gene pool with the newly created gene.

As the genetic algorithm runs, the best genes remain in the gene pool. The worst genes are constantly replaced from variations from the current pool during an evolutionary process. Over time, the "optimal" genes satisfying the cost function remain. The best parameter combination is the experiment with the best out-of-sample test performance.

12.3 TROUBLE-SHOOTING

This section lists problems and suggestions for applying pattern recognition algorithms to problem solving. This trouble-shooting section may give you ideas to overcome some common stumbling blocks. General problems are presented first, followed by algorithm-specific problems.

12.3.1 Training Error Is High

Problem

The training error (performance on the training set) is poor.

Suggestions

- Train incremental algorithms longer

  If you are running an incremental learning algorithm (e.g., MLP/BP, logistic regression, K means), increase the training time. Often algorithms train very slowly and have not yet reached their maximum potential. Plot the training error versus the iteration number to see if the error has converged.

- Increase complexity of the network

  Use a larger network (e.g., increase the number of hidden nodes for MLP/BP, increase the number of radial basis functions for RBF) to increase the complexity of the mapping. For KNN, decrease the value of k.

- Normalize input variables

  If you have a known minimum and maximum value for an input (i.e., you do not care about values above or below particular values), use min-max normalization. If you have outliers, use sigmoidal normalization. Otherwise, use Zscore normalization. Normalization of the inputs helps equalize the ranges of input values and the impact of each input variable.

- For estimation problems, normalize the output variables

  If you have a known minimum and maximum value for an output (i.e., you do not care about values above or below particular values), use min-max normalization. If you have outliers, use sigmoidal normalization. Otherwise, use Zscore normalization. This helps bring the desired output values into a range that can be easily estimated by the network.

- Examine the relationship between model outputs and inputs.

  Using the analysis method described in "Understanding Modeling Results" on page 3-14, examine the relationships between the model output and each input variable. Compare the relationship learned by the model to actual profiled relationships between the output and input variable as reflected by the training data. If the shapes of the relationships differ significantly, this can indicate a lack of data (i.e., the data is spurious), or there is a problem with the training process (see other suggestions in this section). If other suggestions here do not improve the results, try removing the offending input variable.

- Try linear output layer vs. sigmoidal output layer for MLP/BP

  If you are running MLP/BP, normalize your outputs between 0–1 and use a sigmoidal transfer function in the output layer. Also try leaving the output variable(s) unnormalized and using a linear output layer This will allow the network to generate output values over a larger range.

- Collect more input variables

  Does the neural network have sufficient information content in the input variables to be able to model the desired output variable(s)? You may want to look at the problem and add additional input variables to provide critical missing information.

- Restructure an estimation model so there is a single output

  If you have an estimation problem with more than one output node, try redefining the problem with a single output variable. That is, break the problem down from estimating two or more outputs in a single model to estimating one output per model. This can help to simplify the mapping problem.

- For KNN, turn off any data compression

  If you are using data compression (and therefore potentially losing important information), turn off data compression and compare the performance.

- For Gaussian mixture, increase training of initial clusters (so they are better positioned). Also increase the training times of the second phase, where the centers are moved further, the weights of the Gaussians are trained, and the Gaussian shapes (standard deviation) are adjusted.

12.3.2 Test Error Is High

Problem

The training error (performance on the training set) is good, but the test error is poor (i.e., much higher that that for the training set); the network does not generalize well to new data.

Suggestions

- Reduce complexity of the network

  If your model is too complex, it will map the training data very well, but will not generalize well on the test data. Try reducing model complexity by using smaller network configurations until the training and test set errors are almost equivalent.

- Use representative training data

  It is critical that the data in the training set is representative of the data in the test set. Try randomly splitting the data for training and testing, as opposed to using the first part of a sequential training set for training and the remainder for testing. If an inherent ordering of the data set makes the training and test set different, then random selection of patterns can help normalize these differences.

  For classification problems, make sure all desired classes are represented in the training set. For time-series prediction, you may want to consider discarding some data and only using the most recent data. In general, any processing (e.g., throwing out inconsistent data) making the training set patterns more representative will improve the test set error. Oftentimes, using more training data will help. If the available amount of data is small, try using cross-validation methods.

- Reduce the input space

  If the input space is too large with respect to the number of available training patterns, too few examples (points) in the input space are provided to produce a good mapping. Try reducing the number of input variables (e.g., throw away irrelevant or highly correlated inputs, use principal component analysis to reduce the input space, etc.).

- For MLP/BP, stop training early

  For MLP/BP, if the network trains too long, it may overtrain on the training set, producing poor generalization capabilities. Try stopping training at different points to see if test set error is affected.

- For KNN, vary k, the number of nearest neighbors

  Use different values of k. Tuning the number of nearest neighbors used to generate the prediction is critical.

- For unimodal Gaussian, use a diagonal-covariance matrix

  The unimodal Gaussian model may be overfitting the training data. Try a diagonal-covariance matrix instead of a full-covariance matrix. If the input variables are known to be correlated, use PCA first to generate independent inputs.

☞ **NOTE:** If you are performing extremely well on the training and test set, you should be suspicious and check that you are not inadvertently giving the model the answer you are trying to predict. For example, in time-series prediction, predictions in the near future may be trivial if values change very slowly.

Solving Data Mining Problems through Pattern Recognition

12.3.3 Classification Problem Performs Poorly on Some Classes

Problem

A classification model performs accurately for some classes, but performs poorly on others.

Suggestions

- Use more examples of the classes that are performing poorly

  By providing more examples of classes with poor performance, you automatically increase your changes of providing representative data patterns for that class and you increase the importance (in reducing overall RMS error) of predicting that class correctly.

- Adjust the prior probabilities of those classes

  If you increase the prior probability of the classes that are not performing well, you increase the importance (in reducing overall RMS error) of predicting that class correctly. Note, however, that when improving the classification error on a few classes, it is likely you will sacrifice accuracy on other classes and total overall accuracy.

12.3.4 Problems with Production Accuracy

Problem

Running the network in production mode with real data results in worse-than-expected error, or accuracy degrades over time.

Suggestions

- Periodically retrain the model

  It is critical that the data in the training set is representative of the data to be seen in the production environment. If you are running the model in a dynamic environment where the process being modeled changes over time, it is important that you periodically retrain the network on recent data.

- Make sure training set data is representative of real-life data

  You will achieve the best and most predictable performance if the data in your training set accurately represents the data in the production environment.

12.3.5 Decision Tree Works Best by Far

Problem

Decision-tree algorithms (e.g., CHAID or CART) perform extremely well, while other algorithms perform poorly.

Suggestions

This symptom usually indicates that some form of "cheating" is going on. Decision trees are excellent at detecting and taking full advantage of cases where the answer is given away or partially given away by some of the inputs. If you see this situation, examine the top (most important) variables used by the decision tree and verify that they do not contain any information that should not be available.

12.3.6 Backpropagation Does Not Converge

Problem

The training error for the backpropagation algorithm does not decrease over time and converge.

Suggestions

- Normalize the input variables

  Normalize all input variables using Zscore normalization. This helps equalize the ranges of input values and the impact of each input variable.

- Normalize the output variables

  If you have a known minimum and maximum value for an output (i.e., you do not care about values above or below particular values), use min-max normalization. If you have outliers, use sigmoidal normalization. Otherwise, use Zscore normalization. This helps bring the desired output values into a range that can be easily estimated by the network.

- Change the step size of the learning rate

  A correct value of the step size is critical for convergence. The current value may be too large or too small. Try a larger step size if the training error progress is smooth but is not decreasing quickly enough. Try a smaller step size if the training error is bouncing around sporadically. When increasing or decreasing step sizes, try changing the value by a factor of 10 or 100 first. Then fine tune the step size after the training error starts to generate a nice convergence.

☞ **TIP:** Try watching the convergence graph and interactively change the learning rate.

- Increase training times

  Try training the backpropagation algorithm longer. Sometimes algorithm performance can significantly increase with longer training (this appears as a quick drop in the training error progress).

☞ **TIP:** View the convergence graph to see if training has converged. Try training the algorithm overnight or longer.

- Decrease the momentum

  If you are using momentum (non-zero value), try decreasing the momentum or setting it to zero. After the network is able to converge successfully, you can try adding back the momentum term to decrease training times.

- Increase the momentum

  If you have a smooth training error curve but it does not decrease, try increasing the momentum term. This can decrease the time it takes MLP/BP to train.

12.3.7 Backpropagation Finds a Local Minimum Solution

Problem

The backpropagation algorithm converges to a local minimum instead of a global minimum.

Suggestions

- Run multiple experiments with different random seeds

  Try using the same training parameters with different random initial weights, etc. Different initial weight settings help avoid falling into the same local minima.

- Increase the number of nodes in hidden layers

  By allowing the network to be able to create a more complex mapping, local minima are reduced.

- Train weights after each pattern

  Train the weights of the neural network after the presentation of each training pattern, instead of accumulating weight changes over a training epoch. Empirically, training on a per pattern basis produces better results than training once per epoch.

12.3.8 Matrix Inversion Problem

Problem

You are running an algorithm (e.g., linear regression, unimodal Gaussian, Gaussian mixture, RBF) using a matrix inversion implementation and the resulting matrix is singular.

Suggestions

- Check input variables

  A singular matrix means that there are an infinite number of solutions. Check your input variables and make sure there are none with same value throughout (e.g., all zeros). If a variable is always the same value, remove it from the inputs.

- Normalize input variables

  Normalize all input variables (e.g., to a range between 0–1). This helps equalize the ranges of input values and the impact of each input variable.

- Reduce complexity of the network

  By reducing the number of clusters in RBF or Gaussian mixture, you increase the chances of producing an invertible matrix.

- Use gradient descent instead of matrix inversion

  Use an algorithm implementation that uses gradient descent to minimize error instead of matrix inversions. Gradient descent will converge to the same solution (e.g., numerical overflow), except it takes more time.

12.3.9 Unimodal Gaussian Has High Training Error

Problem   The unimodal Gaussian model performs poorly on the training set.

Suggestions
- Reduce the input space

  If the input space is too large with respect to the number of available training patterns, too few examples (points) in the input space are provided to produce a good mapping. Try reducing the number of input variables (e.g., throw away irrelevant or highly correlated inputs, use principal component analysis to reduce the input space, etc.).

- Use a full-covariance matrix instead of a diagonal-covariance matrix

  If you are using a diagonal-covariance matrix and your inputs are not independent, the mapping accuracy will be poor. Try using a full-covariance matrix.

- Use PCA and a diagonal-covariance matrix

  Try running principal component analysis (PCA) on the input variables and then use a diagonal-covariance matrix.

- Use more training data

  Training error may improve with additional training examples.

- Use a global covariance matrix instead of one per class

  If you do not have many examples of a particular class, try using a global covariance matrix instead of generating one per class.

- Use another architecture

  If the data to be modeled is not unimodal Gaussian in its distribution,
  this architecture will perform poorly. Try using another architecture.

See also Section 12.3.1, "Training Error Is High."

12.3.10 Gaussian Mixture Diverges

Problem
A Gaussian mixture algorithm's log-likelihood (the function which
Estimate-Maximize tries to maximize) diverges.

Suggestions
- Use a different number of clusters

Occasionally, in Gaussian mixture, a small number of cluster centers will
dominate the model, causing divergence problems. Try using a different
number of clusters to avoid this condition.

12.3.11 RBF Has High Training Error

Problem
The RBF model performs poorly on the training set.

Suggestions
- Increase training of initial clusters and weights

Solving Data Mining Problems through Pattern Recognition

Increase the training time of the initial clusters (so they are better positioned). Also increase the training times of the second phase, where
the centers are moved further and the weights are trained.

- Adjust the value of h

    RBF's performance is highly sensitive to the value h (the overlap fac-
    tor). Try h values of 0.1, 1, and 10 and values inbetween. Fine-tune the
    h value from the best-performing model and so on.

APPENDIX: ITERATING IN PRW

A.1   Overview of PRW Features

PRW provides many convenient features to simplify the iteration step of the development process:

- **Multiple Spreadsheets** — PRW's unlimited number[1] of spreadsheets allow you to organize your data any way you want. When training an algorithm, you can select patterns to use for training randomly, use the first portion, the last portion, subsample, or specify specific spreadsheets that contain the training data.

- **Multiple Experiment Managers** — One of the most powerful features of PRW is its ability to support an unlimited number of experiment managers.[2] You can set up different experiment managers to organize different experimental branches. For example, one experiment manager might hold experiments using all available input variables. Another might hold experiments where automatic input space reduction is performed using PCA.

- **Multiple Work Sessions** — PRW's ability to save all of your work in a session and to switch among different saved work sessions gives you great flexibility in organizing your work. Since spreadsheets, data, experiments, reports, and user functions can all be individually exported, it is simple to create a new work session and import the necessary components to continue work or explore a different avenue of development.

---

1. The number of spreadsheets in the PRW Professional version is limited only by the resources of your computer. In the PRW Standard edition, you are limited to two spreadsheets.

2. The number of experiment managers in the PRW Professional version is limited only by the resources of your computer. In the PRW Standard edition, you are limited to a single experiment manager.

- **Automated Searches** — PRW supports automated searches for input parameter selection (PCA, sensitivity analysis, forward, backward, forward/backward, and genetic search algorithms) and for algorithm parameter selection (exhaustive, gradient descent, and genetic search algorithms).

- **Data Preprocessing** — PRW has automated data preprocessing for:
  - Modifying class probability
  - Modifying training set size
  - Reducing the input size
  - Normalizing input variables

  This makes it extremely easy to experiment with these commonly used preprocessing steps. Furthermore, complex data manipulation can be performed in PRW spreadsheets using over 100 built-in macro functions and custom-built user functions.

- **Export Experiments and Reports** — Any experiment or report can be exported into a file on disk. This allows you to share experiments and reports among different PRW work sessions.

- **Re-Use Experiment Parameters** — Every report icon contains within it, all the information you need to regenerate the trained model that produced the report. From any report, the **Re-Use Parameters** option automatically generates an experiment icon with the stored experiment configuration. You simply run the experiment to regenerate those results.

- **Building User Functions** — Any function definition in the spreadsheet and any trained experiment can be "wrapped" into a custom user function. A user function can then be used in the spreadsheet, just like a built-in macro function. This allows you to easily build up complex data processing routines (and share them among sessions by exporting them to files). It also allows you to easily evaluate trained experiments by running them on data in the spreadsheet, graphing results, and performing data analysis.

A.2   Creating Multiple Spreadsheets

PRW supports any number of spreadsheets simultaneously, limited only by system resources. This allows you to organize your data into multiple spreadsheets and use data from whatever spreadsheets you want to construct a training and test set.

Creating a New Spreadsheet Window

To create a new spreadsheet window, select **File➔New➔New Data Spreadsheet**.

This will bring up a new **Sheet*n*** window (see Figure 12-5), where *n* increments by one each time (starting with one). You can now import data and build function definitions in the new spreadsheet.

Figure 12-5   Bringing Up a New Spreadsheet Window

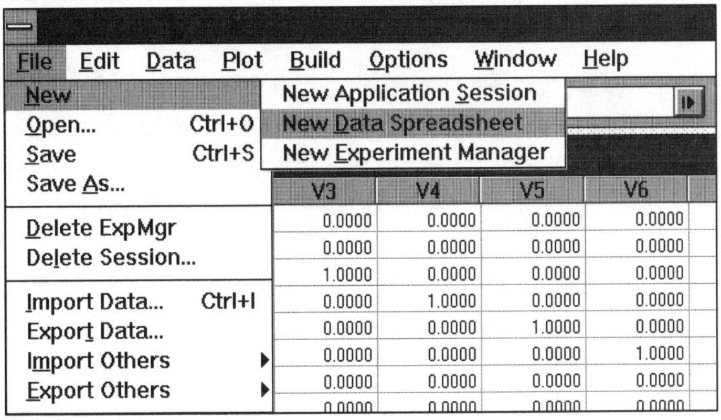

A.3   Creating Multiple Experiment Managers

To create a new experiment manager, select **File➔New➔New Experiment Manager**.

This will create a new **ExpMgr***N* window, where *N* is the next available experiment manager number. If you have more experiment managers than can fit in the **Experiment Manager Icon** area, a horizontal scroll bar will automatically appear.

A.4   Using Multiple Work Sessions

Starting a New Work Session

You can start a new work session at any time with the **New Application Session** command.

> When you begin a new work session, the contents of the current work session will be destroyed. You will be prompted whether to save the current session before beginning a new one. Respond to the **Save Current Session** dialog box (see Figure 12-6) as described above.

To begin a new work session from scratch, select **File➔New➔New Application Session**.

This will begin a new application session with a blank spreadsheet and an experiment manager window.

Loading a Previously Saved Work Session

The five most recently loaded work sessions are listed in the **File** menu for easy access. Simply select the session filename from the **File** menu. You also can load in a previously saved work session at any time using the **Open...** command.

When you load in a previously saved work session, the contents of the current work session will be lost. PRW will ask whether you wish to save the current work session (see Figure 12-6) before loading another one. Select **Yes** to save the current work session, **No** to exit the current session without saving, and **Cancel** to cancel the **Open...** command request.

Figure 12-6   Save Current Session Dialog Box

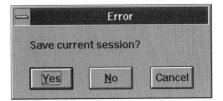

To load in one of the last five most recently used work sessions:

1. **Open the File menu.**

2. **Select the work session filename to load (see Figure 12-7).**

Figure 12-7   File Menu Listing Previously Saved Work Sessions

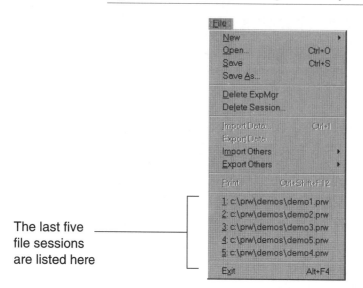

The last five
file sessions
are listed here

To load a work session from a file, select **File→Open...**.

This will bring up the **Open Session File** dialog box shown in Figure 12-8. This is a standard file selection dialog box. Select the filename containing the work session you wish to restore and click the **OK** button.

Figure 12-8 Open Session File Window

Importing and Exporting Sessions

You can export sessions into a single PRW file for easy transport or backup. Importing and exporting session files is like saving and loading session files, except that all data and related files are incorporated into a single file during import and export.

A.5   Using Automated Searches

Setting Up Input Searches

To search for the optimal set of inputs:

1. **Select the Automated Search option (see Figure 12-9).**

   In the **Experiment Configuration** window, enable the **Automated Search** option.

Figure 12-9 Automated Search Tab (Input Selection)

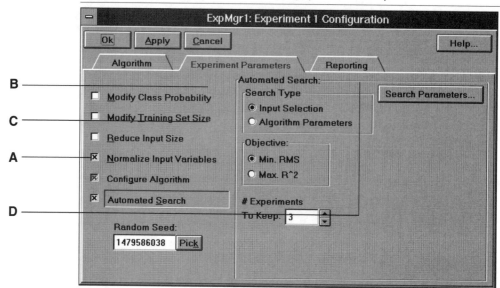

A. Click here to enable automated searches.
B. Click here to perform input selection searches.
C. Select the overall cost function to use for evaluating experiments here.
D. Click here to specify the search parameters.

2. **Enable the Input Selection option.**

3. **Select a cost function for evaluating experiments.**

   In the **Cost Function** area, click the **Min. RMS** or the **Min. R^2** option.

4. **Specify the number of experiments to keep.**

   In the **To Keep** text box, enter the number of experiments to keep (save) in the experiment manager (an integer between 0–16,000 inclusive).

5. Click the Search Parameters... button.

The Input Reduction/Selection Search screen appears (see Figure 12-10).

Figure 12-10   Input Reduction/Selection Search Screen

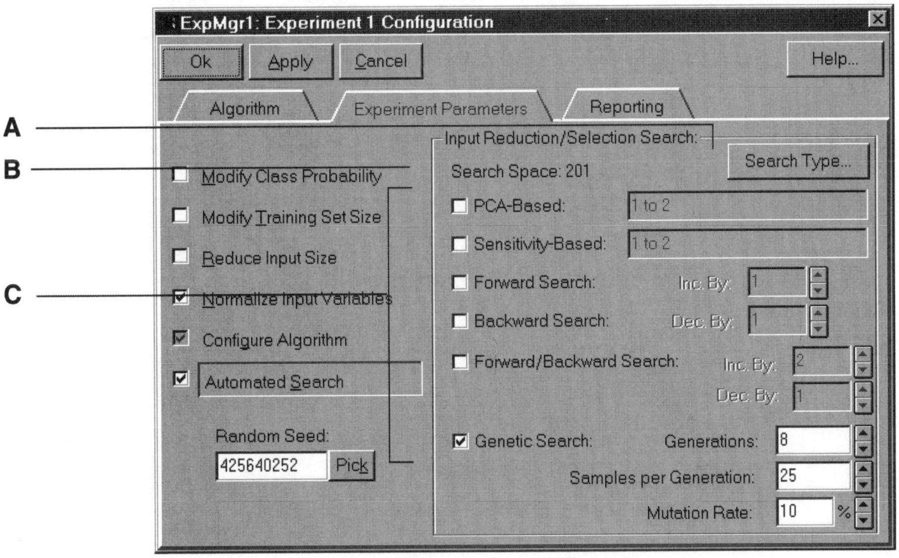

A. Click here to return to the Automated Search screen.
B. The number of total experiment configurations requested appears here.
C. Select one of the search methods here and provide required search parameters.

6. Select one or more of the available search methods.

Click the desired search method(s). The corresponding search parameters are enabled (ungrayed). If you select more than one search method, PRW performs the searches sequentially in the order listed (e.g., PCA-Based search precedes Sensitivity-Based search, etc.).

All search methods have default values based on the number of available inputs. You may use these values or modify them as follows:

a. If you enable the **PCA-Based** option, specify the number of input variables to consider.

b. If you enable the **Sensitivity-Based** option, specify the number of input variables to consider.

c. If you enable the **Forward Search** option, specify the increment value.

d. If you enable the **Backward Search** option, specify the decrement value.

e. If you enable the **Forward/Backward search** option, specify the increment and decrement values.

f. If you enable the **Genetic Search** option, specify the number of generations to run, the number of samples to create per generation, and the mutation rate.

7. **Select Apply.**

Setting Up Algorithm Parameter Searches

To search for the optimal set of algorithm parameters:

1. **Select the Automated Search option (see Figure 12-11).**

In the **Experiment Configuration** window, enable the **Automated Search** option.

Figure 12-11   Automated Search Tab (Algorithm Parameters)

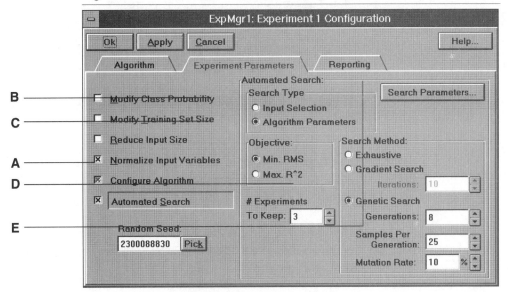

A. Click here to enable automated searches.
B. Click here to perform algorithm parameter searches.
C. Select the overall cost function to use for evaluating experiments here.
D. Specify the search method and search parameters here.
E. Click here to specify the search parameters.

2. **Enable the Input Selection option.**

3. **Select a cost function for evaluating experiments.**

   In the **Cost Function** area, click on the **Min. RMS** or the **Max. R**^{2} option.

4. **Specify the number of experiments to keep.**

   In the **To Keep** text box, enter the number of experiments to keep (save) in the experiment manager (an integer between 0–16,000 inclusive).

5. **Select one of the available search methods.**

   Click the desired search method. The corresponding search parameters are enabled (ungrayed).

   All search methods have default values based on the number of available inputs. You may use these values or modify them as follows:

   a. **If you enable the Gradient Search option, specify the number of iterations.**

      PRW begins with the experiment configuration specified from the **Configure Algorithm** screen. It generates gradient information for each parameter and uses the appropriate value from the allowable parameter values you specify.

   b. **If you enable the Genetic Search option, specify the number of generations to run, the number of samples to create per generation, and the mutation rate.**

6. **Click the Search Parameters... button.**

   The Algorithm Parameters Search screen appears (see Figure 12-12). The current search space size, as configured by the enabled options beneath it, appears at the top of the screen. This lists the number of different experiments PRW will run to complete the algorithm parameters search. To decrease this number, disable one or more of the enabled options or remove some of the parameter values to try.

Figure 12-12   Automated Search Parameters Screen

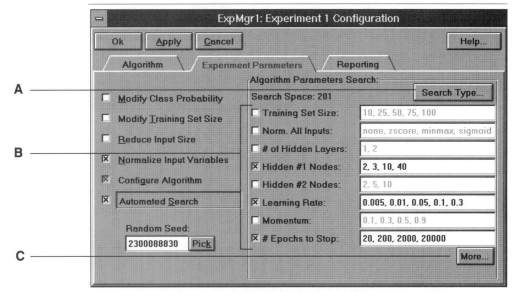

A. Click here to return to the Automated Search screen.
B. Select one of the search methods here and provide required search parameters.
C. Click here to see more algorithm parameters.

7. **Enable one or more of the algorithm parameter options and specify the parameter values to try.**

   Click the the desired search parameter. The corresponding parameters values are enabled (ungrayed).

   The search parameters listed depend on the algorithm selected on the **Algorithm** tab. All search parameters have default values. You may use these values or modify them. In each text box, enter a function definition specifying the parameter value(s) to try. PRW creates experiments using all possible value permutations.

☞   **NOTE:** If a **More...** button appears at the bottom of the screen, click it to view additional algorithm parameters. The **More...** button allows you to cycle through available parameter screens.

---

8. Select Apply.

A.6   Preprocessing Data

PRW's many data preprocessing capabilities are too extensive to detail here. The automated preprocessing options are shown below.

Modify Class Probability

The **Modify Class Probability** data preprocessing option allows you to modify the output class probability (see Figure 12-13). You can choose to set the probability for each class or you can set all classes to have equal prior probability.

Figure 12-13 Modify Class Probability Option

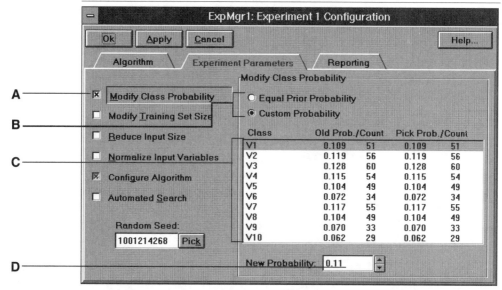

A. Clicking here enables the modify class probability parameters on the right (otherwise, they will be grayed out).
B. Select equal prior probability or custom here.
C. If you choose custom class probability, the old and new probabilities for each output class are displayed here and you can select an output class for which to modify the probability.
D. If you choose custom class probability, you can modify the new probability here.

Modify Training Set Size

This option allows you to change the training set size (see Figure 12-14). You may want to increase the training set size for different statistical runs using a voting scheme for more robust results. You may want to decrease the training set size to reduce training times if many of your training patterns are very similar.

Figure 12-14 Modify Training Set Size Options

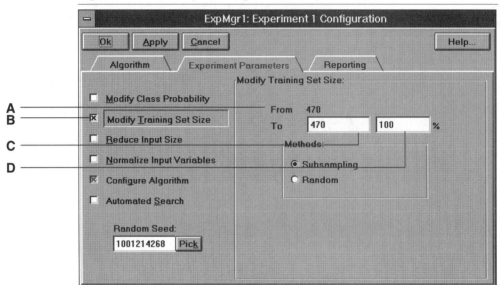

A. The original number of available training set patterns is displayed here.

B. Click here to enable the Modify Training Set Size parameters.

C. Enter the number of training set patterns desired here.

D. Or enter the new percentage desired here.

Solving Data Mining Problems through Pattern Recognition

Reduce Input Size

This option allows you to decrease the input dimensionality (see Figure 12-15). Decreasing the input dimensionality will decrease training times and may result in improved model accuracy.

Figure 12-15 Reduce Input Size Options

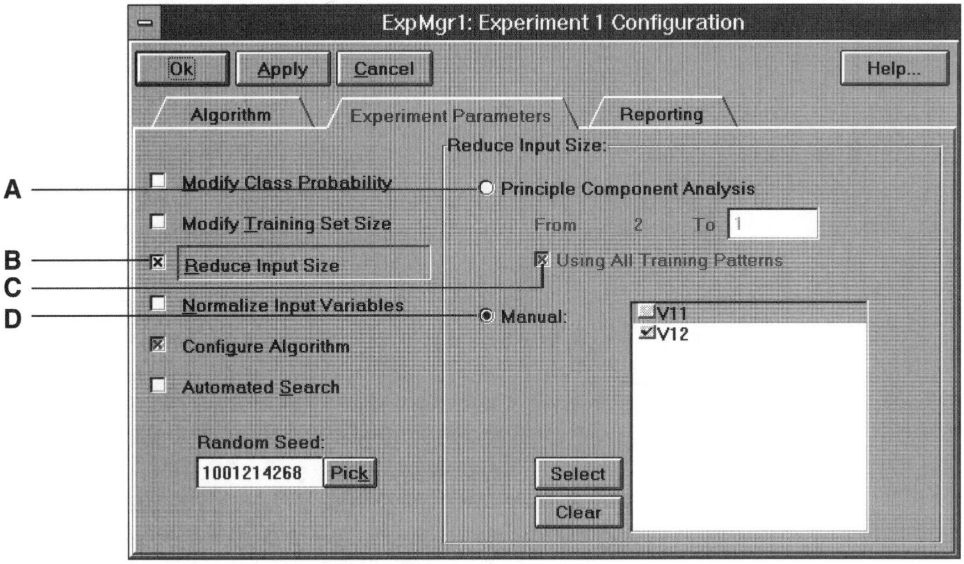

A. Click here to use principal component analysis to automatically reduce the number of input variables.
B. Click here to enable the Reduce Input Size options.
C. Click here to use all training patterns (leave it blank to use a modified training set).
D. Click here to manually select the variables to use from the available input variables.

You can reduce the input dimensions either automatically using principal component analysis or manually. The **Principle Component Analysis** option uses principle component analysis (PCA) to determine the *n* most significant input variables, where *n* is the number of input dimensions specified in the **To** text box below the option.

**Normalize
Input Variables**

This option allows you to normalize the input variables using various normalization algorithms (see Figure 12-16). Use this option to equalize the effect of each input variable during training.[3]

Figure 12-16 Normalize Input Variables

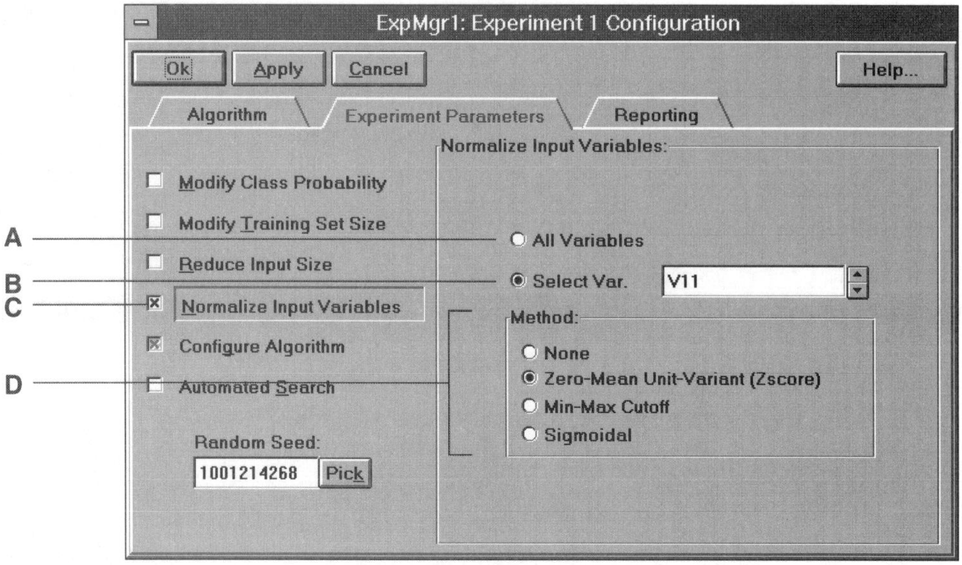

A. Click here to set a normalization method for all input variables.
B. Click here to set a normalization method for a single input variable.
C. Click here to enable Normalize Input Variable options.
D. Select a normalization method here.

You can normalize all input variables, or you can select specific variables to normalize. You can even normalize some variables using one normalization method and other variables using another. You can control the normalization method individually for each input variable.

---

3. When one input variable is many orders of magnitude greater than another, it may unfairly dominate training of some classifiers (e.g., MLP).

A.7   Exporting Experiments and Reports

Exporting an Experiment

Exporting an experiment saves all current experiment information including the names of the input and output variables, all model parameters (including trained state if any), and any notes associated with the experiment (no data is saved with an experiment). This exported experiment can later be imported intact into a PRW experiment manager.

To export the current PRW experiment:

1. Select the experiment to export.

Before exporting an experiment, you must first select the experiment manager (its title bar must be highlighted) and then highlight the desired experiment. If the experiment you want to export is in another session, load the session first using the **Open Session** command.

2. Select the File→Export Others...→Export Experiment command.

This will bring up the **Export Experiment** window shown in Figure 12-17.

Figure 12-17   Export Experiment Window

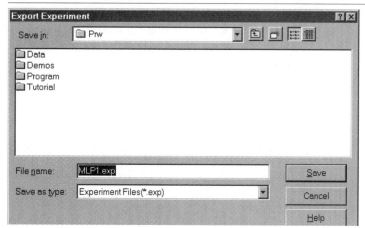

3. **Enter a filename for the saved experiment file.**

If a file extension is not specified, `.exp` will automatically be appended.

4. **Select OK.**

The current experiment will be exported into the specified file.

Exporting a Report

Exporting a report saves all information for the captured reports. This exported report can later be imported intact into a PRW experiment manager. Exporting a report is just like exporting an experiment, except that you use the **File➜Export Others... ➜Export Report** command.

Importing

Any exported object can be easily imported into PRW using the **File➜Import Others...** command. This allows you to easily import an experiment or report into the specified experiment manager.

A.8   Re-Using Experiment Parameters

The **Re-Use Parameters** button, which appears to the right of the **Report...** button, generates a new experiment with exactly the same configuration as the experiment that generated the experiment summary report. The new experiment appears as a new icon in the **Experiments** area and is not trained. The **Re-Use Parameters** button allows you to regenerate results from the report icon only, without having to access the original experiment.

A.9   Building User Functions

Any function definition in a PRW spreadsheet can be wrapped into a user function. This simplifies complex function definitions and allows them to be easily reused, exported, or embedded into still more complex function definitions. The **Build Function From Spreadsheet** window is shown in Figure 12-18. To build a user function, you simply specify the name of the user function and its inputs.

Figure 12-18 Build Function from Spreadsheet Window

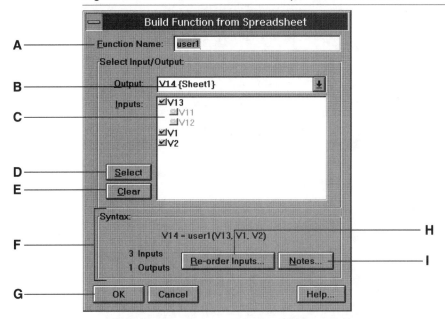

A. Enter a name for the user here followed by TAB.
B. Select the function definition outputs to build here. If more than one spreadsheet is in use, the spreadsheet is identified in braces.
C. Select the inputs here. Alternative ways to generate a column are listed beneath a variable (e.g., V13 can be created from V11 and V12).
D. Click here to select the current variable in the Input area (or double-click the variable name).
E. Click here to clear the current variable in the Input area (or double-click the variable name).
F. The Syntax area displays the current syntax.
G. Click here to build the user or module.
H. Click here to reorder the input variables.
I. Click here to enter a description for the user function.

Similarly, you can build a user function from any trained experiment. Figure 12-19 shows the **Build Function from Experiment** window.

Figure 12-19   Build Function from Experiment Window

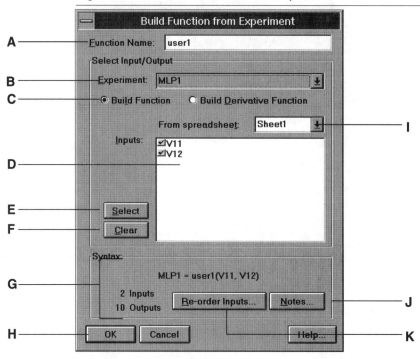

A. Enter a name for the user function here followed by TAB.
B. Select the experiment to build here (ExpMgr name listed in {}'s).
C. Choose to either build the function or the derivative of the function (for sensitivity analysis).
D. Inputs to the experiment are listed in the Inputs area along with alternative ways to generate the column, indented to the right.
E. Click here to select the current variable in the Input area.
F. Click here to clear the current variable in the Input area.
G. The Syntax area displays the current syntax and # of input/ outputs.
H. Click here to build the user function.
I. If more than one spreadsheet is in use, select the one to use.
J. Click here to enter a description of the function being built.
K. Click here to reorder the input variables.

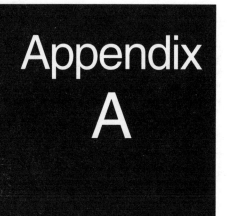

Appendix A

References and Suggested Reading

Review Papers   Elder, John F. IV and Daryl Pregibon, "A Statistical Perspective on Knowledge Discovery in Databases," in *Advances in Knowledge Discovery and Data Mining*, U. M. Fayyad, G. Piatetsky-Shapiro, P. Smyth, and R. Uthurusamy, Editors, AAAI/MIT Press, 1995.

Lippmann, Richard P., "An Introduction to Computing with Neural Nets," *Neural Networks: Theoretical Foundations and Analysis*, C. Lau, Editor, IEEE Press, 1992.

Lippmann, Richard P., "Pattern Classification Using Neural Networks," *IEEE Communications Magazine*, pp. 47–54, 1989.

Hush, Don R., and Bill G. Horne, "Progress in Supervised Neural Networks: What's New Since Lippmann?" *IEEE Signal Processing*, pp. 8-38, January, 1993.

Financial Applications   Bandy, Howard, "Thoughts on Desirable Features for a Neural Network-based Financial Trading System," *Neurovest Journal*, May/June, 1994.

Bandy, Howard, "Neural Network-based Trading System Design: Prediction and Measurement Tasks," *Neurovest Journal*, September/October, 1994.

Bolland, P.J. and Refenes, A.N., "Analysis of the Relationship Between Volume, Open Interest and Futures Prices," in *Proceedings of Neural Networks in the Capital Markets*, London Business School, 1994.

Caldwell, Randal B., "Design of Neural Network-based Financial Forecasting Systems: Data Selection and Data Processing," *Neurovest Journal*, September/October, 1994.

Hutchinson, James M., Andrew W. Lo, and Tomaso Poggio, "A Nonparametric Approach to Pricing and Hedging Derivative Securities Via Learning Networks," *The Journal of Finance*, Vol. XLIX, No. 3, July 1994.

Mizrach, B. "Multivariate Nearest-Neighbor Forecasts of EMS Exchange Rates," *Journal of Applied Econometrics*, Wiley, 1992, 7:151-163.

Otter, Petier, "Feedforward Neural Network and Canonical Correlation Models as Approximators with an Application to One-Year Ahead Forecastin," *Neurovest Journal*, March/April, 1994.

Poddig, Thorsten, "Short-Term Forecasting of the USD/DM-Exchange Rate," *Proceedings of the First International Workshop on Neural Networks in Capital Markets*, London Business School, 1993.

Refenes, Apostolos-Paul, Editor, *Neural Networks in the Capital Markets*, Wiley, 1995.

Refenes, A. N., M. Azema-Barac, L. Chen, and S. A. Karoussos, "Currency Exchange Rate Prediction and Neural Network Design Strategies," *Neural Computing and Applications*, Springer-Verlag, 1993, 1:46-58.

Steurer, E., "Application of Chaos Theory to Predicting the Development of Exchange Rates," *Diplomarbeit*, University of Karlsruhe, 1993.

Thomason, Mark R., "A Basic Neural Network Trading System Development Project #1," *Neurovest Journal*, November/December, 1994.

Thomason, Mark R., "A Basic Neural Network Trading System Development Project #2," *Neurovest Journal*, January/February, 1995.

Thomason, Mark R., "A Basic Neural Network Trading System Development Project #3," *Neurovest Journal*, March/April, 1995.

Thomason, Mark R., "A Basic Neural Network Trading System Development Project #4," *Neurovest Journal*, May/June, 1995.

Trippi, Robert R. and Efraim Turban, *Neural Networks in Finance and Investing: Using Artificial Intelligence to Improve Real-World Performance*, Probus, 1993.

Van Eyden, R. J. and J. J. L. Cronje, "Discriminant Analysis Versus Artificial Neural Networks in Credit Scoring," *Neurovest Journal*, November/December, 1994.

Industrial Applications

Barschdorf, D., L. Monostori, A. F. Ndenge, and G. W. Wostenkuhler, "Multiprocessor Systems for Connectionist Diagnosis of Technical Processes," *Computers in Industry*, 1991, 17:131-145.

Card, Jill, Amy McGowen, and Chris Reed, " Neural Network Approach to Automated Wirebond Defect Classification," in *Conference on Artificial Neural Networks in Engineering*, 1994.

Chitra, Surya P., "Neural Net Applications in Chemical Engineering," *AI Expert*, November, 1992.

Freeman, James A., and David M. Skapura, *Neural Networks: Algorithms, Applications, and Programming Techniques*, Addison-Wesley Publishing Company, 1991.

Gelenbe, Erol, Editor, *Neural Networks: Advances and Applications II*, Elsevier Science Publishers, 1992.

Lee, Yuchun, "Handwritten Digit Recognition Using *k*-Nearest Neighbor, Radial Basis Function, and Backpropagation Neural Networks," *Neural Computation*, Volume 3, Number 3, Fall, 1991.

Lippmann, Richard P., J. Moody, and D.S. Touretzky, *Neural Information Processing Systems 3*, Morgan Kaufmann, 1991.

Lippmann, Richard P., J. Moody, and D.S. Touretzky, *Neural Information Processing Systems 4*, Morgan Kaufmann, 1991.

Lippmann, Richard P., J. Moody, and D.S. Touretzky, *Neural Information Processing Systems 5*, Morgan Kaufmann, 1991.

Peterson, Gorden E., and Harold L. Barney, "Control Methods Used in a Study of Vowels," *Journal of the Acoustical Society of America*, 24(2):175–84, March 1952.

Roscheisen, M., R. Hofmann, and V. Tresp, "Neural Control for Rolling Mills: Incorporating Domain Theories to Overcome Data Deficiency," in *Advances in Neural Information Processing Systems 4*, J. Moody, S. Hanson, and R. Lippmann, Eds., Morgan Kaufmann, pp. 659–666, 1992.

Singer, Elliot, and R. P. Lippmann, "A Speech Recognizer Using Radial Basis Function Neural Networks in an HMM Framework," *Proceedings International Conference on Acoustics Speech and Signal Processing*, San Francisco, IEEE, 1992.

Sobajic, Dejan J., Yoh-Han Pao, and Dennis T. Lee, "Robust Control of Nonlinear Systems Using Pattern Recognition," in *IEEE International Conference on Systems, Man, and Cybernetics*, 1989.

Staib, William E., N. G. Blissand Robert B. Staib, "Neural Network Conversion of the Electric Arc Furnace into the Intelligent Arc Furnace," in *74th AIME Steelmaking Conference*, 1991.

Taylor, J. G. (ed.), *Neural Network Applications*, Springer-Verlag, 1992.

Medical and Biotech Applications

Collins, Mark, "Empiricism Strikes Back: Neural Networks in Biotechnology," *Bio/Technology*, February, 1993, 11:163-166.

Lippman, Richard, Linda Kukolich, and David Shahian, "Predicting the Risk of Complications in Coronary Artery Bypass Operations using Neural Networks," in *Advances in Neural Information Processing Systems 7*, G. Tesauro, D. Touretzky, and T. Leen, Eds., Morgan Kaufmann, 1995.

Weinstein, John N., Lawrence V. Rubinstein, Antonis D. Koutsoukos, Kurt W. Kohn, Michael R. Grever, Anne Monks, Dominic A. Scudiero, Lester Welch, August J. Chiausa, Anthony T. Fojo, Vellarkad N. Viswanadhan, and Kenneth D. Paull, "Neural Networks in the Discovery of New Treatments for Cancer and Aids," *World Congress on Neural Networks*, 1993, I:111-116.

Comparative Empirical Studies

Huang, William Y., and R. P. Lippmann, "Comparisons Between Conventional and Neural Net Classifiers," in *Proceedings of the First International Conference on Neural Networks*, IV-85, 1987.

Kleinbaum, David G., and L. Kupper and K. Muller, *Applied Regression Analysis and Other Multivariable Methods*, second edition, PWS-KENT Publishing Company, Boston, 1988.

Korn, Granino A., *Neural Network Experiments on Personal Computers and Workstations*, Massachusetts Institute of Technology, 1991.

Lee, Yuchun, "Handwritten Digit Recognition Using *k*-Nearest Neighbor, Radial Basis Function, and Backpropagation Neural Networks," *Neural Computation*, Volume 3, Number 3, Fall, 1991.

Lee, Yuchun and Richard Lippmann, "Practical Characteristics of Neural Networks and Conventional Pattern Classifiers on Artificial and Speech Problems," *Advances in Neural Information Processing Systems II*, Morgan Kaufmann, 1990.

Lee, Yuchun, "Classifiers: Adaptive Modules in Pattern Recognition Systems," Master's thesis, Massachusetts Institute of Technology, Department of Electrical Engineering and Computer Science, Cambridge, MA, 1989.

Lippmann, Richard P., J. Moody, and D.S. Touretzky, *Neural Information Processing Systems 3*, Morgan Kaufmann, 1991.

Lippmann, Richard P., J. Moody, and D.S. Touretzky, *Neural Information Processing Systems 4*, Morgan Kaufmann, 1991.

Lippmann, Richard P., J. Moody, and D.S. Touretzky, *Neural Information Processing Systems 5*, Morgan Kaufmann, 1991.

Ng, Kenney, "A Comparison of the Practical Characteristics of Neural Network and Conventional Pattern Classifiers," Master's thesis, Massachusetts Institute of Technology, Department of Electrical Engineering and Computer Science, Cambridge, MA, 1990.

Theory

Barron, Andrew, "Universal Approximation Bounds for Superpositions of a Sigmoidal Function," *IEEE Transactions on Information Theory*, Vol. 40, No. 2, 1994.

Batchelor, B. G., *Practical Approaches to Pattern Classification*, Plennum Press, New York, 1974.

Bertsekas, Dimitri, "A Hybrid Incremental Gradient Method for Least-Squares Solutions,"

Bezdek, James C., R. J. Hathaway, and Vicki J. Huggins, "Parametric Estimation for Normal Mixtures," *Pattern Recognition Letters*, North-Holland Publishing Company, Vol. 3, pp. 79–84, 1985.

Breiman, Leo, Jerome H. Friedman, Richard A. Olshen, and Charles J. Stone, *Classification and Regression Trees*, Wadsworth International Group, Belmont, CA, 1984.

Breimann, Leo, "Hinging Hyperplanes for Regression, Classification, and Function Approximation," *IEEE Transactions on Information Theory*, Vol. 39, No. 3, May 1993.

Broomhead, D. D. and Lowe, D., "Multivariable functional interpolation and adaptive networks," *Complex Systems*, Vol. 2, 321–355, 1988.

Cybenko, G. , "Approximations by Superpositions of a Sigmoidal Function," *Mathematics of Control, Signals, and Systems*, Vol. 2, pp. 303-314, 1989.

Duda, R. O., and P. E. Hart, *Pattern Classification and Scene Analysis*, Wiley, N.Y., 1973.

Dasarathy, Belur V. (ed.), *Nearest Neighbor (NN) Norms: NN Pattern Classification Techniques*, IEEE Computer Society Press, 1991.

Friedman, Jerome H., "Multivariate Adaptive Regression Splines," *Annals of Statistics,* March, 1991.

Friedman, Jerome, H., and W. Stuetzle, "Projection Pursuit Regression," *Journal of the American Statistical Association*, No. 76, pp. 817-823, 1981.

Geman, S., Bienenstock E., and Doursat, R., "Neural Networks and the Bias/Variance Dilemma," *Neural Computation,* January, 1992.

Gersho, Allen, and Robert M. Gray, *Vector Quantization and Signal Compression*, Kulwer Academic Publishers, 1992.

Hathaway, R. J., "Constrained Maximum-Likelihood Estimation for Normal Mixtures," *Computer Science and Statistics: The Interface*, J. E. Gentle, Editor, North-Holland Publishing Company, pp. 263–267, 1983.

Jolliffe, I. T., *Principal Component Analysis*, Springer-Verlag, NY, 1986.

Jones, Lee K., "Good Weights and Hyperbolic Kernels for Neural Networks, Projection Pursuit, and Pattern Classification: Fourier Strategies for Extracting Information from High-Dimensional Data," *IEEE Transactions on Information Theory*, Vol. 40, No. 2, March 1994.

Kanerva, Pentti, *Sparse Distributed Memory*, Massachusetts Institute of Technology, 1988.

Kohonen, T., "An Introduction to Neural Computing," *Neural Networks*, 1:3-16, 1988.

Lippmann, R.P. "Neural Networks, Bayesian a posteriori Probabilities and Pattern Classification," *Proceedings of the 1993 NATO Advanced Studies Institute on Statistics and Neural Networks*, Les Arcs, France, 1993.

Lippmann, Richard P., J. Moody, and D.S. Touretzky, *Neural Information Processing Systems 3*, Morgan Kaufmann, 1991.

Lippmann, Richard P., J. Moody, and D.S. Touretzky, *Neural Information Processing Systems 4*, Morgan Kaufmann., 1991

Lippmann, Richard P., J. Moody, and D.S. Touretzky, *Neural Information Processing Systems 5*, Morgan Kaufmann, 1991.

Nadler, Morton, and E. Smith, *Pattern Recognition Engineering*, John Wiley & Sons, 1993.

Nilsson, N. J., *Learning Machines*, McGraw Hill, N.Y., 1965.

Poggio, Tomaso, and Federico Girosi, "Networks for Approximation and Learning," *Proceedings of the IEEE*, Vol. 78, No. 9, September, 1990.

Richard, Michael D., and Richard P. Lippmann, "Neural Network Classifiers Estimate Bayesian a Posteriori Probabilities," *Neural Computation*, September, 1990.

Rumelhart, David E., and James L. McClelland, *Parallel Distributed Processing: Explorations in the Microstructure of Cognition*, Vol. 1, Massachusetts Institute of Technology, 1986.

Sklansky, Jack, and Gustav N. Wassel, *Pattern Classifiers and Trainable Machines*, Springer-Verlag, 1981.

Special Topics Bradley, Efron, and Robert J. Tibshirani, "An Introduction to the Bootstrap," *Monographs on Statistics and Applied Probability*, 57, Chapman and Hall, N. Y., 1993.

Leonard, J. A. and M. A. Kramer, "A Neural Network Architecture that Computes its own Reliability," *Computers and Chemical Engineering*, August, 1991.

Lippmann, Richard P., L. Kukolich, and E. Singer, "LNKnet: Neural Network, Machine-Learning, and Statistical Software for Pattern Classification," *The Lincoln Laboratory Journal*, Vol. 6, No. 2, pp. 249–268, 1993.

General Andrew, D. F., and A. M. Herzberg, *Dara: a Collection of Problems from Many Fields for the Student and Research Worker*, Springer-Verlag Series in Statistics, 1985.

Bertsekas, Dimitri, *Nonlinear Programming*, unpublished manuscript, 1995.

Cheney, E. W., *Introduction to Approximation Theory*, McGraw Hill, 1966.

Drake, A. W., *Applied Probability Theory*, McGraw-Hill Series in Probability and Statistics, 1967.

Press, William H., B. Flannery, et. al., *Numerical Recipes in C*, Cambridge University Press, 1988.

Sedgewick, Robert, *Algorithms*, second edition, Addison-Wesley Publishing Company, 1988.

Strang, Gilbert, *Introduction to Applied Mathematics*, Wellesley-Cambridge Press, 1986.

Solving Data Mining Problems through Pattern Recognition

Appendix B

Pattern Recognition Workbench

Successful pattern recognition projects demand a rigorous, multi-step approach. Pattern Recognition Workbench (PRW) is unique in providing the comprehensive, integrated tools necessary for the entire process. For the first time, designing advanced data-driven or pattern recognition models no longer requires juggling spreadsheets, compilers, and hard-to-use or toy neural network products.

Using mature neural network, statistical, and machine learning technologies, PRW's easy-to-use Windows interface allows you to develop both pattern classification and function estimation solutions. PRW provides the complete environment for the entire task—from formatting and preprocessing raw data—to searching for the optimal set of input features and algorithm parameters—to running powerful algorithms—to managing experiments—to deploying results.

Figure B-1 PRW Major Components

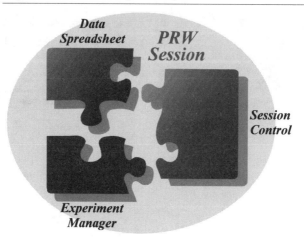

Overview   A PRW session is composed of three major components—data spreadsheet, experiment manager, and session control (see Figure B-1).

PRW uses a familiar spreadsheet environment to organize data. The data spreadsheet is optimized for pattern recognition in both functionality and speed. It supports built-in macro functions and user-defined functions. Once data is prepared in the data spreadsheet, the experiment manager helps guide the user step-by-step through setting up experiments, configuring algorithms, and performing automated searches for the best set of inputs or the optimal algorithm parameter settings. The experiment manager then schedules experiments and organizes results in the form of icons. Experiment progress can be interactively monitored while the experiment is running, and summary results can be viewed when the experiment completes. The user has full control over how experiments and results are organized.

The session control component of PRW provides overall coordination of the PRW session, including base-line support for data/object import and

Solving Data Mining Problems through Pattern Recognition

export, on-line help, real-time data linking, C and Fortran source-code and DLL module generation.

Data Spreadsheets

PRW data spreadsheets are designed specifically to handle a large number of time-series or pattern-oriented data. Each spreadsheet can comfortably handle 16,000 columns and 16 million rows of data. Raw data, either binary or ASCII numerals or text, can be imported and manipulated interactively in the spreadsheet.

PRW supports over 100 built-in macro functions for numerical and text data generation, preparation, and preprocessing. Each formula defined in the data spreadsheet is automatically applied to all rows of patterns, eliminating the tedious task of defining identical formulas, cell-by-cell, thus producing a significant speed advantage over ordinary spreadsheets.

A powerful feature of PRW is the ability to build any formula in the data spreadsheet into a "user-defined function" which can be used later in the session. These user-defined functions can be embedded to create more complex formulas. They also can be exported for use in other PRW sessions. This allows the user to quickly build up a library of useful functions, specific or unique to a problem domain, to share or re-use.

For data analysis, spreadsheet data can be viewed graphically in the form of line graphs, scatter graphs, and histograms. For additional analysis, PRW data spreadsheets fully support cut/copy/paste of data, as well as real-time linking to and from data in other applications using Dynamic Data Exchange (DDE) and Object Linking and Embedding (OLE).

Experiment Managers

Building data-driven financial models for pattern classification and function estimation is highly empirical and often requires an iterative process. In addition, once a data-driven model is selected, the results should be statistically validated. The experiment manager controls this development process, including automated searches for the optimal set of data inputs or algorithm parameters and statistical validation of the model (e.g., cross-validation, bootstrap, and moving-window validation) to help ensure valid results.

An experiment manager guides the user step-by-step through a series of set-up screens. These set-up screens configure the important task- and data-related parameters for experiments. Each experiment can use a different algorithm or the same algorithm with different parameter settings.

All experiments, automated searches, and reports are represented as icons in the experiment manager. Double-clicking an icon displays more detailed information on the experiment, automated search, or report. This icon-based interface simplifies experiment and report file management.

The user can selectively run and rerun experiments. The results of the experiments are kept in corresponding reports, which track information such as error rate, training progress, and algorithm-specific information. Automated searches keep the top n experiments, allowing you to view and use results for these experiments at any time.

The core set of pattern recognition algorithms supported by PRW consists of traditional statistical methods (e.g., linear regression, logistic regression), non-parametric (e.g., k-nearest neighbor, gaussian mixture model), and neural network algorithms (e.g., backpropagation network, radial-basis functions). The algorithm parameters and the most common set of preprocessing steps can be configured using a user-friendly interface.

Automated search methods for input selection include principal component analysis, sensitivity analysis, forward search, backward search, forward-backward search, and genetic algorithm. Algorithm parameter searches can use exhaustive, gradient descent, or genetic search algorithms.

Session Control

PRW session control offers overall integration of data, experiments, and deployment of results. Similar to data spreadsheet formulas, results from any experiment can be built into user-defined functions that can then be used in a spreadsheet. PRW also has extensive peripheral application support, such as C and Fortran source-code generation, DLLs, cut-and-paste, printing, task scheduling, context-sensitive on-line help, and importing and exporting of data, experiments, reports, spreadsheets, and user-defined functions.

Summary

Pattern Recognition Workbench is the most comprehensive tool available for developing neural network, statistical, and machine learning solutions. PRW's data spreadsheet and experiment manager allow quick development and statistical validation of pattern recognition solutions, providing an unparalleled competitive advantage in modeling complex systems for business solutions.

For more information on PRW, please contact:

Unica Technologies, Inc.
Lincoln North
55 Old Bedford Rd.
Lincoln, MA 01773

Tel. (781) 259-5900
Fax. (781) 259-5901

email: unica@unica-usa.com
www.unica-usa.com/~unica

Appendix C

Unica Technologies, Inc.

Unica Technologies, Inc. specializes in the application of data mining to business operations. Unica offers complete solutions through a variety of application products, software tools, Application Programming Interface products, consulting, and technology transfer, Unica is uniquely positioned as a one-stop solution provider.

C.1 ABOUT UNICA

Background

Unica Technologies, Inc. was founded by a few MIT alumni in 1992 with a focus on applying recent advances in machine learning, statistical, and neural network technologies to solve data mining problems in business.

Through extensive involvement with various business applications, Unica can thoroughly understand the process of using pattern recognition and related technologies to solve data mining problems, and the importance of the user interface to expand data mining usage. To facilitate the use of these technologies, Unica has developed comprehensive software systems—MODEL 1™ and Pattern Recognition Workbench™ (PRW™)—to tackle response modeling, cross-selling, segmentation and profiling, customer valuation, and many other common business problems.

For companies desiring custom data mining solutions, access to the Unica Data Mining Engine™ (UDME™) is provided through the UDME API. The addition of MODEL 1 components into new or existing Windows applications can be easily configured using the MODEL 1 API.

Consulting Services

In addition to its acclaimed line of software products, Unica provides consulting services through its Unica Consulting Group. Consultants are available for a wide variety of data mining services including:

- Model building (response, cross-sell, customer valuator, segmentation and profiling, attrition modeling, prospecting, list selection, credit risk analysis, decision support systems, etc.)

- System design and integration using Unica's API products (adding custom data mining components seamlessly to customer's database and production environment)

- Education and technology transfer (to help bring data mining technology in-house)

Finally, through continuing R&D and collaboration with MIT and the National Science Foundation (NSF), Unica is aggressively putting the latest technological advances into easy-to-use data mining solutions.

C.2 UNICA'S SOFTWARE PRODUCTS

Product Summaries

Unica offers a complete array of data mining software solutions, including tools, vertical solutions, and API products for custom development and/or integration:

- Pattern Recognition Workbench™ (PRW™) — A Windows-based toolkit environment for building general pattern recognition and data mining solutions. Designed for the modeler or statistician, PRW provides a variety of statistical, neural network, and machine learning algorithms for hands-on control of the model development process. Built-in productivity-enhancing features include intelligent searches for automatic variable selection and parameter tuning, custom user functions, interactive data visualization, and C-source code/DLL generation.

- MODEL 1™[1] — A Windows-based family of data mining modules for database marketing applications. These modules can be used by marketing analysts and statisticians alike, and are designed to solve specific business problems (e.g., response modeling, cross-selling, customer valuation, segmentation and profiling). A wizard-driven GUI, automated model building process using a variety of algorithms, easy-to-interpret reports, built-in campaign optimization, and run-time module deployment make MODEL 1 a complete data mining solution, deployable without requiring custom integration into your environment.

- MODEL 1™ Application Programming Interface — An API providing access to MODEL 1 components for easy integration into database marketing custom applications. Through a single subroutine call, the application can access the MODEL 1 GUI, a spreadsheet, Data Import wizard, Modeling wizard, Scoring wizard, or reports folder.

- Unica Data Mining Engine (UDME) API — An application programming interface to set of core algorithms and techniques for building data mining applications. Based on pattern recognition technology, the UDME API provides statistical, neural network, and machine learning algorithms to produce data-driven models. Embedded in the UDME are intelligent algorithms for automatic data preprocessing and normalization, variable selection, and algorithm parameter tuning.

---

1. MODEL 1 is a trademark of Group 1 Software.

Advanced features, such as cross validation and campaign optimization, are included to make the UDME a complete solution. These techniques, in conjunction with the suite of data-driven algorithms, provide a powerful core engine for developing the highest performing models as easily as possible.

Product Inter-relationships

Figure C-1 shows the interrelationship among these different products. The UDME API (previously known as the PRW Engine) serves as the data mining engine that can be used to develop a wide range of custom applications, such as Pattern Recognition Workbench (general purpose) or MODEL 1 (vertical focus on database marketing). The MODEL 1 API allows a developer to easily integrate the MODEL 1 software into custom applications or databases.

Figure C-1 Product Relationships

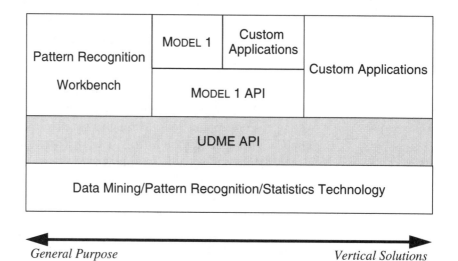

General Purpose   *Vertical Solutions*

Targeted End Users

These different products trade off ease of integration and user friendliness to satisfy different needs. For example, in the marketing space, Table C-1 shows the different target end-users for the various products. The different products are listed across the top in order of ease of integration. Potential end users are listed vertically along the left in order of technical sophistication. The large check marks show the most common end-users of each product.

Table C-1 Product Users

User	Model 1	Model 1 API	PRW	UDME API	Compiler/4GL
Marketing analyst	✓	✓			
Modeler, engineer, statistician	✓	✓	✓	✓	✓
System integrator/ developer		✓		✓	✓

Contact Info

For more information on any of Unica's products or services, please contact:

Unica Technologies, Inc.
Lincoln North
55 Old Bedford Rd.
Lincoln, MA 01773

Tel. (781) 259-5900
Fax. (781) 259-5901

email: unica@unica-usa.com
www.unica-usa.com/~unica

Appendix D

Glossary

Approximation architecture	Approximation architecture is a mathematical structure for non-parametric modeling. It defines parametric models of varying degrees of complexity for use in producing nonparametric models for estimation.
Architecture	Short for approximation architecture
Backpropagation	Backpropagation is an algorithm used for training the multi-layer perceptron that minimizes mean-squared error using via gradient descent.
Causal	A relationship between two variables is causal when manipulating one always affects the other.
Classification	Classification is the act of categorizing an observation into one of a typically finite number of output classes.
Classifier	A classifier is a system that performs automatic classification.

Cluster	A cluster is a set of data points that are grouped by their proximity in a metric space.
Clustering	Clustering is the process of grouping data points into clusters.
Correlation	Correlation is a measurement of the linear dependency between two variables. Correlation between two random variables is mathematically defined as the covariance divided by the product of the standard deviations. *See also* Mutual information.
Cost function	A cost function (or objective function) is used to evaluate and compare results of trained algorithms. Commonly used cost functions include minimum RMS error and maximum R^2 error.
Cross-validation	Cross-validation is a validation technique aimed at maximizing the usage of data for parametric or nonparametric modeling. In cross-validation, the available data is equally divided into n folds. Experiments are run, each using $(n-1)$ folds for training and the other fold for testing.
Data-driven modeling	*See* Nonparametric modeling.
Dependent variable	A dependent variable contains the values (typically representing features or characteristics) to be approximated during the modeling process (same as an output variable).
Epoch	An epoch is one cycle through a training data set made by an iterative training algorithm.
Estimation	Estimation is the act of producing an approximation to one or more desired values based on an observation. The number of possible output values is typically infinite and assumes a logical sequential ordering.
Example pattern	An example pattern is a data pair consisting of an input vector and a corresponding output vector (i.e., the desired output).

Feature extraction

Identifying salient characteristics of an observation that are useful for pattern recognition.

Gradient descent

Gradient descent is a method for minimizing a cost function by tuning parameters that have a nonlinear relationship with the cost. The algorithm works by iteratively taking small steps in the negative gradient direction of the cost function.

Independent variable

An independent variable contains the values (typically representing features or characteristics) used as an input to the modeling process to predict the output or dependent variable (same as an input variable).

Input variable

An input variable is a component of an input vector, typically representing a single feature or characteristic of the pattern recognition problem.

Input vector

A vector of numerical values, derived from an observation, that serve as inputs to a model. This information is used by a model to generate a classification or estimation. *See also* Observation, Raw input vector, Preprocessed input vector.

Learning

Learning is the process of increasing the accuracy of a model through training. This term usually refers to supervised learning from example patterns, but may also encompass unsupervised learning (i.e., clustering).

Model

A model is a characterization of relationships between input and output variables. Given an input vector, a model will generate an output vector.

Multi-layer perceptron (MLP)

Multi-layer perceptron (MLP) is a neural network architecture for nonparametric modeling (applicable to both classification and estimation). It consists of interconnected nodes structured in feed-forward layers. It is commonly trained using the backpropagation algorithm.

Mutual information

Mutual information is a quantity reflecting the degree of relationship between two variables. This relationship can be thought of as information that is simultaneously reflected by both variables and can take on a nonlinear form. *See also* Correlation.

Neural network

Neural network is a term that encompasses many nonparametric architectures consisting of simple nodes in an interconnected network. This term is most often associated with multi-layer perceptron or radial basis function networks. The nomenclature comes from the fact that these architectures are somewhat reminiscent of biological networks in the brain.

Nonparametric modeling

Nonparametric (or data-driven) modeling is an approach to building models that relies heavily on the use of data without using many prior suppositions. Because information is obtained through the use of data, this approach requires less understanding of the specific relationships in the underlying system than other approaches to modeling.

Observation

An observation is a collection of information provided as input to a model. The model bases its output estimation or classification on this input.

Outlier

An outlier is an example pattern that is not representative of the vast majority of observed data (e.g., a signal that is far out of a reasonable range due to a sensor failure or a natural, but rare, event).

Output variable

An output variable is one component of an output vector, typically representing a feature or characteristic to be approximated.

Output vector

An output vector is a vector of numerical outputs. In training, this is a vector of desired values to be generated when a model is exposed to the input vector (i.e., the second part of a data example pair). In classification or estimation, this is the vector of values generated by the model.

Parametric modeling

Parametric modeling is an approach to modeling involving hypothesizing the structure of a model for a system of interest, with several parameters left to be tuned by empirical data. A common example of parametric modeling is linear regression.

Pattern recognition

Pattern recognition is the association of observations with classes or numerical quantities.

Prediction

Prediction is the forecasting of values for some time in the future. Typically, prediction problems are estimation problems that project a future numerical value based on present data.

Preprocessed input vector

A preprocessed input vector is the resultant vector from applying preprocessing to a raw input vector. Preprocessed input vectors are typically presented to a model for learning or classification/estimation.

Preprocessing

Preprocessing is the manipulation of a raw input vector, intended to simplify the task of pattern recognition. This often involves feature extraction geared to either reduce the number of input dimensions or simplify the nature of the model (e.g., making the mapping "smoother," in the case of an estimation task).

Principal component analysis

Principal component analysis (PCA) is a data analysis technique that, presented with a set of input vectors, induces a linear transformation on the input variables so that the new variables are uncorrelated and sorted in order of descending variance. PCA is often used as a dimensionality reduction technique in preprocessing. In this context, only the first few of the post-transformation variables are kept as preprocessed inputs, since their variance dominates that of the other variables, which are disregarded.

Radial basis function network (RBF)

Radial basis function (RBF) network is a neural network architecture for nonparametric modeling based on linear combinations of radial Gaussians (Gaussians with the same standard deviation in all dimensions).

Raw input vector

An encoding of an observation as a vector of numerical values, prior to any preprocessing.

Root-mean-squared error (RMS error)	Root-mean-squared error is a measure of the error of an estimation model on a data set. Mathematically, the square-root of the average, over a data set, of the square difference between model outputs and desired values.
Supervised learning	Supervised learning is the generation of input-output models from data examples.
Test set	A test set is a collection of example patterns used to assess and compare the performance of models in order to select the best performer.
Time series	Time-series refers to a sequence of data collected over time (e.g., a sequence of daily stock prices).
Training	Training is the process of tuning parameters of an approximation architecture to improve accuracy on a training data set.
Training algorithm	A training algorithm tunes the parameters of an approximation architecture to improve accuracy on a training data set.
Training set	A training set is a collection of example patterns used by a training algorithm. Typically, the training algorithm tries to minimize model error on the training set, such that the performance generalizes to example patterns that are representative of but not contained in the training set.
Unsupervised learning	Unsupervised learning is the analysis of a data set with no input-output relationship to ascertain the structure in the Euclidean space (e.g., clustering and principal component analysis).
Validation	Validation is the confirmation of the correctness of an assertion. In pattern recognition, this most often refers to the process of testing a model on a data set that is independent of the data used for training. In statistical validation, multiple experiments are run to statistically verify the correctness of the results.

Weight

A weight is a parameter of a neural network that is tuned during the training process. Weights are typically multipliers of input values to a neuron.

INDEX

A

A posteriori probability, *see* Posterior probabilities

A priori probabilities, *see* Prior probabilities

Accuracy, 7-7
  trouble-shooting, 12-19

Algorithms, 10-1
  backpropagation, 10-23, 10-32
  biases in selecting, 3-13
  CART, 10-56
  CHAID, 10-58
  decision trees, 10-54, 10-59
  Gaussian mixture, 10-41, 10-47
  K means, 10-50, 10-53
  K nearest neighbors, 10-37, 10-41
  logistic regression, 3-13, 10-14, 10-18
  multilayered perceptron, 10-23, 10-32
  nearest cluster, 10-47, 10-49
  parameter searches, 12-12, 12-15
  parameter searches in PRW, 12-36
  parametric vs. nonparametric, 10-2
  radial basis functions, 10-32, 10-35
  selecting, 5-4, 10-1, 10-62
  trouble-shooting, 12-14, 12-26
  types of, 10-2, 10-6
  unimodal Gaussian, 10-18, 10-22

Analytical modeling, 1-12

APIs
  MODEL 1, C-3
  UDME, C-3

Applications of data mining, xix
  database marketing, 4-2, 4-6

Applications of database mining, 6-5
  cross-selling, 4-4
  data compression, 4-10
  detection and inspection, 4-8
  probability estimation, 4-9
  response modeling, 4-2
  sensitivity analysis, 4-11
  time-series prediction, 4-7

Approximation architectures, 2-18, 2-21, 10-1
  choosing one, 2-20

Approximation architectures (*cont.*)
  in classification, 3-12
  practical characteristics, 2-20

ASCII text files (in PRW), 7-13

Automated pattern recognition, 1-3

Automated searches, 12-4–12-5, 12-15
  backward, 12-8
  forward, 12-7
  forward/backward, 12-9
  genetic algorithm, 12-11
  in PRW, 12-28, 12-33, 12-40
  input selection, 12-6, 12-12
  PCA-based, 12-11
  sensitivity-based, 12-11

Averaging data, 9-4

AVG macro function, 8-24, 9-22

B

Backpropagation
  algorithm details, 10-29
  computing back from output layer, 10-28
  defaults, 10-70
  does not converge, 12-20
  gradient descent, 10-25
  local minima, 12-21
  mean-square error, 10-27
  setting parameters in PRW, 10-70
  sigmoidal output nodes, 10-24
  typical settings, 10-30
  updating weights, 10-28
  see also Multilayered perceptron

Backward search, 12-8

Bayesian probability, *see* Posterior probabilities

Benefits
  cross-sell modeling, 4-6
  data mining, xx
  response modeling, 4-2

Biases
  in algorithm selection, 3-13
  preprocessing and, 1-19

Software License Agreement

Dear Evaluator:

Thank you for using Pattern Recognition Workbench. Accompanying this License is the software media containing Pattern Recognition Workbench ("the PRW program") from Unica Technologies, Inc. ("Unica"). By using the PRW program, you will acquire a license to use the PRW Program in accordance with the terms, and subject to the restrictions, contained in this License. You will not acquire ownership of the PRW program; ownership of the PRW program remains with Unica. PRIOR TO USING THE PRW PROGRAM, PLEASE READ THIS LICENSE AGREEMENT CAREFULLY. THE LICENSE AGREEMENT CONTAINS THE TERMS AND CONDITIONS UNDER WHICH YOU ARE ACQUIRING A LICENSE TO USE THE PRW PROGRAM. IF YOU DO NOT ACCEPT THE TERMS AND CONDITIONS OF THIS LICENSE, PLEASE PROMPTLY RETURN THE PRW PROGRAM AND ACCOMPANYING DOCUMENTATION TO UNICA FOR A FULL REFUND OF ANY LICENSE FEES PAID. IF YOU USE THE PRW PROGRAM, YOU WILL BE ACQUIRING A LICENSE TO USE THE PRW PROGRAM IN ACCORDANCE WITH THE TERMS AND CONDITIONS OF THIS LICENSE, AND YOU WILL BE CONSIDERED TO HAVE ACCEPTED AND AGREED TO THESE TERMS AND CONDITIONS.

1. License to Use

a. Unica hereby grants to you a non-transferable and non-exclusive license to use the PRW program, subject to the terms and conditions of this license.

- For the 1-CPU/1-User version, you may install and use the PRW program on the hard disk drive of any single compatible computer that you own. However, you may not under any circumstances have the PRW program installed onto the hard drives of two or more computers at the same time, nor may you install the PRW program onto the hard disk drive of one computer and then use the original diskettes on another computer. If you wish to use the PRW program on more than one computer, you must either erase the PRW program from the first hard drive before you install it onto a second hard drive, or else license an additional copy of the PRW program for each additional computer on which you want to use it.

- The Network/Multiuser version is subject to the same rules and conditions as for the 1-CPU/1-User version, except that it can only be used in conjunction with a valid 1-CPU/1-User computer license. The Network/Multiuser version license gives you the right to run the 1-CPU/1-User installed program from an unlimited number of other computers on a local area network.

b. You may make one (but only one) copy of the PRW program solely for back-up purposes, provided that you reproduce and attach on such copy a Unica copyright notice affixed to the original software media.

c. The license fee for the PRW program shall be payable by you in accordance with the terms of the invoice sent to you by Unica or its authorized distributors and representatives.

d. If the PRW program is an Evaluation Version (as indicated above under "Version Type:"), then the license granted to you on the usage of the PRW program is limited to the evaluation period specified on the label of the software media (or in the accompanying documentation). Upon expiration of the license, you must immediately discontinue use of the PRW program and destroy all other copies of the PRW program and return the accompanied software media and documentation to Unica.

2. License to Develop (PRW PRO+ only)

This License authorizes you to develop PRW-generated modules for deployment in PRW products, DLLs, and C source code generated by PRW. However, this license DOES NOT authorizes you to resell any modules generated by the PRW program.

3. Restriction on Use and Transfer of the PRW Program

You may not copy the PRW program (except as allowed in Section 1.3) or otherwise make the PRW program available, in whole or in part, to any other party, and may not take any action to modify, reverse assemble or reverse compile the PRW program, or any part thereof. You may not sell, assign, give, sublicense in any manner or otherwise transfer by operation of law or otherwise, this license or the PRW program to any third party without prior written approval by Unica.

Unica may from time to time make information about the PRW program available to persons who desire to make the PRW program interoperable with independently created software. For licenses which become subject to the European PRW program Directive implementing laws, you agree that you will inquire of Unica to determine whether we have made or will make such information available which will enable you to achieve the interoperability you require. You may not sublicense, lease, or rent the PRW program.

4. Ownership and Protection of Confidential Information

a. Unica shall at all times retain sole title to and ownership of the PRW Program, except that title to and ownership of any portion of the PRW program that is owned by a third party shall remain with the applicable third party.

b. The PRW program and the associated documentation contains copyrighted and/or proprietary information of Unica. You may not disclose or otherwise make available the PRW Program or the associated documentation to any person other than your employees for the purposes necessary for your use of the PRW program as authorized herein. You may not remove or alter any copyright notices or any other proprietary legends on the PRW program or the associated documentation. You must take such steps as are reasonably necessary to ensure continued confidentiality and protection of the PRW program and the associated documentation as required hereunder and to prevent unauthorized access thereto or use thereof by any of your employees or any other entity. The provisions of this paragraph shall survive any termination of the license granted hereunder.

5. Limited Warranty

a. Unica warrants that (a) the PRW program will perform substantially in accordance with the accompanying documentation for a period of 30 days from the date of receipt; and (b) any hardware accompanying the PRW program will be free from defects in materials and workmanship under normal use and service for a period of one year from the date of receipt. Any implied warranties on the PRW program and hardware are limited to 30 days and one (1) year, respectively. **Some states do not allow limitations on duration of an implied warranty, so the above limitation may not apply to you.**

b. UNICA DOES NOT WARRANT THE RESULT OF ANY SUCH SERVICES OR WARRANT THAT ANY OR ALL FAILURES, DEFECTS OR ERRORS WILL BE CORRECTED, OR WARRANT THAT THE FUNCTIONS CONTAINED IN THE PRW PROGRAM WILL MEET YOUR REQUIREMENTS, OR WILL OPERATE IN THE COMBINATIONS SELECTED BY YOU. UNICA MAKES NO REPRESENTATIONS REGARDING WARRANTY OR LIABILITY OTHER THAN AS STATED IN THIS SECTION 5.

c. THE PROVISIONS OF THE FOREGOING WARRANTIES ARE IN LIEU OF ANY OTHER WARRANTY, WHETHER EXPRESS OR IMPLIED, WRITTEN OR ORAL (INCLUDING ANY WARRANTY OF MERCHANTABILITY OR FITNESS FOR A PARTICULAR PURPOSE). THE FOREGOING WARRANTIES EXTEND TO YOU ONLY AND SHALL NOT BE APPLICABLE TO ANY OTHER PERSON OR ENTITY.

d. Some states do not allow the exclusion of implied warranties, so the above exclusion may not apply to you. This limited warranty gives you specific legal rights, and you may also have other legal rights, which vary from state to state.

6. Remedies

In the event of any breach of any of the warranties set forth in Section 5, Unica shall at its expense fix or replace the defective software or hardware so that they conform to warranty, or at Unica's sole discretion, Unica may terminate this license and refund to you any license fees which you have paid, in which event you shall return to Unica all copies of the PRW program and documentation. The remedies set forth in this Section shall be your sole and exclusive remedy and Unica's sole liability to you.

7. Limitation of Liability

UNICA'S LIABILITY ARISING OUT OF THE MANUFACTURE, SALE OR SUPPLYING OF THE PRW PROGRAM OR ITS USE OR DISPOSITION, WHETHER BASED UPON WARRANTY, CONTRACT, TORT, PATENT OR COPYRIGHT INFRINGEMENT OR MISAPPROPRIATION OF INTELLECTUAL PROPERTY OR OTHERWISE, SHALL NOT EXCEED THE LICENSE FEE PAID BY YOU FOR THE PRW PROGRAM. IN NO EVENT SHALL UNICA BE LIABLE TO YOU OR ANY OTHER PERSON OR ENTITY FOR SPECIAL, INCIDENTAL OR CONSEQUENTIAL DAMAGES (INCLUDING, BUT NOT LIMITED TO, LOSS OF PROFITS, LOSS OF SAVINGS, LOSS OF DATA OR LOSS OF USE DAMAGES) ARISING OUT OF THE USE OR DISPOSITION OF THE PRW PROGRAM. IN NO EVENT WILL UNICA BE LIABLE FOR ANY CLAIM BROUGHT BY YOU MORE THAN ONE YEAR AFTER THE CAUSE OF ACTION AROSE OR REASONABLY SHOULD HAVE BEEN DISCOVERED. **Some jurisdictions do not allow these limitations or exclusions, so they may not apply to you.**

8. Maintenance

You may obtain from Unica, for an annual fee, maintenance services as described in the customer services literature accompanying the PRW program. Software maintenance commences upon the date that the PRW program is licensed from Unica Technologies, Inc.

9. Termination

If the copy of the PRW program is an evaluation copy, the license shall terminate upon the end of the evaluation period. Unica may terminate the license granted hereunder at any time by written notice to you if you (a) fail to pay the license fee when due, or (b) breach any provision of this License and fail to remedy such breach within 15 days after Unica provides you with notice of such breach. in the event of such termination, you must immediately discontinue use of the PRW program and notify Unica in writing that the PRW program has been returned to Unica or destroyed.

10. Export Law

You may not export or otherwise transfer the PRW program outside of the United States unless you do so in full compliance with the U.S. Export Administration Act and any other laws or regulations governing the export of materials of such nature.

11. United States Government Restricted Rights

The PRW program and documentation are provided with Restricted Rights. Use, duplication or disclosure by the U.S. Government or any agency or instrumentality thereof is subject to the restrictions as set forth in subdivision (c)(1)(ii) of the Rights in Technical Data and Computer Software clause at 48 C.F.R. 252.227-7013, or in subdivision (c)(1) and (2) of the Commercial Computer Software — Restricted Rights Clause at 48 C.F.R. 52.227–19 as applicable. Contract Manufacturer is Unica Technologies, Inc. 60 Birmingham Parkway, Brighton, MA 02135.

12. General

If any provision hereof shall be deemed by any court to be invalid, illegal, or unenforceable, such provision will be enforced to the maximum extent permissible by law, and the validity, legality and enforceability of the remaining provisions hereof shall not be affected or impaired.

a. This License supersedes all prior agreements and understandings between you and Unica related to the PRW program and is intended to be the complete and exclusive statement of the terms of your license to use the PRW program.

b. This License shall be governed by, and construed in accordance with the laws of the Commonwealth of Massachusetts and not by the 1980 United Nations Convention on Contracts for the International Sale of Goods, as amended. This is the entire agreement between us relating to the contents of this package, and supersedes any prior purchase order, communications, advertising or representations concerning the contents of this package. No change or modification of this Agreement will be valid unless it is in writing, and is signed by us.

LICENSE AGREEMENT AND LIMITED WARRANTY

READ THE FOLLOWING TERMS AND CONDITIONS CAREFULLY BEFORE OPENING THIS CD PACKAGE. THIS LEGAL DOCUMENT IS AN AGREEMENT BETWEEN YOU AND PRENTICE-HALL, INC. (THE "COMPANY"). BY OPENING THIS SEALED CD PACKAGE, YOU ARE AGREEING TO BE BOUND BY THESE TERMS AND CONDITIONS. IF YOU DO NOT AGREE WITH THESE TERMS AND CONDITIONS, DO NOT OPEN THE CD PACKAGE. PROMPTLY RETURN THE UN-OPENED CD PACKAGE AND ALL ACCOMPANYING ITEMS TO THE PLACE YOU OBTAINED THEM FOR A FULL REFUND OF ANY SUMS YOU HAVE PAID.

1. **GRANT OF LICENSE:** In consideration of your purchase of this book, and your agreement to abide by the terms and conditions of this Agreement, the Company grants to you a nonexclusive right to use and display the copy of the enclosed software program (hereinafter the "SOFTWARE") on a single computer (i.e., with a single CPU) at a single location so long as you comply with the terms of this Agreement. The Company reserves all rights not expressly granted to you under this Agreement.

2. **OWNERSHIP OF SOFTWARE:** You own only the magnetic or physical media (the enclosed CD) on which the SOFTWARE is recorded or fixed, but the Company and the software developers retain all the rights, title, and ownership to the SOFTWARE recorded on the original CD copy(ies) and all subsequent copies of the SOFTWARE, regardless of the form or media on which the original or other copies may exist. This license is not a sale of the original SOFTWARE or any copy to you.

3. **COPY RESTRICTIONS:** This SOFTWARE and the accompanying printed materials and user manual (the "Documentation") are the subject of copyright. The individual programs on the CD are copyrighted by the authors of each program. Some of the programs on the CD include separate licensing agreements. If you intend to use one of these programs, you must read and follow its accompanying license agreement. If you intend to use the trial version of Pattern Recognition Workbench, you must read and agree to the terms of the notice regarding fees on the back cover of this book. You may not copy the Documentation or the SOFTWARE, except that you may make a single copy of the SOFTWARE for backup or archival purposes only. You may be held legally responsible for any copying or copyright infringement which is caused or encouraged by your failure to abide by the terms of this restriction.

4. **USE RESTRICTIONS:** You may not network the SOFTWARE or otherwise use it on more than one computer or computer terminal at the same time. You may physically transfer the SOFTWARE from one computer to another provided that the SOFTWARE is used on only one computer at a time. You may not distribute copies of the SOFTWARE or Documentation to others. You may not reverse engineer, disassemble, decompile, modify, adapt, translate, or create derivative works based on the SOFTWARE or the Documentation without the prior written consent of the Company.

5. **TRANSFER RESTRICTIONS:** The enclosed SOFTWARE is licensed only to you and may not be transferred to any one else without the prior written consent of the Company. Any unauthorized transfer of the SOFTWARE shall result in the immediate termination of this Agreement.

6. **TERMINATION:** This license is effective until terminated. This license will terminate automatically without notice from the Company and become

null and void if you fail to comply with any provisions or limitations of this license. Upon termination, you shall destroy the Documentation and all copies of the SOFTWARE. All provisions of this Agreement as to warranties, limitation of liability, remedies or damages, and our ownership rights shall survive termination.

7. **MISCELLANEOUS:** This Agreement shall be construed in accordance with the laws of the United States of America and the State of New York and shall benefit the Company, its affiliates, and assignees.

8. **LIMITED WARRANTY AND DISCLAIMER OF WARRANTY:** The Company warrants that the SOFTWARE, when properly used in accordance with the Documentation, will operate in substantial conformity with the description of the SOFTWARE set forth in the Documentation. The Company does not warrant that the SOFTWARE will meet your requirements or that the operation of the SOFTWARE will be uninterrupted or error-free. The Company warrants that the media on which the SOFTWARE is delivered shall be free from defects in materials and workmanship under normal use for a period of thirty (30) days from the date of your purchase. Your only remedy and the Company's only obligation under these limited warranties is, at the Company's option, return of the warranted item for a refund of any amounts paid by you or replacement of the item. Any replacement of SOFTWARE or media under the warranties shall not extend the original warranty period. The limited warranty set forth above shall not apply to any SOFTWARE which the Company determines in good faith has been subject to misuse, neglect, improper installation, repair, alteration, or damage by you. EXCEPT FOR THE EXPRESSED WARRANTIES SET FORTH ABOVE, THE COMPANY DISCLAIMS ALL WARRANTIES, EXPRESS OR IMPLIED, INCLUDING WITHOUT LIMITATION, THE IMPLIED WARRANTIES OF MERCHANTABILITY AND FITNESS FOR A PARTICULAR PURPOSE. EXCEPT FOR THE EXPRESS WARRANTY SET FORTH ABOVE, THE COMPANY DOES NOT WARRANT, GUARANTEE, OR MAKE ANY REPRESENTATION REGARDING THE USE OR THE RESULTS OF THE USE OF THE SOFTWARE IN TERMS OF ITS CORRECTNESS, ACCURACY, RELIABILITY, CURRENTNESS, OR OTHERWISE.

Solving Data Mining Problems through Pattern Recognition

IN NO EVENT, SHALL THE COMPANY OR ITS EMPLOYEES, AGENTS, SUPPLIERS, OR CONTRACTORS BE LIABLE FOR ANY INCIDENTAL, INDIRECT, SPECIAL, OR CONSEQUENTIAL DAMAGES ARISING OUT OF OR IN CONNECTION WITH THE LICENSE GRANTED UNDER THIS AGREEMENT, OR FOR LOSS OF USE, LOSS OF DATA, LOSS OF INCOME OR PROFIT, OR OTHER LOSSES, SUSTAINED AS A RESULT OF INJURY TO ANY PERSON, OR LOSS OF OR DAMAGE TO PROPERTY, OR CLAIMS OF THIRD PARTIES, EVEN IF THE COMPANY OR AN AUTHORIZED REPRESENTATIVE OF THE COMPANY HAS BEEN ADVISED OF THE POSSIBILITY OF SUCH DAMAGES. IN NO EVENT SHALL LIABILITY OF THE COMPANY FOR DAMAGES WITH RESPECT TO THE SOFTWARE EXCEED THE AMOUNTS ACTUALLY PAID BY YOU, IF ANY, FOR THE SOFTWARE.

SOME JURISDICTIONS DO NOT ALLOW THE LIMITATION OF IMPLIED WARRANTIES OR LIABILITY FOR INCIDENTAL, INDIRECT, SPECIAL, OR CONSEQUENTIAL DAMAGES, SO THE ABOVE LIMITATIONS MAY NOT ALWAYS APPLY. THE WARRANTIES IN THIS AGREEMENT GIVE YOU SPECIFIC LEGAL RIGHTS AND YOU MAY ALSO HAVE OTHER RIGHTS WHICH VARY IN ACCORDANCE WITH LOCAL LAW.

ACKNOWLEDGMENT

YOU ACKNOWLEDGE THAT YOU HAVE READ THIS AGREEMENT, UNDERSTAND IT, AND AGREE TO BE BOUND BY ITS TERMS AND CONDITIONS. YOU ALSO AGREE THAT THIS AGREEMENT IS THE COMPLETE AND EXCLUSIVE STATEMENT OF THE AGREEMENT BETWEEN YOU AND THE COMPANY AND SUPERSEDES ALL PROPOSALS OR PRIOR AGREEMENTS, ORAL, OR WRITTEN, AND ANY OTHER COMMUNICATIONS BETWEEN YOU AND THE COMPANY OR ANY REPRESENTATIVE OF THE COMPANY RELATING TO THE SUBJECT MATTER OF THIS AGREEMENT.

Should you have any questions concerning this Agreement or if you wish to contact the Company for any reason, please contact in writing at the address below.

Robin Short
Prentice Hall PTR
One Lake Street
Upper Saddle River, New Jersey 07458

What's On This CD

The CD-ROM at the back of this book contains a fully functional evaluation copy of Unica Technologies, Inc.'s Pattern Recognition Workbench™ (PRW™) PRO+ software (see product summary in Appendix B).

You may install this software and use it on your own data sets to evaluate the software. Terms of the software licensing agreement are in the file LICENSE.TXT on the CD-ROM.

New Release Available

NOTE: A new version of PRW especially designed for solving database marketing problems will be released by press time. Call Unica at (781) 259-5900 for a free update!

Requirements

To install this software, you need the following:

      Intel-based PC 486+
      8+ MB RAM
      5+ MB free disk space
      MS-Windows 95 or Windows NT 3.51+

Quick Installation

To install PRW on your computer:

1. **Insert the CD-ROM into your CD-ROM drive.**

2. **Select the Start→Run command (Win 95 or Win NT 4.0) or select File→Run from the Program Manager (Win NT 3.51).**

3. **Type D:\setup.exe and click OK.**

   Use the appropriate drive letter for your CD-ROM drive (the example uses D:).

4. **Follow the directions that appear on your screen to complete the installation.**

Full installation instructions are available on the README.TXT file on the CD-ROM.

Software Registration

Once you have successfully installed the software, you will need to call Unica Technologies, Inc. at (781) 259-5900 to register the software. Please have the PRW registration screen displayed on your computer when you call in and use a phone located next to your computer. You will be given a 60-day trial license to use and evaluate PRW software.

Contact Information

Please contact Unica Technologies, Inc. for additional information on PRW and related products or for purchase information:

Unica Technologies, Inc.
Lincoln North
55 Old Bedford Rd.
Lincoln, MA 01773

Tel. (781) 259-5900
Fax. (781) 259-5901

email: unica@unica-usa.com
www.unica-usa.com/~unica

☞ **NOTE:** The area code provided for Unica Technologies on the CD has been changed since the CD was created. Please use (781) instead of (617) as indicated here.

Prentice Hall does not offer technical support for this software. However, if there is a problem with the media, you may obtain a replacement copy by emailing us with your problem at discexchange@phptr.com